THE PURPOSEHOOD® METHOD FOR A LIFE WORTH LOVING

EASE

EXISTENTIAL HEALTH IN THE AGE OF OVERWHELM

AMMAR CHARANI

EASE: Existential Health in the Age of Overwhelm

Published by Purposehood Publishing
Printed in the United States and worldwide.
Hardcover ISBN: 978-1-7349629-2-5
Paperback ISBN: 978-1-7349629-3-2
Ebook ISBN: 978-1-7349629-4-9

Library of Congress Control Number: 2026911281

PHD
publishing

www.purposehood.org

DEDICATION

For those becoming

and those who walk beside them.

INSCRIPTION

This EASE journey belongs to:

____

TABLE OF CONTENTS

PART I: AWAKENING

PART II: THE PURPOSEHOOD® METHOD FOR EXISTENTIAL HEALTH

BONUS CHAPTER

PART I:

AWAKENING

WHY THIS BOOK MATTERS

There are moments in life when the noise quiets and a deeper question rises to the surface: *Is this all there is?*

I asked myself that question when my heart literally stopped during a medical test. In those suspended seconds between beats—between life and whatever comes next—everything became clear. I needed more than good intentions. I needed a way to create not just a life I could manage, but a life worth loving.

That moment became both an ending and a beginning. It compelled me to codify what I had witnessed for decades sitting with people in their most vulnerable moments—as their friend, spiritual guide, teacher, employer, or mentor. Again and again, I had watched ordinary people discover extraordinary capacity for growth, meaning, and joy they never knew they possessed. One woman, after facing her greatest challenge, smiled and said, *"Maybe now I can finally begin."* And she did.

Through these encounters I began noticing patterns. Beneath the surface differences, the same struggles appeared: people drowning in too many solutions, succeeding at things that left them empty, or struggling because their lives weren't aligned with their deeper purpose. Yet those who truly transformed seemed to follow remarkably similar paths whether they realized it or not. They all seemed to have the ability to navigate life's challenges with ease; they had a deeper sense of health—a sense of existential health.

From this convergence of personal necessity and professional observation, I developed The Purposehood® Method for Existential Health. It wasn't invented so much as discovered—a compass through uncertainty, a way of finding meaning in struggle, and a practice of ease, which is not the absence of challenges but the ability to navigate them with grace. At its foundation are three principles: WholeBeing, seeing ourselves as complete, interconnected systems rather than fragments; RootHealing, addressing sources of existential suffering rather than symptoms; and EASE Leadership, a four-phase process—Engage, Assess, Support, Enact—that shifts us from passive recipients of solutions to active architects of our own transformation.

This journey is for you if you're ready to move beyond managing life to consciously creating it. If you want systematic tools rather than inspirational quotes. If you sense you're capable of more joy and meaning than you're currently experiencing.

You are exactly where you need to be. And something beautiful is waiting to unfold.

My friend, may you heal and grow with ease.

Ammar

A NOTE ON THE STORIES

The stories and case studies you'll encounter throughout this book are drawn from real people and real experiences. Some names and details have been changed to protect privacy. In a few cases, conversations are reconstructed from memory, and certain events are edited for clarity or flow. What remains true is the heart of each journey—the struggles, insights, and transformation that shaped them.

CHAPTER 1

THE PARADOX OF PLENTY
WHY WE STILL STRUGGLE
IN AN AGE OF SOLUTIONS

In a quiet suburb not far from where I live, I visited a friend whose thirteen-year-old son, Adam, had all the signs of a comfortable life: a warm home, loving parents, and good schools. But Adam rarely came out of his room. He spent most of his time immersed in video games. Not out of laziness or even for fun, but because he preferred that world over his own.

Curious, I asked him, "What do you like most about the game?"

"I matter in there," he said without turning from the screen.

That simple answer stopped me cold. Adam wasn't escaping boredom. He was escaping insignificance. He was retreating from a world that had forgotten how to help him matter as a whole human being.

And he's not alone.

From Tokyo to Toronto, from dense cities to quiet suburbs and rural towns, more and more people are retreating. The teenager disappearing into social media. The executive achieving everything on paper while feeling empty inside. The parent going through the motions that once felt meaningful. The retiree wondering what any of it was for.

They're all experiencing the same fundamental disconnection Adam felt: the sense that the world sees them as fragments—as students to be educated, workers to be productive, consumers to be exploited, problems to be solved—rather than as complete beings with inherent worth and purpose.

In Japan, more than a million young adults have disappeared into their bedrooms, becoming *hikikomori*, social recluses who isolate themselves for months or years. Their basic needs are met, but their sense of purpose is not.

We're living in a paradox, a time of overwhelming abundance and growing inner emptiness. The more access we have, the more we seem to disconnect. The more comfort we acquire, the more we quietly suffer.

You've done everything right. You've built the life you were told would fulfill you—success, security, solutions at your fingertips. And yet something feels off. A strange quiet hum beneath the noise. A dissonance you can't explain.

This isn't a flaw in you. It's a signal. A signal that something deeper is misaligned in the system shaping your life.

WHEN ABUNDANCE DOESN'T END SUFFERING

We're the most connected generation in history—more informed, more equipped, more optimized than any other. And somehow we're also more anxious, more burned out, more alone.

This is the paradox of plenty: a world overflowing with tools, options, and comforts but starving for meaning, clarity, and purpose—like an experiment in abundance gone wrong. We've never had more tools to support well-being, and yet we aren't well.

The problem affects every aspect of our health:

Physical health: Chronic illnesses due to lifestyles now account for 75 percent of deaths worldwide. Incidence of conditions like heart disease, obesity, and diabetes is growing faster than our treatments can manage them. We track our steps, scan our bodies, and swallow our medications, but vitality—the experience of feeling alive—is fading.

In some wealthy countries, life expectancy is no longer rising. In others it's falling, especially due to "deaths of despair"—suicides, drug overdoses, and diseases of disconnection.

Mental and emotional health: One in eight people on this planet now lives with a diagnosed mental disorder, and depression and anxiety are soaring, especially among the young.

There are now more than 450 documented therapies designed to heal our minds and emotions, and yet burnout and overwhelm are becoming our new normal. We scroll endlessly, we perform wellness routines, but beneath the surface many feel emotionally hollow, stuck in cycles of worry, stress, or regret.

Social health: Technology connects us in seconds, but more than one in five people say they feel lonely every day. Social media offers likes, not belonging. Cities are crowded but feel empty. Traditional sources of connection—extended families, spiritual communities, neighborhood networks—are fading.

Existential health: What haunts us most may be the loss of meaning—the absence of a reason to wake up, to endure, to give, to grow. Suicide is now the third leading cause of death among young people worldwide. Many who don't take their lives simply report feeling invisible—disconnected, unanchored, lost in a world that seems to offer everything except clarity.

In light of this, Adam's words ring all the louder: "I matter in there." In a simulated universe, he could build, achieve, and belong. In this one, he wasn't sure who he was, or if he mattered at all.

This isn't a crisis of access. It's a crisis of alignment.

A SYSTEM MISALIGNED

This misalignment is embedded in the very systems supposedly built to help us, systems that profit more from managing our problems than from solving them.

In 2018, Goldman Sachs released a report with a chilling question at its core: *Is curing patients a sustainable business model?* The report, aimed at biotech investors, acknowledged that one-time gene therapy cures carry immense value for patients and society, but pose a financial problem. Case in point: Gilead's revolutionary hepatitis C treatment. After it cured thousands, demand dropped. The virus lost its grip. Revenue fell from $12.5 billion to under $4 billion in a few years.

The Goldman Sachs report's implied conclusion: cures aren't good for business.

This misalignment shapes the systems we rely on to heal and grow within ourselves, our families, our work, our communities, and our relationship with nature. Take health care. It's where we invest enormous resources, yet where so many continue to suffer. In many systems, suffering generates more economic value than recovery. There's no money in the healthy, no gain in the dead; the profit lies in those who live long and suffer. And the incentives—often invisible and unintentional—keep us focused on managing symptoms rather than resolving causes.

Even the most well-meaning professionals work in such systems. Specialists treat organs, not people. Therapists treat minds, not beings. Coaches focus on performance, not healing. And the person suffering gets lost in the handoffs in between.

The breakdown isn't random. It's the result of three core misalignments built into the way modern systems approach care:

1. FRAGMENTATION

Modern systems of care split us into parts: mind, body, emotion, spirit, and more. We see different specialists for different symptoms—psychologists for thoughts, doctors for bodies, coaches for goals—but no one sees the whole picture.

The danger isn't just poor coordination; it's that fixing one fragment often damages another. Vioxx relieved arthritis pain but destroyed hearts, killing an estimated 60,000 people before being pulled from the market. SSRIs lift mood but dull emotional range. Therapy that excavates trauma can heal one wound while rupturing current relationships.

Performance coaching that ignores burnout creates success at the cost of health.

When you're treated as disconnected fragments rather than as an integrated WholeBeing, the underlying patterns that connect across all areas of your life remain invisible and unaddressed. You can "fix" one part while the whole system continues to suffer or even deteriorates further.

This fragmentation exists not just in treatment but also in identity. We start believing we're just our roles, just our diagnoses, just our problems.

2. SURFACE-LEVEL FIXES

We've grown accustomed to quick wins and instant relief, but treating symptoms without addressing root causes leads to recurring struggle. Whether it's numbing anxiety without exploring existential purpose or addressing a key performance indicator without also addressing company culture, the approach remains shallow. We become experts at coping but not at transforming.

3. DEPENDENCY INSTEAD OF LEADERSHIP

The system is built on repeat customers. We're conditioned, subtly and systemically, to rely on professionals, programs, and products for our well-being. Over time, we lose trust in our own capacity to heal, grow, and lead ourselves. Dependency becomes normalized, and empowerment becomes rare.

WHEN SUFFERING BECOMES PROFITABLE

You'd think a nation investing more in health care than any other would be a global model of well-being, but in the United States, we spend the most while achieving some of the poorest outcomes among wealthy nations. Rates of chronic illness, preventable death, suicide, and maternal mortality remain alarmingly high. The health outcomes are poor, the experience is fragmented, and the system leaves people feeling disempowered.

This isn't coincidental. It's by design.

Our healthcare system is designed to sustain revenue. It treats symptoms, not systems. It manages illness, not health. It promotes dependency, not empowerment. And at its core, it reinforces a deeper disconnection—from our WholeBeing, from our purpose, and from the healing power of meaning and relationship.

In a widely circulated article for *Harvard Health Publishing*, Dr. Robert Shmerling writes: "I don't know anyone who would design the system we currently have—well, other than those who are profiting from it." Even physicians, who often enter the field with a desire to serve and heal, are gradually conditioned to uphold this design. He writes: "During my medical training, I received relatively little instruction in nutrition, exercise, mental health, and primary care, but plenty of time was devoted to inpatient care, intensive care units, and subspecialties."

Doctors are trained to diagnose and treat within fragments—organs, symptoms, specialties—not within the wholeness of a human life. Meanwhile, the pharmaceutical industry—a profit engine that thrives on long-term customers rather than root-cause healing—shapes not only what gets prescribed but how suffering itself is classified and sustained.

If a human condition like grief, anxiety, or disorientation can be pathologized, it can be medicated. And if it can be medicated, it can be monetized. The result is a system where existential suffering is medicalized but not truly addressed, where the deeper disconnections of purpose, identity, and meaning are silenced by prescriptions instead of explored through healing relationships.

All the while, care itself is deeply fragmented. Patients bounce among specialists, clinics, and systems that rarely communicate. One doctor prescribes, another adjusts, a third repeats the same test—all without an integrated understanding of the WholeBeing they're trying to treat.

"People tend to get care in a variety of settings that may have little or no connection to each other," Shmerling notes. Innovative approaches like home-based care, telehealth, and prevention-first models often fail to scale because they aren't easily reimbursed. They threaten the business model. "Innovative approaches may never become widespread... because current payment systems don't routinely cover this care," he adds.

This system perpetuates strain rather than ease. It rewards compliance more than empowerment and treats symptoms in isolation instead of restoring WholeBeing. At its core, it functions less like healthcare and more like a profit system—one that manages the suffering of fragmented beings rather than helping them heal.

But healing is possible.

FROM CONSUMER TO CONTRIBUTOR

This book introduces a different path: a structured, practical approach called The Purposehood Method for Existential Health. *Existential health is the ability to navigate life's challenges with ease.* The method is built around a foundational concept, Purposehood—your existential purpose, your reason for being that goes beyond roles, achievements, and external validation. Not just goals or ambitions, it's the coherent direction that emerges when you align with what truly matters to you and how you're called to contribute to life itself.

It begins with a simple truth: You aren't just a body, a mind, or a role. You're a WholeBeing.

Each person is made of interwoven dimensions—physical, emotional, mental, spiritual, existential, relational—and each part affects the others. And each must be seen, heard, and aligned.

This method flips the system by restoring three principles:

Wholeness over fragmentation: As a WholeBeing, you're made of interconnected dimensions across life's five extensions—Self, Family, Work, Communities, and Nature.

RootHealing over surface fixes: At the root of our modern struggles lie five recurring sources of misalignment. The Purposehood Method for Existential Health helps you go deeper to resolve them, not just treat their symptoms.

Leadership over dependency: This method invites you to lead your own healing and growth instead of relying passively on external systems. With guidance and practice, you develop the capacity to navigate struggle, retain progress, and inspire others through your example.

This process is called EASE: Engage, Assess, Support, and Enact, and it's designed to help you assess your whole life, identify what's truly misaligned, and create lasting change that builds into a life worth loving.

This isn't a quick fix. It's a map and compass. A way to move from fragmentation to alignment. From dependency to leadership. From suffering to ease.

Because the opposite of suffering isn't comfort. It's ease—ease when you're enduring, ease when you're healing, ease when you're content, and ease when you're growing.

⏸ PURPOSEHOOD PAUSE

Reflect on your own paradox of plenty.

When have you had "everything" but felt emptier than ever?

What modern "solutions" may be part of your disconnection?

What do you long for beyond success or achievement?

Take a moment to sit with these questions. Your answers aren't problems to solve right now—they're doorways to understanding.

AN INVITATION TO BEING

Three months after our conversation, I saw Adam again. This time he wasn't in his room. He was in the backyard, teaching his younger sister how to build something—not in a virtual world but with wood and nails and their own hands.

"What changed?" I asked his mother.

"He started to feel like he mattered out here too," she said.

That transformation, from isolation to engagement and from insignificance to impact, is available to anyone willing to understand themselves as a WholeBeing and commit to the process of aligned growth.

If you've ever felt like Adam—successful on paper but empty inside, surrounded by solutions yet still struggling—this book is for you. If you're ready to move beyond managing symptoms to transforming causes, the journey begins now.

Let's discover how you can heal and grow at home, at work, in your community, and within yourself.

THE PURPOSEHOOD® METHOD FOR EXISTENTIAL HEALTH

CHAPTER 2

WHOLEBEING
YOUR LIFE AS AN INTEGRATED SYSTEM

Anna prided herself on being a well-balanced person. She was active, ate healthily, meditated regularly, and enjoyed meaningful relationships with her friends and family. Life was good, until it wasn't. One small thing began to unravel everything: a toothache.

When one of her teeth started hurting, she brushed it off as an inconvenience. Soon, the dull ache became a sharp pain. When she bit into something hot or cold, the effect was like a blaring trumpet disrupting her life's symphony, but she told herself it would get better on its own.

What Anna didn't realize was that her decision to avoid this one issue would cascade through every extension of her being. The throbbing pain in her jaw kept her awake. She woke up feeling tired, and her exhaustion followed her through the day, making it harder for her to function. Her usual routine of morning exercise began to slip, and without the energy to hit the gym, she felt lethargic.

Since it hurt to chew, she was eating a lot of soft carbs instead of the crunchy vegetables that had been the foundation of her healthy diet. Instead of being nourished and energized by her meals, she felt sleepy and sluggish.

And as her physical health declined, so did her mood. Typically calm and cheerful, Anna became easily irritated, mentally foggy, and emotionally drained. She started snapping at small things like her employees' innocent questions and her partner's well-meaning advice, and those relationships started to suffer. As her spiritual meditation—the practice that kept her centered—became a chore, she started skipping it, depriving herself of the peace she cherished.

When a mutual friend referred Anna to me, she came seeking help with her relationships and work stress, never mentioning her tooth. She talked about feeling disconnected from her partner, frustrated with her team, and unable to find the peace she once had in meditation.

This is classic WholeBeing disruption. The real problem was hidden while the symptoms spread across multiple extensions. I didn't need to psychoanalyze her entire past or spend months exploring relationship dynamics to identify the source of her struggles. The clue came when she winced while taking a sip of tea.

"What's wrong?" I asked.

"Oh, it's just this toothache I've had for a while."

"Anna, I think we need to start there."

"I would," she said, "but I hate going to the dentist. The idea of going gives me so much anxiety that I'd rather put up with the pain."

I understood exactly what she was experiencing. I'd lived through the same cycle myself. For years I avoided visits to the dentist because of intense anxiety rooted in a painful childhood experience, convincing myself that any discomfort would somehow resolve on its own. When I finally faced my fears, I used every coping strategy I could—meditation before appointments, noise-canceling headphones during procedures, even anti-anxiety medication.

But when I discovered The Purposehood Method, I learned to go deeper, to address the real source of my suffering: the limiting belief that I couldn't handle the discomfort and uncertainty. Once I replaced that belief with the empowering truth that I could endure temporary discomfort in service of long-term health, my attitude changed.

That experience taught me something crucial that Anna's story confirmed: the bigger issue isn't the challenge we face but how suffering in one area, left unaddressed, can quietly infect every part of life.

"I understand that your anxiety seems overwhelming," I said to Anna, "but what about all the effects on your partner and employees and on your sleep and nutrition that are disrupting the inner peace you used to feel?"

She was quiet for a minute as her shoulders sagged with recognition. "I'm embarrassed that my fear is affecting the people around me, and I know I need to get myself to go to the dentist."

Anna's story illustrates something profound about how we function as human beings. Her tooth was just one small element of her physical self, but when left unaddressed, it disrupted every component of her being: her relationships, her work performance, her emotional state, her spiritual practice, and even her connection to the healthy lifestyle she valued.

Through our session together, Anna came to understand that in avoiding what she feared, she was creating far more suffering than facing it ever could. We worked together to help her identify the limiting belief that was keeping her trapped—*I can't handle dental procedures*—and trained her in a practical process for replacing it with an empowering belief—*I can handle temporary discomfort to protect my long-term health.* This process gave her tools she could use for any challenge where fear was creating more problems than the thing she feared.

She picked up the phone and made a dentist's appointment on the spot. And when she finally went to the dentist, the procedure was straightforward—a cavity that had turned into an infection, easily treatable but long overdue.

As the infection cleared, so did Anna's pain. And as the pain subsided, she could sleep again, eat without discomfort, and exercise without exhaustion. Her mood lifted and she returned to her meditation practice, reconnecting with the peace that had been lost in the chaos. She had to work to rebuild the relationships that her irritability had strained, but because she'd addressed the root cause, her healing was genuine and lasting.

WHAT'S YOUR HIDDEN 'TOOTHACHE'?

Anna's story isn't unique. We've all experienced how one unaddressed issue can create cascading effects throughout our lives. Maybe you recognize some of these situations in your own experience:

A difficult conversation you've been avoiding that's creating tension in multiple relationships

A health concern you keep postponing that's affecting your energy, mood, and productivity

A career decision you're delaying, leaving you feeling stuck and unfulfilled

A financial issue you're not facing that's creating stress in your family and limiting your choices

A habit you know isn't serving you but feels too hard to change, affecting your self-respect and well-being

The specific issue doesn't matter as much as understanding this truth: in an interconnected system like your WholeBeing, there are no truly small problems. What seems like an isolated challenge in one area is often disrupting the harmony of your entire life's symphony.

Sometimes the most important work we can do is facing what seems like the smallest problem, because the reality is it's the avoidance, not the problem itself, that's creating the chaos in our lives.

Anna's recovery followed a three-part shift:

First, she recognized herself as a WholeBeing—an interconnected system that can't be well if any part is suffering.

Then, she addressed the root cause of her suffering: a limiting belief that quietly kept her from seeking help.

Finally, she learned an empowering process—one she could use not only to navigate future challenges, but to help others in her life do the same.

These three shifts form the principles of The Purposehood Method for Existential Health:

- *WholeBeing:* seeing your life as an interconnected system

- *RootHealing:* identifying and treating the actual sources of your suffering

- *EASE Leadership:* a process to initiate and sustain lasting change

Once you understand your WholeBeing, you stop approaching life as a series of problems to fix and start conducting a life that's in tune with who you truly are. Like a conductor who needs to understand the full orchestra before leading the music, you need to recognize your complete "I"—the totality of your being—before you can create harmony, meaning, and ease.

YOUR LIFE AS A SYMPHONY

Your life is a symphony waiting to be conducted. Every day, whether you're aware of it or not, you stand before an orchestra of interconnected elements, each playing a role in the music of your existence. When these elements play in harmony, the result is extraordinary: a life rich in meaning, gratitude, ease, and abundance. But when even one section falls out of tune, the whole experience suffers.

Just as a grand symphony depends on the coordinated rhythm of many instruments, your sense of fulfillment and harmony depends on how well the parts of your being are aligned. These parts—what The Purposehood Method calls the Five Extensions of Being—are Self, Family, Work, Communities, and Nature.

THE FIVE EXTENSIONS OF BEING

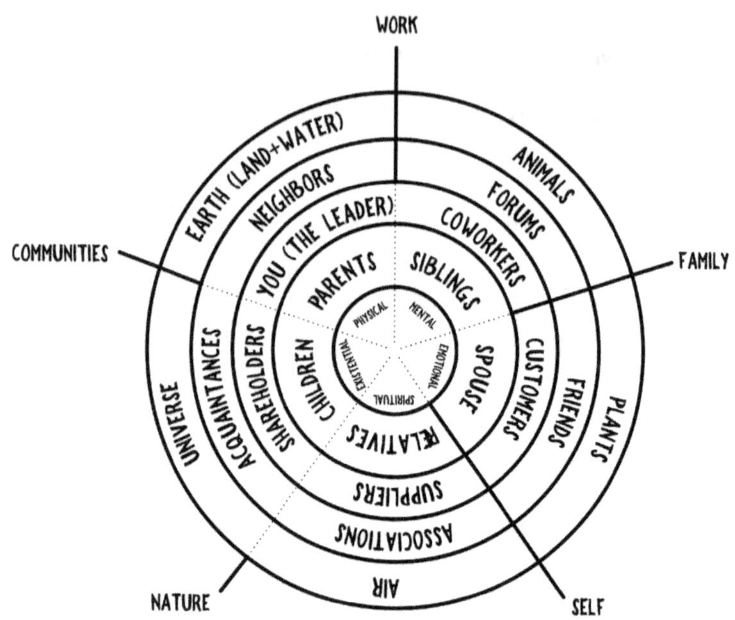

SELF EXTENSION—YOUR INNER CONDUCTOR

At the center of it all is the Self, the conductor who sets the tempo and direction. Like a conductor who doesn't make a sound but influences every note, your self-awareness and Purposehood shape how your life plays out. The orchestra relies on the conductor to unify the whole, just as your extensions rely on your core alignment.

The Self is called an extension because while it feels like our core identity, it's not a fixed or isolated entity. Instead, it's an evolving, expansive part of your being, shaped by your thoughts, emotions, and experiences and deeply influenced by your interactions with family, work, communities, and nature. This perspective empowers you to see the Self not as a static "I" but as an adaptable, ever-growing presence that both directs and is shaped by the harmony of your life.

Your Self extension encompasses five essential components: your thoughts, your emotions, your body, your spiritual self, and your existential self—the part of you that seeks meaning, not just goals or success, but a deeper *why* behind how you live, give, and grow. This is your existential purpose, the inner compass that aligns your values, decisions, and direction with meaning. When that purpose is clear and integrated, it brings coherence to your life and anchors you in Purposehood, the lived state of alignment with your deepest reason for being.

When all five components of the Self are attuned to one another and aligned with your values, they provide the clarity and intention needed to guide all other extensions of your life toward meaning, growth, and ease.

FAMILY EXTENSION—YOUR FOUNDATION

Your Family extension represents the string section—the orchestra's foundation, providing richness, depth, and stability to your life's melody. Like the backbone of any great symphony, your relationships with parents, siblings, partner, children, and other close relatives create the emotional bedrock on which everything else is built.

When your family relationships are in harmony, they offer strength, support, and grounding. When discord arises in this section, its effects ripple through your entire symphony, affecting your confidence, peace of mind, and ability to thrive in other areas.

WORK EXTENSION—YOUR CONTRIBUTION

Your Work extension is like the orchestra's brass section: bold, purposeful, and designed to project your contribution into the world. The trumpets, trombones, and other horns represent your professional duties, your co-workers, the shareholders who depend on your performance, the customers or audiences you serve, and the suppliers or partners who enable your work. Together, these components form the resonant force of your contribution—your career, projects, and creative pursuits that allow you to make your mark on the world.

When this section is aligned with your existential purpose, work becomes energizing and meaningful. But when it's disconnected from your deeper values, even the most impressive achievements can sound hollow, leaving you successful on paper but empty inside.

COMMUNITIES EXTENSION—YOUR CONNECTIONS

Your Communities extension represents the woodwind section—the flutes, clarinets, and oboes that create connection and emotional texture throughout the symphony. Though they may not dominate like the bold brass or anchor like the foundational strings, woodwinds are essential for the music's richness, flow, and nuanced beauty.

Similarly, your relationships with friends, neighbors, small groups focused on goals like healing and growth, associations, and acquaintances may seem secondary to family and work, but they're vital for your well-being. These components of social connection offer perspective, support, and diversity of thought that enrich your entire life experience.

Research on relational diversity shows that people who engage with a broad range of social connections—from close friendship ties to casual acquaintances—experience greater happiness and life satisfaction than those with narrower social networks. Like a well-orchestrated woodwind section, these varied relationships allow your life's music to breathe, adapt, and move with greater ease through every transition.

NATURE EXTENSION—YOUR GROUNDING

Your Nature extension is the heartbeat of your orchestra, the percussion section that sets the rhythm and grounds the entire performance. Just as percussion anchors the tempo and structure of a symphony, your connection to the natural world anchors your balance, energy, and vitality.

This connection includes your relationships with the air you breathe, the animals and plants you interact with, the land and water that sustain you, and the universe that evokes awe and perspective. When you're in sync with nature's rhythm, you feel emotionally steadied, physically restored, and spiritually reconnected.

THE 25 COMPONENTS OF WHOLEBEING

Here's the complete orchestration of your being—twenty-five components across five extensions that make up your WholeBeing:

SELF	FAMILY	WORK	COMMUNITIES	NATURE
Existential	Parents	Job	Friends	Air
Physical	Partner	Coworkers	Neighbors	Plants
Mental	Children	Shareholders	Circles	Animals
Emotional	Siblings	Customers	Associations	Earth
Spiritual	Relatives	Suppliers	Acquaintances	Universe

For a complete exploration of each component, see Appendix A.

This system of components serves as your foundational map for understanding and nurturing your WholeBeing. Each component has its own unique strengths and potential challenges, and by understanding, nurturing, and tapping into the components' superpowers, you unlock the potential for sustained growth and inner harmony across all areas of your life.

When all five extensions are aligned and their components are healthy, you experience WholeBeing, a state where your life operates as a coordinated symphony rather than a collection of competing solos. Challenges don't derail you because your entire system is resilient. Growth accelerates because all parts of your life support rather than compete with each other.

Most important, you're no longer trying to fix problems in isolation. Instead, you're conducting your life with intention, creating harmony where there was discord, and composing a masterpiece that reflects your deepest values and highest aspirations.

When we begin to see ourselves as systems, not symptoms, we realize the power of alignment. And few stories reveal this transformation more clearly than Andre's. Where Anna unraveled under hidden misalignment, Andre rebuilt through conscious orchestration of his WholeBeing.

ANDRE'S WHOLEBEING JOURNEY

Sometimes the most successful people face the deepest struggles with WholeBeing. From the outside, their lives appear perfectly orchestrated—thriving businesses, impressive achievements, respected reputations—but beneath that polished exterior, many quietly grapple with disconnection, anxiety, or profound imbalance. Andre's journey powerfully illustrates that even those who seem to be winning at life can face hidden challenges that disrupt their entire symphony.

Like many of the extraordinary leaders I've had the privilege of knowing through the Young Presidents' Organization (YPO)—a global network in which CEOs meet in chapters and small expansion circles known as forums for deep personal exchange—Andre was driven, brilliant, and successful by every external measure. The CEO of a rapidly growing combat sports company and a member of several prestigious boards, he'd earned more accolades by his late thirties than most people collect in a lifetime.

But when we met, there was something in his eyes that hinted at a different story, and he walked as if he were shouldering an invisible weight.

"This," Andre said, holding up my book *Purposehood: Transform Your Life, Transform the World* as he settled into a chair across from me, "connected so many dots. It's like it gave me the framework I've been searching for my entire life." He flipped through the worn pages, showing me they were filled with scribbled notes and divided with colorful tabs.

"I'm glad it resonated," I said. "Tell me about your journey."

He took a deep breath. "I've been on a quest for meaning since I was a kid. Growing up in a deeply religious Orthodox Christian family, I always felt there was more to explore. I delved into Buddhism, Islam, various philosophies—I was searching for something that could help me make sense of the world and my place in it. I've been meditating since I was sixteen, and I studied political science to understand societies and human behavior." He paused, his gaze distant for a moment. "But despite all that exploration, I felt like I was missing a unifying system, a way to integrate everything I was learning and experiencing. My life became this patchwork of insights without a connecting thread."

"What led you to my book?"

"My forum friend Katya invited me to join the Purposehood Engineering training you conducted last year, but when I got back to her, it was already full. I was disappointed, so she sent me a copy of your book as consolation. It sat on my shelf for months—life was busy, as usual. Then, during a vacation, I finally picked it up and couldn't put it down."

He flipped through the marked-up pages and pointed to a highlighted line. "'If any extension is toxic, then all will have some level of toxicity.' The idea that we can't be well if any component is unwell resonated deeply. I was so focused on career success that I neglected everything else."

"Which areas felt most out of tune?"

"My family, for one. I haven't been very present with them. Physically, I might be there, but I'm always thinking about the next business move, the next project. And I've lost touch with my spiritual practices. I used to meditate every day, spend time in nature, have philosophical discussions with friends. Now it's all about work."

"People sometimes have this realization after struggling," I said. "Is that what brought you to this point?"

"Exactly," he said. "I'd been mentoring other people, helping them find their path, but I hadn't fully aligned my own life with my purpose. Your explanation of WholeBeing—that neglecting even one component affects the whole—helped me finally make sense of what I'd been feeling."

Andre's situation was a perfect example of what happens when one extension dominates all others. His work extension was thriving—he was successful, respected, financially secure—but this success had become a craving that consumed his attention and energy, pulling him away from the other extensions that desperately needed nurturing.

"I want to realign my life," he said. "I want to live my Purposehood, not just think about it."

Together, we mapped out Andre's 25 Components of Being. What we discovered was telling: while his Work extension showed strength in most areas, his Self extension was struggling with existential misalignment, his Family extension showed strain in multiple relationships, his Communities extension had shrunk to business contacts only, and his Nature extension was virtually neglected.

"The goal isn't to diminish your professional success," I said. "It's to let that success flow from and support your WholeBeing rather than consuming it."

Andre began making deliberate changes in the extensions where he'd been struggling:

- Self extension: He returned to his meditation practice, starting with just ten minutes every morning, and scheduled monthly solo retreats for philosophical reflection.

- Family extension: He established boundaries around work hours and began having weekly one-on-one conversations with each family member about their lives, not just logistics.

- Communities extension: He began volunteering to mentor young entrepreneurs, sharing his wisdom in a way that connected him to his Purposehood beyond just business networking.

- Nature extension: He started taking walking meetings outdoors and planned family nature trips.

Most important, he stopped seeing these changes as taking away from his professional success. He discovered that when all extensions of his being were aligned, his leadership actually improved. He became more present in meetings, more creative in problem-solving, and more inspiring to his team.

When we met again a few months later, Andre reflected on his transformation: "I realize now I wasn't really successful; I was just busy. Real success is when all parts of my life work together and strengthen each other, instead of one part taking over everything else."

His story illustrates a crucial truth about WholeBeing: external success without internal integration is ultimately hollow. When we neglect any extension of our being, we create discord that ripples through everything else, no matter how well other areas appear to be functioning.

Andre's journey from fragmented success to integrated fulfillment demonstrates that true prosperity comes not from maximizing one area of life but from conducting all areas in harmony. When we understand ourselves as WholeBeings, we stop sacrificing our relationships for our careers, our health for our ambitions, our inner peace for our external achievements. Instead, we learn to create a life where every extension supports and enhances the others, where success means achieving our goals in a way that honors all aspects of who we are and who we're called to become.

Like Andre discovered, when you align your entire being with your Purposehood, you don't just achieve success—you create a masterpiece.

⏸ PURPOSEHOOD PAUSE

Take a moment to consider your whole system, not just your symptoms.

Which extension of your life do you attend to most? Which extensions do you neglect?

When was the last time you felt fully integrated, with all areas of your life supporting rather than competing with each other?

How might fragmentation be feeding your fatigue or struggles?

Notice without judgment. Your awareness is the first step toward wholeness.

Anna's and Andre's stories reveal a truth: whether life is unraveling or flourishing, lasting transformation begins with existential alignment. WholeBeing is the foundation—recognizing yourself as a connected system, not a collection of parts.

But even the most beautiful system can fall out of tune if its roots are diseased. In the next chapter, we'll explore the hidden sources that disrupt our harmony.

CHAPTER 3

ROOTHEALING ADDRESSING SOURCES, NOT SYMPTOMS

Two patients walk into different cardiologists' offices with the same complaint: their blood pressure has been rising.

Patient A spends less than fifteen minutes with his doctor. The physician quickly reviews the chart, asks a few routine questions, and prescribes a second medication. There's no time—or incentive—to go deeper. The visit ends with a new pill and the scheduling of a follow-up in six weeks.

Patient B's doctor takes a different approach entirely. He spends whatever time is needed (which turns out to be ninety minutes) and asks a fundamentally different question: "What's changed in your life?" He doesn't just look at lab results. He explores the patient's stress levels, emotional patterns, eating habits, sense of overwhelm, and unspoken fears. Together they trace the blood pressure spikes back to a deeper root: a life increasingly out of alignment—too much urgency, not enough recovery, too much responsibility, not enough meaning.

Six months later, Patient A is on more medication but still feels anxious and out of control. Patient B is still on the same medication but with lower readings, steadier emotions, a clearer sense of self, and renewed motivation. His health didn't change because of a pill. It changed because he addressed what the symptom was trying to say.

The difference? One doctor treated the symptom, and the other practiced RootHealing.

I know because over the years, I was both patients.

WHEN I WAS PATIENT A

For years I was Patient A in my own story. After that twelve-minute cardiologist visit—another prescription and a follow-up in six weeks—I thought the problem was solved.

But my body wasn't fooled. The medications managed the numbers for a while, but my blood pressure kept spiking. Each subsequent appointment felt more rushed, more disconnected from what was actually happening in my life. I was experiencing the system's trap at every level:

A healthcare system that profited more from managing my blood pressure than from resolving what was creating it

Doctors who, though well-intentioned, were trained to match symptoms to quick fixes in brief windows, not to explore deeper patterns

And myself, conditioned to expect instant relief rather than do the uncomfortable work of examining what my body was trying to tell me

The pharmaceutical industry had spent billions convincing me that pills were the solution. My doctors, constrained by packed schedules and billing codes, offered the fastest answers that fit the system. And I'd learned to prioritize relief over the deeper questions: Why was my nervous system in constant overdrive? What was my body responding to that my mind refused to acknowledge?

Two years in, I was experiencing "solution fatigue," exhausted from managing a problem instead of understanding it.

Why? Because no one—not the system, my doctors, or even myself—ever asked the RootHealing question: "What's creating this pressure in the first place?"

And I wasn't alone. Countless others, maybe including you, have lived some version of this same trap.

THE THREE-LAYER TRAP

What caught me wasn't just personal bad luck; it was a systemic trap designed around wrong incentives with three reinforcing layers that keep millions stuck in cycles of temporary relief instead of lasting transformation:

LAYER 1: THE FINANCIAL LAYER
Managing Symptoms Pays Better Than Solving Problems

My doctors weren't malicious—they were working within a system that rewarded them for managing my numbers, not for understanding what drove them up. But this reflects a much deeper problem with how treatment decisions are actually made: insurance companies reimburse providers based on procedures performed and medications prescribed, not on patient outcomes or long-term health improvements.

The numbers reveal the stark mismatch: while Americans spend $4.3 trillion annually on health care, less than 4 percent goes toward identifying and addressing root causes of illness. The rest funds symptom management through an endless cycle of tests, procedures, and prescriptions.

Pharmaceutical spending alone has increased 76 percent in the past decade. Americans now take an average of 4.7 prescription medications each. Meanwhile, chronic diseases—many preventable through lifestyle changes—affect 60 percent of adults and account for 90 percent of health care spending.

The system rewards volume over value. A doctor who spends forty-five minutes helping a patient understand the lifestyle roots of their diabetes earns far less than one who schedules three fifteen-minute medication adjustments. Root-cause interventions like nutrition counseling, stress management, and addressing social isolation aren't profitable enough to sustain most practices.

LAYER 2: THE TIME PRESSURE LAYER
Symptom Relief in 15 Minutes or Less

Those twelve-minute appointments I experienced aren't unusual—they're structural necessities. Even the most dedicated health care professionals face an impossible challenge: they're expected to identify and treat complex interconnected health issues in impossibly brief time slots.

The average primary care appointment lasts just thirteen to sixteen minutes. In that window, doctors have to review medical history, conduct examinations, address multiple concerns, document everything for insurance, and develop treatment plans. Research shows that when patients start to describe their symptoms, physicians interrupt them within eighteen seconds.

This time pressure creates a predictable pattern: focus on the most obvious symptom, prescribe the most direct treatment, schedule a follow-up to monitor, repeat. There's simply no time to explore whether a patient's anxiety might stem from work stress, relationship conflict, or existential confusion. No time to investigate whether their chronic pain connects to unresolved trauma, poor sleep, or social isolation.

The result is what health care experts call "symptom whack-a-mole": treating each complaint as it surfaces without ever asking why so many symptoms keep appearing in the same person.

LAYER 3: THE CULTURAL LAYER
We've Lost Faith in Our Own Healing Capacity

My own conditioning to expect instant relief reflects a broader cultural problem: we've been conditioned to see ourselves as passive recipients of health rather than active participants in healing. We've outsourced our well-being to systems that profit from our continued need for their services.

Modern culture has normalized a troubling belief that sustainable change is nearly impossible. Despite living in an age of unprecedented personal development resources, 92 percent of people fail to achieve their stated goals within a year. We've developed what psychologists call "learned helplessness" about our own capacity for transformation.

This helplessness extends to health. Seventy-three percent of adults say they believe their health problems are "just part of getting older" rather than conditions that could be improved through sustained effort. We've accepted chronic fatigue, persistent anxiety, and relationship problems as inevitable rather than addressable.

The culture of impatience and quick-fixes compounds the problem. Americans change television channels every two and a half seconds when surfing and expect websites to load in under three seconds. But meaningful health improvements typically require months of consistent effort. In a culture optimized for instant gratification, the patience required for root-level healing feels impossibly demanding.

These three layers reinforce each other in a destructive cycle: Financial pressures force providers to offer quick symptom relief rather than comprehensive healing. Time constraints prevent professionals from exploring root causes even when they want to. Cultural conditioning leads patients to expect instant results and doubt their capacity for sustained change.

This demand for quick fixes justifies the supply, and the cycle continues. What makes the trap so insidious is that each layer affects everyone. Financial pressures not only shape the system but also limit your doctor's options and your insurance coverage. Time constraints aren't just about rushed appointments; they're built into medical training, billing requirements, and our own impatience. Cultural conditioning hasn't only shaped patients; it has shaped how medicine is taught, practiced, and paid for.

Every participant is caught in all three layers simultaneously. Your doctor may want to spend more time with you but risks financial penalties for being labeled 'inefficient.' You might be ready to do deeper healing work but find no insurance coverage, no time with providers, and cultural messages that you are being 'difficult' for wanting more than a prescription. The result? We spend more on healthcare than ever before while feeling less healthy and whole. We have access to miraculous treatments for acute conditions, yet chronic diseases, mental health struggles, and existential emptiness continue to rise.

But what if there were a different way, one that didn't treat symptoms in isolation but addressed the deeper sources of struggle across your WholeBeing? What if, alongside medical or therapeutic care, you could also be trained to strengthen your existential health, so that lasting well-being becomes possible?

This is the promise of RootHealing, and it begins with understanding a fundamental truth the three-layer trap obscures: most of what they call disorders are natural human conditions—ones that can be transformed, not just managed, when existential health is addressed alongside other care.

RootHealing is, at its core, the work of restoring existential health—the roots of meaning and direction that nourish every other dimension of well-being.

WHAT IS ROOTHEALING?

What if Patient A's doctor had asked a different question? Instead of "What medication can help your blood pressure?" imagine if he'd asked, "What pattern in your life keeps elevating your blood pressure?"

That single shift from managing symptoms to understanding sources is the essence of RootHealing. RootHealing isn't another treatment modality—it's a fundamentally different approach, one that asks, "What's creating this struggle in the first place?"

While traditional approaches focus on the *what* (the symptom) and the *how* (the treatment), RootHealing focuses on the *why*, the underlying sources that, when left unaddressed, keep generating the same problems over and over.

Every day, millions of people struggle with anxiety, stress, regret, sadness, guilt, grief, and disconnection, but these aren't always pathologies requiring medical intervention. They're often signals, natural human responses pointing to something deeper that needs attention.

Even many chronic physical conditions are influenced by similar dynamics. While biology and genetics play essential roles, persistent stress, emotional strain, relational conflict, and loss of meaning often shape how illness develops, progresses, and heals. When these underlying patterns remain unexamined, treatment may control symptoms without restoring vitality.

We don't call someone a patient because they're hungry. We understand that hunger is a natural signal of a need that arises, becomes acknowledged, and then is met. We learn to eat with rhythm, balance, and awareness so hunger doesn't become a crisis. The same is true for many mental, emotional, existential, and even some physical struggles. They come and go. They point to something deeper. And they can be *trained for.*

But modern systems have pathologized normal human experience. They've medicalized sadness, spiritual confusion, and even the natural fear of meaninglessness. Health care professionals find themselves treating struggles that would be better addressed through existential alignment rather than medical intervention.

This is where RootHealing diverges from the three-layer trap. Instead of profiting from dependency, RootHealing creates empowerment. Instead of fragmented symptom management, RootHealing addresses the deeper sources of suffering that affect the whole person. Instead of quick fixes, RootHealing builds lasting capability.

In a word, RootHealing transforms you from a patient consuming treatments to a person developing mastery.

FIVE SOURCES OF EXISTENTIAL SUFFERING

Across decades of work with hundreds of people spanning diverse cultures, backgrounds, and life conditions, I've consistently found that nearly all human struggle traces back to five deeper patterns. These aren't just emotional or behavioral issues—they're root sources of existential suffering, described in ancient traditions and confirmed by recent scientific research. They are the persistent ache beneath the surface that no amount of success, comfort, or achievement can resolve. When left unaddressed, they quietly shape our thoughts, sabotage our efforts, and keep us cycling through symptoms without real healing.

THE FIVE ROOT SOURCES AT A GLANCE

Root Source	Core Experience	Typical Result
Misdirection	Emptiness, confusion	Drifting
Disorientation	Panic, identity loss	Resignation
Limiting Beliefs	Shame, fear, guilt	Dependency
Stagnation	Apathy, boredom	Complacency
Cravings	Anxiety, addiction	Excess

1. MISDIRECTION

I'm living someone else's life.

The absence of true north.

What it sounds like: *I'm successful but feel empty. I don't know what I actually want. I'm going through the motions.*

How it shows up daily: chronic indecision, scrolling endlessly instead of engaging, achieving goals that feel hollow, saying yes to everything because you have no clear priorities, feeling like you're living someone else's expectations.

The deeper pattern: Without an existential direction, life becomes reactive. You chase what others value, follow paths that don't fit, and wonder why success doesn't satisfy.

2. DISORIENTATION

I don't know where I fit.

Lost in time, role, and goals.

What it sounds like: *I feel stuck in the past. I don't know who I am anymore. Everything feels overwhelming and confusing.*

How it shows up daily: dwelling on past mistakes, feeling paralyzed by future uncertainty, confusion about your role in relationships or work, difficulty making decisions because nothing feels clear, constant anxiety about "falling behind".

The deeper pattern: When your sense of identity, timing, or place becomes unclear, even stable circumstances feel chaotic and threatening.

3. LIMITING BELIEFS

I'm not capable of more.

The invisible chains.

What it sounds like: *I need someone else to fix me. I can't trust my own judgment. I have to follow the expert's plan exactly. I'm too broken to heal on my own. What if I make the wrong choice?*

How it shows up daily: waiting for others to validate your progress, seeking constant reassurance that you're "doing it right," abandoning efforts when initial results don't meet expectations, believing you need more credentials/therapy/preparation before you can act, looking for external experts to fix what only you can heal.

The deeper pattern: Subconscious beliefs about your limitations operate like invisible software, automatically blocking empowerment and keeping you dependent on others for your healing and growth.

4. STAGNATION

Nothing ever changes.

Resistance to natural growth.

What it sounds like: *This is just how life is. I'm too comfortable or maybe too scared to change. Why bother trying? I used to care about things, but now...*

How it shows up daily: going through the same routines without engagement, avoiding new experiences or challenges, feeling bored but not taking action, relationships that lack depth or growth, work that feels like sleepwalking.

The deeper pattern: When you resist life's natural flow of evolution, vitality drains away and existence becomes mechanical rather than meaningful.

5. CRAVINGS

I need more to feel complete.

When desires become compulsions.

What it sounds like: *I'll be happy when I get/achieve/become... I need this in order to feel okay. More, better, sooner. I can't stop checking/buying/consuming...*

How it shows up daily: endless scrolling on social media, shopping for things you don't need, working compulsively even when exhausted, constant comparison with others, feeling like you're running on a treadmill that never stops, brief satisfaction followed by immediate wanting.

The deeper pattern: Healthy desires become compulsive when disconnected from Purposehood, creating cycles of temporary satisfaction followed by deeper emptiness.

What makes these sources of existential suffering so destructive is that they don't stay contained. Remember from Chapter 2 that you're a WholeBeing—when one source takes hold, it spreads. Misdirection in work creates stress that strains family relationships. Disorientation about your role creates confusion in multiple relationships. Limiting beliefs about worth affect how you show up in your community. Stagnation in one area creates restlessness that bleeds into everything. Cravings for achievement consume time meant for rest and connection.

This is why surface-level solutions fail—they treat symptoms while root sources continue generating problems everywhere else.

RootHealing makes you a different promise than symptom management:

Instead of: "We'll help you cope with your anxiety," RootHealing says: "We'll help you identify and resolve what's creating your anxiety."

Instead of: "Here's how to manage your stress," RootHealing says: "Here's how to eliminate the sources of unnecessary stress."

Instead of: "This will make you feel better temporarily," RootHealing says: "This will teach you to create lasting well-being."

When you address root sources rather than symptoms, something remarkable happens: Healing accelerates across your entire WholeBeing. Energy that was trapped in managing problems gets freed up for growth and fulfillment.

This is the power of RootHealing: address the source, and symptoms resolve themselves.

WHY MOST CHANGE EFFORTS FAIL

After undergoing lifesaving heart surgery, patients are given a stark warning: "If you don't change your lifestyle, you will die." The diagnosis is clear, the stakes are ultimate, the path forward is obvious. And yet nine out of ten don't change their lifestyles. They return to old eating habits, sedentary routines, and unchecked stress despite knowing the cost could be fatal.

This isn't a medical failure. It's an existential one.

The phenomenon reveals the invisible architecture of human suffering. Through the lens of RootHealing, we can see exactly how the five sources of existential suffering conspire to keep people trapped even when their life depends on breaking free. Heart surgery patients' experiences and my own blood pressure journey reveal how the five root sources create invisible barriers to change even when people intellectually and emotionally understand what needs to happen:

Misdirection means the missing why: Patients are told what not to do but not what to live for. They receive lists of restrictions—stop smoking, stop eating poorly, stop being sedentary—but restriction without direction is unsustainable.

Without a Purposehood rooted in meaning, fear becomes the only motivator. And fear fades.

The cardiologist says: "Avoid these foods or you'll have another heart attack." RootHealing asks: "What do you want to be healthy for? What matters enough to make these changes worthwhile?"

People don't change to avoid death. They change to pursue meaning.

Disorientation shatters identity. Heart surgery shatters more than arteries; it fractures identity. Patients lose their bearings. *Who am I if I can't eat what I love? How do I relate to my spouse as a "cardiac patient"? What does my future look like now?*

Without guidance to rebuild a coherent sense of self, patients drift in limbo, knowing they "should" change but unsure who they're becoming.

The medical system stabilizes the body but abandons the story. Patients are discharged with pill schedules but no narrative for their new life. RootHealing restores the narrative: this isn't the end of who you are—it's the beginning of who you're meant to become.

Limiting beliefs become inner saboteurs. Many patients carry unspoken scripts that doom change before it can begin: *I'm too old to change. It's too late for me. I've always been like this. I don't have the willpower.* These beliefs are rarely challenged in clinical settings. Doctors address cholesterol levels, not the internal narratives that drive behavior.

RootHealing rewrites the script. Change begins not with information but with permission—permission to believe in your own potential again.

Stagnation sets in when there's no vision for growth. Even patients who make initial changes often plateau. The medical system monitors vitals but offers no vision for what's possible beyond "normal" numbers. And in the absence of growth, stagnation sets in. Without new mountains to climb, old valleys become appealing again.

Recovery is just the starting line. RootHealing asks: Now that you have more time, what will you do with it? What would make this second chance meaningful?

Cravings return when Purposehood is absent: When Purposehood is absent, old cravings fill the vacuum. The comfort foods, numbing routines, and familiar vices all return because they're known, immediate, and available. Unless desires are realigned with a deeper why, patients inevitably relapse.

The answer is to redirect cravings toward something worth craving. What if the energy that once went toward food went toward grandchildren? What if the time spent watching TV became time in the garden?

RootHealing doesn't eliminate desire—it elevates it.

WHEN HEARTS BREAK FROM LOST PURPOSEHOOD

At a longevity workshop in Dubai, Dr. Hassan Sannoufi invited me to share the stage to discuss the importance of existential health. Dr. Sannoufi, a Purposehood-driven physician who had become a friend through our shared passion for holistic healing, had a story that illustrated the deeper complexities of healing.

He shared the case of a forty-five-year-old woman who came to his clinic a few months after her husband's sudden death from a heart attack. She arrived with chest pain, fatigue, and shortness of breath. Like many grieving patients, she'd been to several doctors, all of whom diagnosed her with stress or depression caused by grief. But Dr. Sannoufi's instincts told him there was something more.

He ran tests and discovered she had *takotsubo* cardiomyopathy, more commonly known as broken heart syndrome, a condition triggered by intense emotional trauma that can mimic a heart attack. But as the patient sat in Dr. Sannoufi's office, completely consumed by her loss, she said something that revealed the deeper crisis.

"He was my whole world," she told him, tears in her eyes. "I don't know who I am anymore without him. What's the point of all this?"

Dr. Sannoufi realized she wasn't just mourning her husband, she was mourning the loss of her own life's direction. Her identity and reason for being had been so closely tied to someone else that when he passed away, her purpose vanished along with him.

In her case, the unaddressed pain revealed all five sources of existential suffering at once:

Misdirection (primary): complete loss of life direction when her husband died. Her purpose was entirely external and dependent

Disorientation: lost in time (dwelling on the past), confused about her role (widow vs. wife), unclear about future goals

Limiting beliefs: *I can't exist without him. I'm nothing on my own. Love means total dependency*

Stagnation: stuck in grief, unable to move forward or envision growth

Cravings: excessive attachment to the relationship as her sole source of meaning and identity

Her broken heart syndrome was the physical manifestation of complete existential collapse. When external-dependent purpose disappears, the body itself can break down. But this story doesn't end in tragedy. Dr. Sannoufi understood that healing her heart required rebuilding existential health from the ground up.

EXISTENTIAL HEALTH—THE FOUNDATION OF ALL WELL-BEING

Dr. Sannoufi's widow patient reveals a profound truth: The strength of your existential foundation determines whether you rise or fall when life tests you. But what exactly is this foundation? And how do you build it strong enough to withstand any storm?

When we speak of health, most people immediately think of physical fitness—strong muscles, clear arteries, the absence of disease. Others might also think of mental and emotional wellness—managing stress, processing emotions, maintaining positive relationships. But there's a deeper dimension that underlies and influences all others: existential health.

Existential health is your ability to live with direction and meaning while navigating life's challenges with ease. It's what helps you overcome misdirection, disorientation, limiting beliefs, stagnation, and cravings, while staying rooted in core values like patience, gratitude, and connection—strengthening every other form of health.

As the foundation on which all other forms of well-being rest, existential health shapes our relationship with our place in the larger story of existence. While physical symptoms can be treated and emotional wounds can heal, existential misalignment creates a persistent ache that no amount of success, comfort, or achievement can ease.

Think of existential health as the root system of a mighty tree. Your physical, mental, emotional, spiritual, and relational health are like the branches—they can grow and bear fruit when conditions are right, but without deep, strong roots, even the most beautiful branches will topple when storms arise. Existential health provides those roots, drawing nourishment from what truly matters and keeping you grounded regardless of external circumstances.

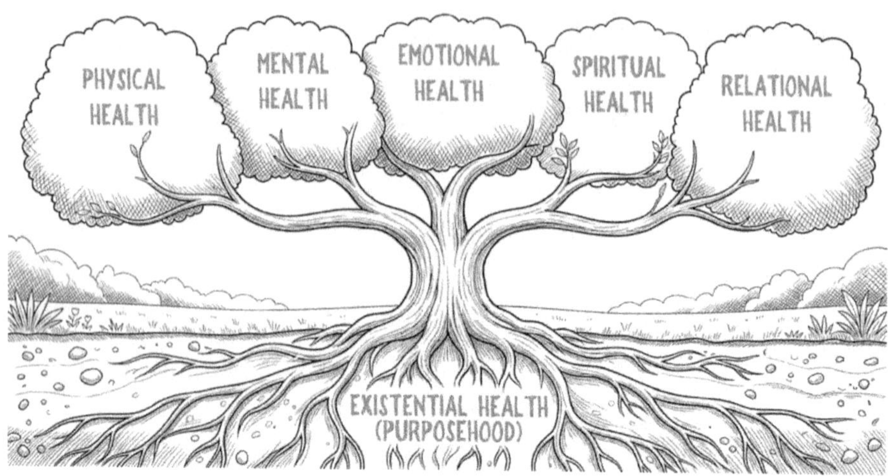

At the heart of existential health lies Purposehood—your unique existential purpose that gives life meaning and direction. This isn't simply about having goals or ambitions; it's about understanding your fundamental why—the reason you exist and the contribution you're called to make to life itself. When this foundation is strong, it influences every other aspect of your well-being:

Physical health becomes purposeful: Self-care transforms from a chore into an act of stewardship. Exercise, nutrition, and rest become ways of honoring your body as the vessel through which you express your Purposehood.

Mental health gains clarity: With existential direction, your mind has a filter for what deserves attention. Instead of being overwhelmed by endless options and obligations, you can focus on what aligns with your deeper values.

Emotional health finds stability: While still fluctuating, emotions are contextualized within a larger framework of meaning. Joy becomes gratitude for alignment; struggle becomes an opportunity for growth and deeper understanding.

Spiritual health deepens: Your connection to something greater than yourself becomes more authentic and grounded. Whether through meditation, prayer, or contemplation, spiritual practices gain deeper meaning when rooted in your life's purpose, creating a sense of transcendence that supports resilience and inner peace.

Relational health strengthens: When you're clear on your life's purpose, you approach relationships with intention. You attract people who share or support your values, and you contribute to others' well-being from a place of abundance rather than need. Your relationship with nature also transforms. The natural world becomes a source of healing, an inspiration for resilience, and a wellspring of creativity as you recognize your place in the larger web of life.

Without a foundation, people often experience what Viktor Frankl—founder of logotherapy and the third school of Viennese psychiatry—called an "existential vacuum," a profound sense of meaninglessness that can't be filled by external achievements. This shows up both in existential ways and in daily emotional struggles you might recognize:

Existential symptoms: feeling successful by external measures yet hollow inside, chronic restlessness despite having "everything you need," decision paralysis when faced with choices, relationships that feel superficial, work that pays well but drains your soul, a persistent question: "Is this all there is?"

Daily emotional symptoms: persistent anxiety that doesn't match your circumstances, stress that feels disproportionate to actual problems, depression that medication doesn't fully resolve, regrets that cycle endlessly, a nagging sense that you're living someone else's life.

These different types of symptoms are different expressions of the same underlying disconnection from existential health. The anxiety, stress, and depression are often symptoms of the deeper vacuum that Frankl identified.

This isn't a character flaw or a sign of weakness; it's a signal that your existential health needs attention.

When existential health is strong, the effects ripple outward through every extension of your being. People with robust existential health naturally:

Navigate crises with steady resolve because they see challenges as chapters in a larger story, not threats to their identity

Make difficult decisions without endless second-guessing, because they have an internal compass calibrated to what truly matters

Attract and build relationships that energize rather than drain because they engage from wholeness, not neediness

Find purpose even in mundane work because they connect daily tasks to their larger contribution to the world

Maintain energy and focus without constant willpower because their choices flow from deep alignment rather than forced discipline

Experience spiritual practices as nourishment, not obligation, because their inner work connects to lived meaning

Feel restored by nature rather than just entertained by it because they recognize their place in the larger web of existence

Sleep better, worry less, and laugh more freely because their foundation is solid enough to support true joy

Developing existential health isn't about finding your "one true calling" or having a dramatic revelation about your life's purpose. It's about consistently aligning your daily choices, relationships, and commitments with your deepest values, your understanding of what it means to live a meaningful life.

This alignment creates *ease,* the ability to navigate life's inevitable difficulties from a place of groundedness and clarity. When you're existentially healthy, you don't drain energy resisting reality or doubting your direction; you meet life as it is, with clarity and conviction.

But what are the specific qualities that support existential health and help us navigate the sources of suffering that can knock us off course?

This is where the Ten Purposehood Pillars of Existential Health become essential to creating unshakable holistic well-being from the inside out.

TEN PURPOSEHOOD PILLARS OF EXISTENTIAL HEALTH

Through decades of walking alongside people on their journeys of healing and growth, informed by both ancient wisdom and modern research, I've identified ten universal qualities that form the pillars of existential health. These aren't personality traits you're born with—they're capacities you can develop, strengthen, and rely on throughout your life.

Think of these as the pillars supporting the foundation of your Whole-Being:

PILLAR 1: DIRECTION—KNOW YOUR PATH

Direction is about having a clear sense of where you're headed in life. It's the ability to define your Purposehood—your personal guiding star that informs your actions and decisions. When you have direction, everything you do is aligned with your overarching goal, providing life with coherence and deep purpose.

Without direction, you may feel lost, drifting aimlessly, vulnerable to distractions and overwhelmed by the pressures of daily life. Studies show that people with a clear sense of purpose tend to experience higher levels of resilience, better mental health, and overall life satisfaction. Direction gives us clarity, helping us make choices that feel meaningful and aligned with our values.

You don't have to have every detail mapped out. Direction is about knowing your true north. Your sense of direction keeps you oriented toward what matters most, even when the path becomes complicated or unclear.

PILLAR 2: ENDURANCE—EMBRACE THE LONG JOURNEY

Endurance is the strength to persist when life gets tough. It's the ability to stay committed to your path even in the face of challenges and setbacks. Life is full of difficult moments, and existential health requires the resilience to push through them, trusting that your journey is worth it.

Research published in the *Journal of Positive Psychology* shows that people who develop endurance tend to experience greater emotional resilience and mental well-being. Endurance is about embracing life's long journey, knowing that obstacles are part of growth. By strengthening this pillar, we cultivate the stamina needed to maintain our sense of Purposehood, no matter how difficult.

Endurance doesn't mean gritting your teeth and pushing through pain; it means finding the deeper meaning in your struggles that gives you strength to continue. It's the difference between surviving and thriving through adversity.

PILLAR 3: EMPOWERMENT—RECLAIM CONTROL

Empowerment is about taking ownership of your life. It means recognizing that while you can't control every external circumstance, you have agency over your thoughts, actions, and responses. Empowerment isn't about controlling what happens to you—it's about controlling how you respond to what happens. This includes taking charge of your own healing and growth rather than remaining dependent on others to fix or improve your situation.

A study in *Psychological Review* found that people who feel empowered are more likely to achieve their goals, experience satisfaction in their work, and have healthier relationships. Empowerment enables us to take meaningful steps toward growth and fulfillment, all while aligning with our Purposehood.

True empowerment comes from understanding that your response to any situation is always within your control. This realization is liberating; it means you're never truly powerless, even in the most challenging circumstances.

PILLAR 4: CONTENTMENT—FIND PEACE IN THE PRESENT

Contentment is about finding peace and satisfaction in the present moment. It allows us to appreciate where we are while still being open to growth. Contentment isn't complacency; it's experiencing joy and fulfillment without constantly striving for more.

Research from the *Journal of Happiness Studies* reveals that people who practice contentment experience lower levels of stress and anxiety and are more resilient to life's ups and downs. By nurturing contentment, we create emotional balance and promote mental well-being, allowing us to enjoy life as it unfolds.

Contentment provides the emotional stability needed for sustainable growth. When you're not constantly anxious about the future or regretful about the past, you can be fully present to the opportunities and relationships in front of you.

PILLAR 5: AMBITION—STRIVE FOR GROWTH

Ambition is the drive to reach beyond your current circumstances. It's not just about material success but about striving for growth, learning, and achievement in a way that aligns with your values and Purposehood. While contentment provides peace, ambition pushes you forward, challenging you to evolve and fulfill your potential.

Research reported in the *Personality and Social Psychology Bulletin* suggests that people who pursue ambitious, value-aligned goals experience higher life satisfaction. Healthy ambition isn't about endless striving; it's about meaningful progress toward your personal aspirations while staying rooted in your Purposehood.

The key to healthy ambition is ensuring it serves your Purposehood rather than your ego. When ambition is aligned with meaning, it becomes a powerful force for positive change in your life and the lives of others.

PILLAR 6: PATIENCE—TRUST THE PROCESS

In our fast-paced world, patience is often undervalued, but it's essential for long-term success. Patience is the ability to trust the process, allowing things to unfold in their own time without rushing or forcing outcomes. It's about understanding that growth, healing, and progress take time and that sometimes the best outcomes come from waiting.

According to research in the *Journal of Behavioral Science,* people who cultivate patience experience lower levels of stress and greater success in achieving their long-term goals. Patience allows us to approach life with greater clarity and minimizes impulsivity, helping us make decisions aligned with our deeper purpose.

Patience isn't passive waiting; it's active trust. It's maintaining clarity in your direction and continuing to take meaningful action even when results don't come immediately.

PILLAR 7: GRATITUDE—CULTIVATE APPRECIATION

Gratitude is the practice of recognizing and appreciating the good in your life. It shifts your focus from what's missing to what's present, helping you build emotional resilience and find joy in the everyday. Gratitude creates a mindset of abundance, making it easier to experience fulfillment even in difficult times.

A study published in *Psychological Science* found that gratitude enhances emotional well-being and strengthens social bonds. By regularly practicing gratitude, we can lower stress, ease feelings of anxiety, and build stronger emotional resilience. Gratitude also shifts our perspective, allowing us to see abundance where cravings might have taken hold.

One of the most transformative of all practices, gratitude reshapes the brain, activating regions linked to reward, optimism, and connection, and strengthening the neural pathways that support lasting well-being.

PILLAR 8: CONNECTION—BUILD MEANINGFUL RELATIONSHIPS

Our relationships form the foundation of our emotional, mental, and spiritual well-being. Whether with family, friends, colleagues, or community members, meaningful connections provide us with support, belonging, and fulfillment.

The Harvard Study of Adult Development, one of the longest-running studies on happiness, found that the quality of our relationships is the most important factor in predicting long-term happiness and health. Nurturing relationships where you can be loving and supportive and grow together strengthens our sense of self and enhances overall well-being. These connections become sources of strength during challenges and joy during celebrations.

PILLAR 9: MATTERING—KNOW YOU MAKE A DIFFERENCE

Mattering is the belief that your life and actions are significant. It's the feeling that you have an impact on others, your community, or the world at large. When we feel like we matter, we're more likely to engage in meaningful work and contribute to the well-being of those around us.

Research from *Social Psychology Quarterly* found that people who believe they matter to others experience higher levels of life satisfaction and are more likely to engage in altruistic behavior. This pillar is key to feeling purposeful and connected to life's bigger picture.

Far from egotistic, the sense that you matter is about understanding that your unique contribution to the world is needed and valued. This understanding drives engagement and creates a sense of responsibility for making a positive difference.

PILLAR 10: MEANING—LIVE A PURPOSEFUL LIFE

Meaning is the pillar that ties everything together. It's the deep sense that your life, actions, and experiences are aligned with something greater. When we live a meaningful life, we find purpose in the everyday and feel connected to something bigger than ourselves.

Viktor Frankl's *Man's Search for Meaning* argues that the pursuit of meaning is essential for enduring life's challenges and finding fulfillment. Research reported in the *Journal of Positive Psychology* confirms that people who have a strong sense of meaning are more resilient and experience greater life satisfaction.

Meaning emerges when all the other pillars work together—when your direction is clear, your endurance is strong, your connections are deep, and your actions reflect your values. It's the integration of everything into a coherent whole that makes life feel worth living.

These ten pillars work together to create an unshakable foundation for existential health. They work together like interconnected beams, each one reinforcing the others to support holistic well-being.

DIRECTION + ENDURANCE + EMPOWERMENT + CONTENTMENT + AMBITION + PATIENCE +GRATITUDE + CONNECTION + MATTERING + MEANING = EXISTENTIAL HEALTH

This equation represents the existential health components within The Purpose-hood Method for Existential Health—ten interconnected pillars that, when culti-vated together, create optimal existential health and a life worth loving.

When the pillars are strong, the five root sources of suffering can't take hold. Misdirection is impossible when you have direction. Disorienta-tion dissolves with endurance and patience. Limiting beliefs crumble before empowerment and mattering. Stagnation can't survive ambition balanced with contentment. Cravings transform into purposeful pur-suit when meaning and gratitude guide them.

When you understand and strengthen these pillars, you create the con-ditions for navigating any challenge with ease and growing through any circumstance with intention. But how does this work in real life? How do these pillars manifest when someone faces ultimate challenges? Let's return to our widow story to see RootHealing in action.

WHEN PURPOSEHOOD BECOMES MEDICINE

Dr. Sannoufi's widow patient reveals a profound truth about healing: When existential health collapses, physical and mental symptoms fol-low. But her transformation didn't happen through medication alone. It required rebuilding the very foundation of her being. Her journey illustrates how the Purposehood Pillars work together to restore not just emotional balance but physical health itself.

Dr. Sannoufi didn't dismiss his patient's grief or rush her through it. He recognized that her healing required rebuilding existential health from the ground up. Her broken heart syndrome had revealed something deeper than medical textbooks typically address—when life's purpose becomes entirely external, its loss can be literally heartbreaking.

"She wasn't just mourning her husband," Dr. Sannoufi said. "She was mourning the loss of her entire reason for being."

Rather than treating only her physical symptoms, Dr. Sannoufi began addressing the existential sources of her suffering. Looking back, we can see that five of the Ten Purposehood Pillars of Existential Health were especially active in her healing:

Direction: He helped her discover intrinsic values that existed independently of any relationship—her deep capacity for care, her ability to create safety for others, her gift for understanding pain.

Empowerment: Instead of remaining passive in grief, she began taking small steps toward rebuilding, first reaching out to friends, then joining a support group.

Patience: She learned to trust the slow process of healing, understanding that grief has its own timeline and that recovery can't be rushed. She allowed her heart to heal at its natural pace, maintaining faith that meaning would emerge from her suffering in time.

Mattering: Through supporting other widows, she began to see that her significance extended beyond being someone's wife. Her survival and healing could serve something larger.

Meaning: Gradually, she began to see that her capacity to love deeply—the very thing that made her husband's loss so devastating—could become the foundation for service to others facing loss.

The transformation wasn't quick, but these five pillars of existential health worked together to help her rediscover a sense of Purposehood, one that wasn't dependent on any single person. RootHealing addressed the existential collapse at the source, and she slowly built an existential purpose that was broader than any single relationship could contain, one that could carry her through whatever life might bring in the future. Within two months, her chest pain had resolved, her energy returned, and her heart had healed.

While her case showed Purposehood being reconstructed after collapse, Dr. Sannoufi had once witnessed something even more remarkable in his practice.

A DIFFERENT KIND OF PATIENT

"One of the most impactful stories in my career happened fifteen years ago," Dr. Sannoufi began as he addressed the audience at our Dubai workshop.

A fifty-six-year-old life insurance broker had come to his clinic in Ontario, Canada, with facial numbness and brief speech loss. "I lost my speech for a few moments, but I'm fine now," he said. "Maybe I'm just stressed."

Dr. Sannoufi's instincts told him to dig deeper and he ordered an MRI.

The results were devastating: glioblastoma multiforme, one of the most aggressive and deadly brain cancers. Most patients with this diagnosis don't survive long.

"Delivering this news is never easy," Dr. Sannoufi said. "I sat him down and explained the situation, preparing to offer support. 'You have a bad cancer,' I said, 'but we'll get through this together.'"

The patient listened calmly, then surprised Dr. Sannoufi completely with his response.

"I can't die now. I have too many life insurance policies sitting on my desk. I need to close them."

Dr. Sannoufi was taken aback. "I was thinking, 'This man has terminal cancer and he's worried about work?' I didn't say it out loud, but I couldn't help thinking it."

He asked the patient more about his work and why it mattered so much.

At fourteen, the patient had lost his father unexpectedly. His mother, a homemaker with no income, was left with a mortgage and no financial resources. They had to sell their home and move into a one-bedroom apartment. It was a painful and traumatic time in his life, and he made a vow—he wouldn't let another family go through what his family had.

"I've spent my whole life making sure families are protected if something happens to their loved ones," he explained. "That's my purpose. That's why I get up every day."

"In that moment, I realized his work wasn't just a job," Dr. Sannoufi told us. "It was his existential purpose, the very thing that gave his life meaning. He wasn't just fighting cancer for himself—he was fighting for the families he had promised to protect."

Against all odds, he survived. He beat one of the deadliest cancers known to medicine. His oncologists, radiologists, and surgeons were baffled by his recovery.

Dr. Sannoufi asked what had kept him going.

"Every morning, I woke up and asked God for just one more day," he said. "I needed another day to finish my work, to protect more families."

Fifteen years later, a few days after sharing these stories at our Dubai workshop, Dr. Sannoufi sent me a WhatsApp message from his clinic in Ottawa:

> *Something unexpected happened yesterday. I saw the hero of my story, the life insurance broker, sitting in our clinic waiting room with his wife.*

Without even thinking for a second, I came to him and hugged him. I normally don't hug patients. The first thing that came out of my mouth was, 'Are you still in the business of protecting families?' He responded with a smile, 'Yes, and I'm still not ready to die.'

His survival wasn't a medical miracle; it was a Purposehood miracle. His rooted existential purpose activated every pillar of existential health, making his spirit stronger than the statistics.

While the widow's case shows what happens when Purposehood becomes externally dependent, requiring intentional reconstruction of existential health through the Ten Purposehood Pillars, the insurance broker's case demonstrates what happens when all pillars are naturally aligned through authentic existential purpose—it can create existential health so robust it can sustain life against impossible odds. Both cases reveal that existential health isn't about avoiding suffering but about having sufficient meaning and Purposehood to transform suffering into healing and growth.

Dr. Sannoufi himself is a purpose-driven professional who has been prescribing my book *Purposehood: Transform Your Life, Transform the World* to his patients to help them discover their life purpose on their journey to healing and holistic well-being. He once remarked that the book can feel heavy for some patients, and he wished there were an easier version to prescribe.

Well, Dr. Sannoufi, I hope this book will do.

⏸ PURPOSEHOOD PAUSE

Reflect on your personal pillars of existential health.

Assessment: Which pillars feel strongest in your life right now? Which ones feel underdeveloped or strained?

Integration: How do these pillars influence one another in your life? For example, how does your sense of direction shape your ambition? How does gratitude affect your connections?

Action: Choose *one* pillar to intentionally strengthen this month. What is one concrete practice or habit that would support it?

Let your answers guide your next steps, not just in thought but in daily alignment.

FROM INSIGHT TO TRANSFORMATION

You now understand the profound truth behind RootHealing. Most suffering stems not from circumstances but from five deeper sources that create symptoms across your entire WholeBeing. You've seen how addressing misdirection, disorientation, limiting beliefs, stagnation, and cravings at their source can literally heal hearts and sustain life against impossible odds. Let that awareness settle; it is already medicine. The widow's transformation and the insurance broker's survival happened through awareness and systematic engagement with what was actually creating their suffering. When you're ready, we'll turn next to the process that makes change sustainable.

CHAPTER 4

EASE LEADERSHIP
TAKING CHARGE OF YOUR CHANGE

Nora had spent a decade building a successful therapy practice. Her clients trusted her, her techniques were evidence-based, and her schedule was always full. But sitting in her car after another session with David, a tech executive who'd been coming for two years of regular sessions, she felt something she'd never expected: guilt.

"I don't feel broken," he told her in session forty-seven, "but I also don't feel alive. I've read all the books, done the journaling, the breath work, the coaching. I understand my past and my triggers, but I still feel lost."

David had gained tremendous insight into his patterns, understood his triggers, and could articulate his challenges with remarkable clarity, but between appointments, he'd find himself right back where he started: anxious, overwhelmed, and unable to make lasting changes on his own. Two years of sessions had given him tremendous insight but zero capability to transform his daily experience independently.

"I've become addicted to therapy," he confessed to Nora. "Not because it was helping me heal but because it was the only place I felt capable of healing. The moment I leave your office, I feel powerless again."

That night, Nora scribbled on her whiteboard: "What if the goal of therapy is graduation—and the beginning of contribution?"

From that moment, her entire approach shifted.

That moment revealed a truth most people never see—we've been taught that healing happens *to* us, not *through* us.

THE TREATMENT TRAP

David's struggle is systemic. It reveals a troubling truth that affects not just health care but therapy, coaching, and every form of personal development.

Think about it. When you're struggling, what's the first thing people tell you to do? "Go see someone." Find a therapist. Hire a coach. Take this medication. Follow this program. The underlying message is always the same: you need someone else to fix you.

This creates a dependency cycle, a pattern where people become passive recipients of care rather than active participants in their own transformation. They learn to wait for appointments, rely on prescriptions, and look to experts for answers that only they can ultimately provide.

The statistics are staggering. Despite the fact that we spend more on mental health services than ever before, rates of anxiety, depression, and existential emptiness continue to climb. Why? Because traditional approaches, however well-intentioned, often reinforce the very helplessness they're trying to heal.

Nora knew this pattern all too well. She'd watched it play out with countless clients over the years. They'd make progress in sessions, gain insights, and develop coping strategies but somehow remained fundamentally unchanged in their capacity to handle challenges on their own.

"I started noticing that many of my clients weren't stuck because of their trauma," she told me. "They were stuck because no one had taught them how to heal themselves."

They had insight, even courage, but no process. Nora realized she had unintentionally become a crutch. Clients like David returned for years, not because they hadn't made progress but because they hadn't been empowered to sustain that progress alone or share it with others. They'd built homes in the waiting room of healing.

When we position ourselves as patients who need to be "fixed" by experts, we unconsciously surrender our agency. We learn to depend on external validation, professional guidance, and prescribed solutions rather than developing our own capacity for healing and growth. This learned helplessness becomes self-reinforcing.

Nora's realization hit her hardest when she picked up my earlier book, *Purposehood: Transform Your Life, Transform the World.* One key insight stood out: "You are not a problem to be solved. You are a potential to be unleashed."

This reflects a broader challenge facing many well-meaning professionals in the healing and growth space.

WHEN HELPING CREATES DEPENDENCY

Even well-meaning professionals can inadvertently perpetuate this cycle. When therapists become the sole source of insight, when coaches position themselves as the experts with all the answers, when programs promise instant transformation if you just follow their prescribed steps, they're reinforcing dependency, not leadership.

This isn't to diminish the valuable role professionals play. The best therapists, coaches, and healers understand that their job isn't to fix their clients but to guide them toward fixing themselves. They know that sustainable change comes from within and that their role is to facilitate that inner transformation, not replace it.

But too many approaches still operate from the old paradigm: expert knows best, patient follows instructions, healing happens through treatment. This model might work for broken bones, but it fails miserably when it comes to broken spirits, confused purposes, and misaligned lives.

What if there were a different way? What if instead of creating patients, we created existential leaders—people skilled in the art of their own healing and growth? What if instead of offering temporary relief, we provided lasting capability to lead themselves and eventually guide others?

This is the promise of the third principle of The Purposehood Method for Existential Health: EASE Leadership. EASE Leadership is existential leadership made practical, a process that teaches you how to lead your own healing and growth. It's built on a radical premise that flies in the face of conventional wisdom. You already have everything you need to heal and grow; you just need the right process to access it.

You don't need someone to fix you. You need someone to show you how to systematically engineer your own transformation. You don't need another treatment. You need training in the art of leading yourself toward wholeness.

Nora overhauled her model. She created Purposehood Expansion Circles, small group programs built around structure, growth, and eventual independence. Each participant learned to understand their WholeBeing and apply practical tools to their lives. After nine sessions, they began preparing to guide others.

Nora no longer saw herself as the healer. She became a facilitator of existential leadership development—and it worked. Her clients didn't just feel better; they became capable of helping others feel better.

This is the essence of EASE Leadership.

TREATMENT VS. TRAINING

There's a fundamental difference between a doctor and a fitness trainer that exposes what's flawed in how we approach healing and growth.

When you go to a doctor with a broken arm, they set the bone, apply a cast, and send you home. You're passive in the process—the doctor does the work, and your body heals. This is treatment, and it works perfectly for acute physical problems.

But when you work with a fitness trainer, something entirely different happens. The trainer doesn't get strong for you. They don't lift your weights or run your miles. Instead, they teach you how to lift correctly, how to push your limits safely, and how to build strength systematically over time. They're training you to become your own expert. This is training, and it's the only thing that works for lasting transformation.

Most approaches to mental, emotional, and existential challenges still operate like the doctor model. You show up with your "broken" life, the expert applies their technique, and you're expected to feel better. The problem? You remain fundamentally unchanged in your capacity to handle challenges.

Of course, there are serious clinical conditions, such as bipolar disorder, severe depression, or suicidality, that require medical treatment, professional care, and sometimes urgent intervention. Here, I'm speaking about the more universal struggles of living where training in existential leadership becomes not only possible but essential.

Consider what happens in traditional therapy:

Sessions 1-10: You learn to identify your patterns. Sessions 11-20: You gain insights about your past. Sessions 21-30: You develop coping strategies. Sessions 31+: You keep coming back because you haven't learned to be your own therapist.

Don't get me wrong. Therapy, in most cases, can be incredibly valuable. But too often, it creates therapeutic dependency. Clients feel capable only within the safety of the therapeutic relationship but remain helpless in their daily lives.

What if we approached healing the way we approach fitness? Instead of treating people, what if we trained them to lead themselves through the process? A great trainer doesn't just help you lose weight—they teach you how to maintain a healthy lifestyle forever. They help you understand your body well enough to trust it, read it, and lead it. Their goal isn't dependency; it's capability.

That's what's missing from most approaches to personal transformation. People don't just need treatment—they need training in existential leadership and the skills to navigate life's challenges on their own.

The treatment model assumes the professional knows better than you do. But no one has lived your life except you. A trainer understands this. They don't tell an athlete what to feel; they teach them how to listen. They don't impose a universal program; they help someone discover what works for their body, their history, and their goals.

> **TREATMENT MODEL:** EXPERT HAS THE ANSWERS → CLIENT RECEIVES SOLUTIONS → FOCUS ON FIXING PROBLEMS → CREATES DEPENDENCY → TEMPORARY RELIEF → CLIENT REMAINS HELPLESS WITHOUT EXPERT.
>
> **TRAINING MODEL:** EXPERT PROVIDES PROCESS → CLIENT DISCOVERS SOLUTIONS → FOCUS ON BUILDING LEADERSHIP CAPACITY → CREATES EXISTENTIAL LEADERSHIP → LASTING CAPABILITY → CLIENT BECOMES ABLE TO LEAD THEMSELVES AND GUIDE OTHERS

The same is true for existential health. You don't need someone to hand you a purpose or manage your life for you. You need the capacity to discover meaning, build healthy relationships, and lead your own well-being.

Support still matters—even Olympic athletes have coaches. But the aim is different: to develop people who can move through life with skill, confidence, and wisdom, and who naturally become guides for others along the way.

BEYOND MOTIVATION TO CAPABILITY

The word *leadership* often evokes images of people in positions of power—CEOs, presidents, team captains. But leadership in the context of healing and growth is something deeper and more universal. As I wrote in *Purposehood*: "Everyone is a leader, and their responsibility is to unleash the potentiality of those they influence."

But that influence begins with how you lead yourself.

Most people think leadership is about making decisions or influencing others. That's not wrong, but it's incomplete. True leadership starts with choosing how you respond to life. It's about commanding your own process of becoming. Before you lead anyone else, you must lead yourself through pain, through uncertainty, and toward growth.

In our culture, leadership has become confused with charisma and motivation. We're sold inspiration as if it were transformation. We feel fired up by a speech, a resolution, or a morning ritual and we mistake that fire for real change. But inspiration without structure is like a spark with no wood: bright for a moment and then gone.

Existential leadership isn't about how loudly you roar on January 1. It's about what you're still doing on February 15. That's why EASE begins with building capability, confidence, and process—systematically, one step at a time.

THE THREE STAGES OF EASE LEADERSHIP DEVELOPMENT

EASE Leadership follows a natural progression, much like growing from child to adult to parent:

Stage 1: The Child – *Someone else needs to lead me.* Like a child who depends on parents for guidance, direction, and care, you look to others for answers about your healing and growth. It's a natural starting point. Children need loving guidance to develop their own capabilities; you seek therapists, coaches, and programs to help you understand yourself and navigate your challenges.

Stage 2: The Adult – *I can lead my own life.* Like an adult who's learned to make their own decisions and take responsibility for their choices, you develop the capability to navigate your own challenges and create sustainable change. You still seek wisdom from others, but you're the primary author of your life. You've learned to be your own most reliable source of direction and growth.

Stage 3: The Parent – *I can help others grow.* Like a parent who guides children by helping them discover their own capabilities, you naturally become someone others turn to for support because you've learned how to help people find their own answers. You unleash the potentiality of those you influence, just as loving parents do.

EASE Leadership = Capability × Confidence × Process

EASE leadership in your own life depends on three essential components:

Capability: the skills and knowledge to create change

Confidence: trust in your ability to navigate challenges

Process: a systematic approach you can repeat and refine

Remove any one of these and existential leadership collapses:

Capability without confidence leads to self-doubt and hesitation

Confidence without capability leads to reckless decisions and eventual failure

Process without the other two becomes empty ritual

Any two without the third creates temporary success that doesn't last

WHAT SEPARATES LEADERS FROM HOPEFUL STARTERS

We see it everywhere: gyms full in January and empty by March. People start strong, but without structure their efforts dissolve. Belief without process isn't leadership—it's hope—and while hope is a beautiful thing, leadership is what builds.

The fitness industry perfectly illustrates why willpower-based approaches don't work. The people who fill the gyms every January are highly motivated and rely purely on willpower to change their bodies. They don't have a systematic process, they don't understand proper form, and they don't know how to build capability gradually.

What happens? They burn out, get injured or simply lose motivation when results don't come fast enough. The ones who succeed are the ones who develop a systematic approach to building fitness over time.

The same principle applies to every area of life. You can't will your way to better relationships, meaningful work, or inner peace. You need a process that builds your existential leadership capability systematically while reinforcing your confidence through small consistent wins.

When you lead yourself with capability, confidence, and a clear process, you become the kind of person who naturally influences others by example. You don't have all the answers, but you know how to systematically find them. This is EASE Leadership.

THE EASE PROCESS

The third principle of The Purposehood Method for Existential Health, EASE transforms insight into action—and action into a life worth loving.

Each of the four steps is designed to develop specific existential leadership skills that compound over time:

E – Engage: building authentic commitment to change

A – Assess: creating clarity through systematic observation

S – Support: tailored guidance that make change sustainable

E – Enact: embedding transformation into daily life

1. ENGAGE – ARE YOU READY TO TRANSFORM?

Genuine engagement begins with three essential questions that determine your readiness for EASE Leadership:

- Am I open to change? Without genuine openness to transformation and willingness to receive help, nothing meaningful can begin.

- Do I trust this method or guide? Change requires trust in something—a process, a system, or a person. Without trust, every step forward feels unstable.

- Am I willing to do the work? Not once, but consistently. When it's hard. When it's inconvenient. When no one else is watching.

These aren't screening questions—they're activation tools designed to help you step fully into leadership rather than just participating intellectually. Engagement is about existential commitment that endures regardless of how you feel on any given day.

2. ASSESS – WHERE ARE YOU IN YOUR WHOLEBEING?

You can't navigate to where you want to go without knowing exactly where you are. Assessment means mapping your current state across all five extensions of your being—Self, Family, Work, Communities, and Nature—to understand which areas are thriving and which need attention.

The REVEAL360™—Purposehood® WholeBeing Assessment reveals which components of your life are in different zones of well-being: contracting, healing, comfortable, or growing. When you understand your whole situation accurately, you can finally stop scattered efforts and start making strategic moves that honor your actual readiness for effective leadership.

3. SUPPORT – TAILORED HELP THAT MATCHES THE ZONE

Different zones require different types of support. Someone struggling needs different assistance from someone who's comfortable but stagnant. Using the ART framework—Attain, Retain, Train—you'll learn to shift from negative states to positive ones, stabilize your progress, and build resilience for whatever comes next.

4. ENACT – TURN PRACTICE INTO LIFESTYLE

Implementation is about turning insights into sustainable change through three dynamics: Do it. Habitually. Together. You'll learn to take zone-aware action, integrate practices across your WholeBeing, and build community support that makes transformation feel natural rather than forced.

This is how understanding becomes embodiment and how temporary changes become permanent ways of being.

True existential leadership extends beyond yourself. When you develop real capability in healing and growth, you naturally become someone who can support others in their journeys too. It isn't about becoming a professional coach or therapist. It's about becoming the kind of person others turn to when they're struggling—a parent helping a child, a teacher guiding students, a manager supporting coworkers, a community member lifting neighbors, or a group moderator holding space for their circle group.

That's what happened for Nora, who now trains people in EASE Leadership in schools, parenting workshops, and organizations. Instead of offering endless sessions, she offers frameworks for self-guided transformation.

"I'm not here to fix you," she tells her circles. "I'm here to train you to guide yourself—and eventually someone else."

Real leadership creates a ripple effect. Leaders develop other leaders, not through preaching or advice-giving but through modeling what's possible and sharing practical processes that work.

Before I could teach this to others, though, I had to live it myself.

WHEN MY HEART STOPPED, EVERYTHING STARTED

I learned the hard way that transformation isn't something that happens *to* you—it's something you must systematically create. The lesson came in the most unexpected way: through death itself.

"Can you open your eyes?" The nurse's voice seemed to come from far away. I didn't want to open my eyes. For the first time in years, I was at peace. My body was still on the table in the clinic where they'd been running tests to figure out why I'd been fainting, but my mind was elsewhere. In that moment, I felt no fear or anxiety, just a deep serene calm. Even now, recalling that feeling gives me goosebumps.

The nurse held the phone to my ear. "Ammar, you need to go to the hospital right away," I heard my doctor say. But even then I wasn't worried. All I wanted was to stay in that peaceful state.

Months earlier, I'd stood in the mountains of Switzerland surrounded by breathtaking views, but all I could think about were the challenges in my life. It had been years since I'd felt anything remotely close to peace. Business stress had slowly invaded every aspect of my existence: my relationships, my family, and ultimately, myself. I was easily irritated and unable to focus, and my spiritual practices felt empty. My body had started reacting with fainting spells, as if the weight of life had become too heavy to carry.

When the doctor showed me the printed results of my cardiogram, I saw that I'd flatlined. My heart had stopped. And in that moment of clinical death, one question had echoed in my mind: What was it all for? If my life had ended that day, what would it have all been about? And now that I'm alive, what should it be all about?

That question became the catalyst for everything that followed, not just my personal transformation but also the systematic approach that would eventually become EASE. It was as if my entire operating system had been wiped clean, like a computer reformatted. All the old labels, expectations, and corrupt files were erased. What remained was a blank slate.

The question—*What should it all be for?*—cut through all the noise, all the distractions, all the surface-level concerns that had been consuming my energy. Suddenly, nothing mattered except finding an authentic answer. I realized I'd been living reactively, responding to whatever crisis or opportunity presented itself, without ever truly engaging with my deeper purpose. Now I was engaging with the fundamental question of existence.

Real engagement, I discovered, is about asking the hard questions and being willing to face whatever answers emerge. It's about commitment born from clarity, not enthusiasm born from desperation. And the flatlining experience taught me that it begins with a moment of radical honesty: Am I living the life I actually meant to live, or am I just surviving the life that happened to me?

Coming back from that experience, I realized I needed to understand my entire situation—not just the business stress that triggered my health crisis but everything. My relationships, my work, my spiritual life, my physical health, my connection to community and nature. I needed to see the whole picture. I needed to take an honest inventory, like a business owner conducting an audit. What was working? What wasn't? Where were the real problems hiding? What strengths did I have to build on?

What I discovered was that my crisis wasn't really about business stress; that was just the symptom. The real issues were deeper: I'd lost connection with my Purposehood, I was trying to be everything to everyone, and I had no systematic way to maintain balance across all areas of my life.

Most important, I learned that you can't fix what you can't see clearly. I needed to develop the clarity to understand my whole situation so I could make intelligent decisions about where to focus my energy. And I needed a way to systematically address what I discovered.

My engineering background taught me that any complex system requires structured design and reliable processes, but I'd never applied that thinking to my own life. I realized that sustainable transformation requires systematic support: structures, practices, and processes that support change even when you don't feel like changing.

This meant developing specific practices for different aspects of my life, creating accountability systems, and learning to make tiny adjustments consistently rather than attempting dramatic overhauls that never lasted. The key insight was that support isn't just about getting help from others, though that's important. It's about creating a systematic approach to supporting your own transformation. It's about becoming your own best coach, your own most reliable source of guidance and encouragement.

The final piece of the puzzle was the hardest: turning insights and practices into a sustainable way of life. I'd gained clarity about my purpose, I understood my whole situation, and I'd developed supportive practices, but would I actually live differently six months later?

This is where most transformation efforts fail. People have breakthrough moments, they create beautiful plans, and they start strong, but they don't build the daily systems that make change inevitable rather than optional. Enacting transformation means embedding new ways of being so deeply into your daily life that they become automatic, creating systems that help you quickly return to alignment when you drift off course. I learned to see setbacks not as failures but as information. Every time I slipped back into old patterns, I could use that experience to strengthen my systems rather than beating myself up for not being perfect.

What emerged from my personal crisis was a recognition that transformation follows discoverable patterns. The same systematic approach that helped me rebuild my life could help anyone navigate their own challenges and growth. The four elements I discovered weren't unique to my situation: Everyone needs genuine engagement with their deeper questions. Everyone benefits from clear assessment of their whole situation. Everyone requires systematic support to create lasting change. And everyone has to learn to enact transformation as a way of life.

EASE became that systematic approach.

WHY EASE SUCCEEDS

EASE works because it addresses the four most common reasons that transformation efforts fail:

Lack of authentic commitment (solved by "engage")

Unclear understanding of the real situation (solved by "assess")

No systematic approach to creating change (solved by "support")

Inability to sustain new behaviors (solved by "enact")

Most important, EASE treats you as the leader of your own life. The process provides structure, but you provide the content. This ensures that your transformation is authentically yours, not someone else's vision imposed on your life.

One of the most powerful aspects of EASE is that it's not a one-time program you complete and move on from. It's a cyclical process that deepens and evolves as you do. As you master each phase, you'll find yourself naturally cycling through them again at deeper levels:

Engage: reengaging with new aspects of your Purposehood as you grow

Assess: reassessing your situation as circumstances change

Support: creating more sophisticated support systems as your capabilities expand

Enact: enacting transformation at levels you couldn't previously imagine

This is why people who master EASE often say it becomes a way of life, a systematic approach to continuous growth that works regardless of what challenges or opportunities arise.

EASE is a new process to heal and grow. It starts with engagement, not persuasion. It offers clarity, not diagnosis. It empowers with tools, not just talk. It ends with contribution, not just insight. Whether you're a coach, a parent, a teacher, a community leader, a manager, or simply someone who wants to live with more clarity and ease, this process is yours to use.

This is leadership that doesn't depend on perfect circumstances, endless motivation, or having your life "figured out." It's existential leadership that grows stronger through practice, turns obstacles into opportunities for growth, and enables you to guide others who are struggling with similar challenges.

Your transformation doesn't begin when you've figured everything out. It begins the moment you genuinely engage with the first question: What do I really want to change, and am I willing to do the systematic work required to change it? Everything else builds from there, one step at a time, one day at a time, until the life you're living becomes the life you're meant to live.

That's the real birth of EASE Leadership.

⏸ PURPOSEHOOD PAUSE

Think of something you've been avoiding or delaying—a conversation, a decision, a change that keeps calling to you.

Engage: Are you ready to stop managing this and start transforming it? What would authentic commitment look like?

Assess: Where is this challenge showing up in your life? Is it affecting just one area or creating ripples through your relationships, work, or sense of self?

Support: What kind of help do you actually need—internal shifts, external resources, or both? What would make this change feel more possible?

Enact: What's one small action you could take today that would move you toward what you want rather than away from what you fear?

Remember: EASE isn't about having perfect answers. It's about engaging with the right questions and trusting the process to unfold.

Now let's dive deeper into each step, beginning with the foundation for all transformation: learning how to truly engage with your desire for change. Because without genuine engagement, even the most sophisticated tools become empty techniques.

CHAPTER 5

ENGAGE AUTHENTIC READINESS FOR CHANGE

There's a particular kind of exhaustion that comes from knowing your own patterns so clearly that you could teach a class on them but feel powerless to change them.

Amy, a mid-career professional in her forties, came to me for an existential health coaching session after years of searching. She had tried everything: Tony Robbins seminars, months with various therapists, even studying with a guru in India. Each gave her moments of insight, but she still felt stuck. "I learn, I grow, I feel better for a while," she admitted, "but then I'm back to the same patterns, the same emptiness. It's like I'm collecting techniques without ever really changing."

Her real struggle wasn't lack of knowledge or methods; it was that she had never crossed the threshold from *wanting* change to *committing* to it. In our session she experienced, maybe for the first time, what it meant to step fully into readiness rather than hovering on the edge of it. That recognition shifted something deep inside her.

Months later Amy wrote to tell me she was finally living the transformation she had sought for years, because she had at last learned how to engage, not just to experiment.

Her struggle is remarkably common. Research shows that half of therapy clients drop out by session three, and most self-help readers quit long before finishing their programs. It's rarely because the methods don't work; it's because people approach them intellectually without ever crossing the threshold into true transformation, emotionally, existentially, and practically.

WHY ENGAGEMENT COMES FIRST

Change is seductive in theory and demanding in practice. We live in a culture that celebrates transformation stories: the dramatic before-and-after, the sudden breakthrough, the life-altering epiphany. But these stories skip over the most critical element: the moment when someone moves from wanting change to being ready for it.

The difference is what truly matters. Wanting change is passive. It's wishing things were different, hoping circumstances will shift, or waiting for motivation to strike. Being ready for change is active. It's making a conscious decision to step into uncertainty, to do things differently, and to persist when the initial enthusiasm fades.

Research from the field of behavioral psychology reveals that readiness for change accounts for more variance in successful outcomes than the intervention itself. You can have the best methodology, the most skilled practitioner, and unlimited resources, but if someone isn't engaged, none of it matters.

Without engagement, assessment produces insight without action. With engagement, support becomes empowerment and change becomes sustainable.

Engagement is different from motivation. Motivation is emotional and fluctuates. Engagement is existential and endures. Motivation says, "I feel like changing today." Engagement says, "I'm committed to this process regardless of how I feel on any given day."

Engagement is also different from compliance. Compliance is following someone else's agenda. Engagement is aligning with your own Purposehood. When someone is merely compliant, they're borrowing someone else's reasons for change. When they're engaged, they've found their own.

The threshold of engagement can be distilled into three simple but demanding agreements. They're not screening tools; they're activation tools:

Am I open to change? Without openness, nothing can begin. And part of that openness is recognizing that change rarely happens in isolation—you may also need to be open to help. You need to be willing to let go of what's familiar even if it's uncomfortable.

Do I trust this method or the person who might help guide me? Change requires trust in something: an idea, a system, or a person. Without trust, every step forward will feel unstable.

Am I willing to do the work? Not once but again and again. When it's hard. When it's inconvenient. When no one else is watching.

These questions aren't optional; they're foundational. Because without clarity on these, nothing else works—not fully and not sustainably. This is where we begin. Not with hope but with agreement. Agreement to openness, trust, and commitment.

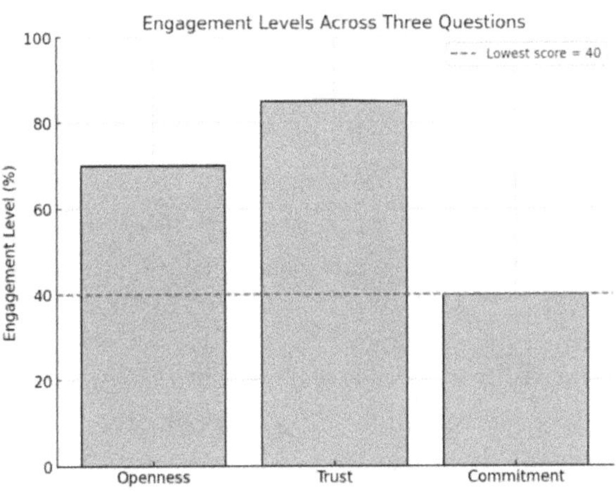

Overall Engagement

Your engagement is only as strong as its weakest link. Even if two answers are high, the lowest answer sets the true level.

```
Overall Engagement = min(Openness, Trust, Commitment)
```

Most approaches to change assume engagement and focus on technique. The Purposehood Method for Existential Health recognizes that engagement *is* the technique. Master this foundation and everything else becomes possible. Skip it and even the most sophisticated tools will leave you exactly where you started.

You met David in the previous chapter, the tech executive who'd been working with therapist Nora for two years. His story shows exactly what happens when engagement shifts from theory into lived reality. He gained deep self-understanding through their sessions and tried every tool (journaling, breath work, coaching), but nothing in his life had truly shifted. His breakthrough came when Nora shifted her approach and introduced him to the three engagement questions.

She asked him directly: "Are you truly open to change and open to help? Do you trust this process and me as your guide? And are you willing to do the work even when it's uncomfortable?"

That moment cracked something open. David realized he hadn't truly engaged. He'd been managing discomfort, not stepping into change. He was participating intellectually, not existentially. He knew what to do but hadn't committed to doing it.

Once he answered the three engagement questions (honestly, not performatively), his behavior changed. He began tracking his well-being weekly instead of just talking about it. He stopped holding back and began showing up with presence and vulnerability at home. He mentored younger colleagues, not as a polished expert but as someone walking the path himself.

Like Amy, David didn't need more insight. He needed to cross the threshold from passive reflection into active engagement. And when he did, change became inevitable.

THREE QUESTIONS OF READINESS

Each of the three questions that determine readiness for transformation targets a different dimension of engagement, helping you distinguish between surface-level interest and the deeper readiness that sustains meaningful transformation. These questions are meant to center you, helping ensure that your desire for change isn't just emotional but existentially anchored and practically supported.

1. AM I OPEN TO CHANGE?

This question sounds simple, but it's the foundation of everything that follows.

Many people say they want change, fewer are truly open to it, and even fewer are open to being guided through the process. Sometimes we confuse discomfort with openness to change. We feel restless, stuck, or overwhelmed and think, *I just need things to be different.* But deep down we may still be hoping for improvement without involvement. Without vulnerability. Without effort.

That's normal. It's human. But it's also where transformation stalls. You can't heal what you won't name. You can't grow if you refuse help.

The first engagement question is an invitation to step into your own readiness. When you ask yourself about openness, you're asking whether you've noticed a part of your life that's no longer sustainable as is. You're wondering if you're willing to move from coping to changing. Most important, you're deciding whether you're open not just to change but also to receiving help as part of that change.

This isn't about confidence. It's about willingness. You don't have to be certain. You just have to be willing to begin and to be guided along the way, if needed.

Common resistance excuses include: *I'm fine; I just wish things around me would change. I've been through worse; I'll figure it out eventually. I don't like it, but I'm not sure I want to get into it yet.* These aren't wrong answers. They're honest signals that you're not ready to engage fully, and acknowledging that truth is more powerful than pretending otherwise.

But if you *are* ready (even cautiously), then this is the true beginning. You don't need total clarity. Just a clear yes: *I'm open to change. And I'm open to help.* Openness is the first door, and you've just placed your hand on the handle.

2. DO I TRUST THE METHOD OR GUIDE?

Openness opens the door, but trust is what allows you to walk through it. Even when someone knows they're open to change, transformation rarely begins until they find something or someone they're willing to trust. Not blindly, but enough to try.

Trust is the bridge between openness and action. It doesn't require full confidence, but it does require willingness. Willingness to explore, to participate, to be guided even when you're uncertain.

When you ask yourself about trust, you're asking whether you believe that the method or the person guiding you has something of value to offer. You're wondering if you're open to being challenged, supported, and stretched by that process. You're deciding whether you can give this a real chance, rather than staying on the sidelines.

Sometimes resistance to the method sounds like: *I'll try this, but I doubt it will work.* Or: *I've done so many programs… This feels like more of the same.* Or: *I'll go along with it, but I don't want to get my hopes up.* Protective responses like these often stem from disappointment, betrayal, or burnout, and the question is whether you're willing to trust again.

Trust doesn't require certainty. It asks only for willingness. But that willingness has to be real. Ask yourself now: *What would it take for me to trust The Purposehood Method for Existential Health enough to engage with it? Am I keeping one foot out the door even as I say I want change? And what would trust look like in practice: honesty, consistency, openness?* If even a tentative yes arises—to trusting the method and the one guiding you—you're no longer standing at the edge. You're stepping in.

3. AM I WILLING TO DO THE WORK?

Trust gets you into the room. Commitment is what keeps you there when the work gets real.

You've recognized your openness to change. You trust the method enough to step in. Now comes the final and most practical question: Am I willing to do the work?

This is where lasting change takes root: through the willingness to show up repeatedly, even when the process becomes uncomfortable. Transformation is about consistency. It's about choosing to apply the tools you've been given even on the days when it's easier to avoid them.

When you ask yourself about willingness, you're asking whether you're prepared to show up even when it feels repetitive or uncertain. You're wondering if you'll reflect honestly, act consistently, and remain accountable. Most important, you're deciding whether you can commit to progress.

This doesn't mean pushing yourself to exhaustion. It means building the muscle of participation, step by step. Engagement is a discipline, not a spark.

Lack of willingness might sound like: *I'll do it when I have time.* Or: *This just feels like a lot right now.* Or: *I already know what I need. I just don't do it.* These are all signs that you may want change but haven't yet committed to the process. Sometimes the most powerful move is to admit, *I'm not ready to do the work yet.* That honesty gives you a real starting point.

But when you are ready, willingness has its own quiet signature. You find yourself clearing time in your calendar. Instead of avoiding the uncomfortable conversations or insights, you lean toward them with curiosity. Most telling of all, you're no longer looking for quick fixes or immediate results. You understand that this is a process, and that doesn't discourage you. It grounds you.

This is where the journey truly begins: with action. If your answer is yes to doing the work, even imperfectly, then you're engaged.

Fully. Willingly. Consciously.

IF YOU'RE GUIDING OTHERS

Whether you're a parent, friend, manager, coach, therapist, mentor, or facilitator, keep in mind that engagement isn't a given. Openness and willingness must be invited with respect, not pressure. Trust must be earned and re-earned. It grows through transparency, clarity, and presence. The more you honor someone's pace and agency, the more likely they are to engage fully.

⏸ PURPOSEHOOD PAUSE

Take a deep breath. Can you feel your readiness to engage?

- Am I genuinely open to change and to receiving help along the way?

- Do I trust the EASE process enough to stay with it even when it gets uncomfortable?

- Am I willing to do the work consistently, not just when I feel motivated?

- Can I say with honest self-awareness, "I am open, I trust, and I am willing to do the work"?

You don't need perfect readiness. You need genuine engagement. This is where transformation becomes inevitable.

DAILY ENGAGEMENT PRACTICE

Now that you understand the three questions, the next step is learning how to use them as an ongoing rhythm of self-awareness. Self-engagement is a daily and weekly habit of checking in with your openness, your trust, and your willingness as life evolves.

Most people skip this step. They assume that because they picked up the book or started the assessment, they're automatically engaged. But engagement is layered, and it shifts.

You might start with high commitment but low trust. Or deep openness but wavering willingness. Or complete trust in the method but resistance to specific parts of the work. That's why engagement is a discipline. It begins with a willingness to change but deepens through trust and consistent action.

The most effective way to stay engaged is to build regular check-ins into your process.

Every morning, pause and ask yourself:

Am I open to life today?

Do I trust my plan for today enough to take one step?

Am I willing to follow through on even one small action?

On a weekly basis, take ten minutes with a journal or reflection tool and go deeper into each area:

Openness: *What am I noticing about my readiness this week?*

Trust: *How is my confidence in the process that's supporting me? What's strengthening it or shaking it?*

Commitment: *How consistent have I been with the work? What's supporting or undermining my follow-through?*

Honest engagement might sound like: *I'm open to change, but I'm scared of what I might discover about myself.* Or: *I trust the method, but I don't trust my ability to stick with it.* Or: *I'm willing to do the work, but only if I can control the timeline.* These aren't obstacles. They're starting points. Engagement begins with naming what's true, not with having it all figured out.

WHEN ENGAGEMENT WAVERS

Everyone's engagement fluctuates. The question isn't whether you'll have moments of doubt, resistance, or fatigue. It's what you'll do with them.

Common wavering points include the time after initial enthusiasm fades (week 2-3), when the work reveals something uncomfortable, when progress feels slower than expected, and when old patterns resurface despite effort.

Engagement recovery practices include:

- Returning to your original "why" — what brought you to this work in the first place

- Lowering the bar temporarily — finding the smallest step you can take to stay connected

- Reaching out to someone — someone who can remind you why this matters

- Trusting the process — knowing that engagement naturally ebbs and flows

If you're struggling with any of the three dimensions of engagement, here are specific approaches for each:

For low openness: Journal about what isn't working. Don't try to solve anything. Just notice.

For low trust: Research the method more. Read testimonials. Talk to someone who's been through it.

For low commitment: Start smaller. What's one tiny practice you can maintain consistently?

Start with honest self-reflection. Spend time with the three questions to understand what readiness would look like for you. What would need to shift for you to feel committed?

Identify what you're protecting. Resistance often protects something valuable—your energy, your hope, your sense of control. Understanding what you're protecting helps you engage in a way that honors those needs.

Create small experiments. Try engaging with just one aspect of readiness, perhaps by sitting with the three questions for a week without pressure to come up with perfect answers. Small experiments can build confidence and clarify your willingness.

Address practical barriers. Sometimes resistance is logical rather than emotional. If time, money, or energy are genuine constraints, acknowledge them with honesty and compassion. Then ask, *What's one small way I can begin anyway, even within these limits?*

The goal isn't to force readiness. It's to create conditions where readiness can emerge naturally.

OVERCOMING RESISTANCE TO CHANGE

Not everyone comes to this work from the same place. Some people are naturally inclined toward introspection and change. Others have been conditioned (by family, culture, or painful experience) to view seeking help as weakness or vulnerability as danger.

If engagement feels difficult for you, you're not broken. You're human. And you're not alone. Over the years, I've noticed three common resistance patterns. Recognizing your own can help you find the most effective way forward.

The Independent Type: *I should be able to figure this out myself.*

You've learned to rely on yourself, and that's served you well. But independence can become isolation when it prevents you from accessing help that could accelerate your growth.

Reframe: Engagement isn't dependence; it's intelligence. Using effective tools and guidance isn't giving up your autonomy; it's exercising it more skillfully.

The Skeptical Type: *I've tried things before and they didn't work.*

Sometimes resistance isn't about self-reliance but self-protection. Past disappointments have taught you to guard your hope. That wisdom matters, but it can also keep you stuck in old patterns.

Reframe: Skepticism can be an asset if it helps you engage more thoughtfully. Ask yourself, *What would this need to include for me to give it a real chance?*

The Overwhelmed Type: *I don't have the bandwidth for one more thing.*

And sometimes it's not independence or skepticism, it's sheer exhaustion. Your life is already full, and adding anything feels impossible. But often, the overwhelm is exactly what needs addressing, and engagement is the path to less struggle, not more.

Reframe: Engagement isn't adding to your burden; it's reorganizing it. The work creates space rather than consuming it.

Some families or cultures view seeking help as shameful, self-focus as purely selfish, and personal struggles as something to keep private. These protective systems often served a purpose in the past, but they can make it harder to engage now. Honor them, and then ask: *What would it mean to take care of myself in a way that actually serves my family and community better?*

If you find yourself comparing—*People my age have this figured out. I should be past this by now. I'm too old/young/educated/successful to be struggling with this*—remember that these thoughts aren't facts. They're comparisons. And comparisons are almost always based on incomplete information about other people's inner lives.

Where you are is where you are. The only question that matters is: *What's the next right step from here?*

You don't have to commit to everything at once. Sometimes the path to engagement is through the back door—small, safe actions that build trust over time:

- Choose one small area of your life to observe with curiosity

- Sit with one reflection question without pressure to act on the answer

- Share one honest insight with someone you trust

Small steps build trust—in yourself, in the process, and in your ability to handle what you discover. Our culture celebrates rapid transformation, but sustainable change often happens slowly. There's no timeline you need to match, no pace you need to maintain except the one that feels right for you. Some people dive in completely from day one. Others wade in gradually over months. Both approaches can lead to profound change.

Finally, note that sometimes barriers to engagement are about capacity, not willingness. If you're dealing with active trauma, severe depression, addiction, or other clinical concerns, professional support may need to come first. Getting the support you need to be able to engage is part of the engagement process itself.

WHEN READINESS FEELS ELUSIVE

True engagement has distinctive markers that go beyond intellectual agreement or temporary motivation. It has a quality you can feel. The work starts showing up in your daily life as a natural part of how you think about challenges and opportunities. When resistance arises, instead of battling it or giving up, you find yourself becoming curious: *What is this protecting? What might it be trying to tell me?*

You stop waiting for perfect conditions or perfect execution. Progress becomes more interesting than perfection, and you begin taking genuine ownership of both your breakthroughs and your setbacks.

You'll recognize genuine readiness by several distinctive shifts:

You've moved from *I should* to *I will.* When engagement is real, the language changes. Instead of *I should probably work on this* or *I need to get my life together,* you find yourself saying *I will take this step* or *I'm ready to see what this reveals.* This shift from obligation to intention signals genuine commitment.

Your curiosity outweighs your fear. You're more interested in what you might discover than worried about what it might cost you. While some anxiety about change is normal, genuine engagement means your desire to heal and grow is stronger than your need to stay safe.

You can tolerate uncertainty about outcomes. You don't need guarantees about how this will unfold or what you'll discover. You're willing to engage with the process itself, trusting that clarity will emerge through action rather than planning.

You feel ownership over your decision. This isn't something you're doing because someone else thinks you should or because you've run out of other options. You understand this as your choice, made for your reasons, aligned with your values.

SIGNALS OF INAUTHENTIC READINESS

Sometimes what feels like engagement is actually something else: pressure, desperation, or people-pleasing. The following signals suggest you may need to slow down and build genuine readiness:

You're doing this primarily for someone else. If your main motivation is to get someone off your back, save a relationship, or prove something to others, the foundation isn't solid enough for sustainable change.

You expect this to be easy or quick. If you're looking for a painless solution or expecting transformation without discomfort, you may not be prepared for the reality of meaningful healing and growth.

You can't identify what you want to change. Vague dissatisfaction isn't the same as readiness. If you can't articulate what's not working in your life, you need more clarity before proceeding.

You're in active crisis. If you're in the middle of a major life crisis (acute depression, active addiction, relationship crisis, job loss), you may need stabilization before you can engage meaningfully with healing or growth work.

You think you "have to" do this. Genuine engagement feels like choice, even when it's motivated by pain or struggle. If this feels like something you have no choice about, explore what's driving that feeling.

READY TO BEGIN

When you know you're engaged, you'll naturally want to understand your current state. The assessment phase will deepen this engagement by providing clarity about your WholeBeing. That work requires the foundation you've built here: genuine participation in your own transformation.

You don't need perfect engagement. You need enough to begin. If you can answer yes to the three questions with genuine intention, you're ready for the next step. Your engagement is the soil in which all other growth happens. Tend it well, trust it enough to proceed, and let it guide you into the discovery that awaits.

Once you've engaged with the three questions, you're ready for something most people never receive: a complete map of your WholeBeing.

CHAPTER 6

ASSESS
REVEAL360 WHOLEBEING MAPPING

You've engaged. Now comes what might be the most important question you've never been asked: "Where exactly do you stand right now?" Not where you wish you were. Not where others think you should be. Not where you imagine you'll be six months from now. But where you actually are, right now, across every extension of your life.

This isn't a question most of us spend time with. We're usually focused on where we're going or where we've been. We set goals for the future or analyze mistakes from the past. Rarely do we pause to take a comprehensive, honest look at our present reality. And yet this question, this moment of clear seeing, changes the whole trajectory.

When you use GPS navigation, the first thing it does is locate where you are. Where you want to go comes second. Where you are is the starting point without which no navigation system in the world can help you. Your life works the same way. It helps to have a clear vision of where you want to be—healthier, more fulfilled, better connected to the people you love—but if you don't know your exact starting point across all extensions of your being, you'll keep taking steps that feel like progress but don't actually get you where you want to go, because you might be starting your journey from the wrong coordinates.

When you truly know where you stand, something shifts. You stop guessing about what's wrong and start knowing exactly where to focus your energy. You stop trying random solutions and start making strategic moves. You stop feeling overwhelmed by everything that needs to change and start seeing the specific steps that will actually make a difference.

That's what assessment is really about—creating the clarity that makes real change possible, the kind of clarity that transforms confusion into direction, overwhelm into strategy, and scattered efforts into focused growth.

WHY CHANGE EFFORTS USUALLY FAIL

If you're reading this, chances are you've tried to change before. Maybe you've worked on your career, your relationships, your health, or your mindset. Maybe you've tried to support your children, your spouse, or even colleagues at work. Maybe you've seen some progress—even significant progress—but somehow the changes didn't last the way you hoped they would.

You're not alone in this experience, and there's nothing wrong with you.

Here's what most approaches miss: they try to create change without first understanding your unique starting point. Although they offer solutions—often good solutions—they're working with incomplete information about your actual situation.

It's like going to a doctor who prescribes treatment without running any tests. They might give you medicine that works for most people with your symptoms, but without understanding your specific condition, body chemistry, and health history, even good medicine might not work for you. Or worse, it might help one issue while creating problems elsewhere.

The same thing happens with personal change. You focus on improving your work life and your relationships suffer from neglect. You work on your physical health, but your sense of Purposehood remains unclear. You develop better emotional habits, but your family dynamics are stuck in old patterns. That's what happens when you treat symptoms instead of understanding the whole system.

Most of us have been conditioned to think we already know what's wrong. *I need to exercise more. I should spend more time with my family. I have to find work that's more meaningful.* And often, we're not wrong about these things. But knowing what's wrong isn't the same as understanding the whole picture.

You might know that you need to exercise more, but do you understand why you're not exercising? Is it because your work schedule is overwhelming? Because you're dealing with family stress that drains your energy? Because you've lost touch with activities that used to bring you joy? Each of these root causes would require a different approach.

Without comprehensive understanding, even correct insights lead to incomplete solutions. You join a gym without addressing the time management issues that prevent you from going. You try to improve communication with your spouse without recognizing the work stress that's affecting your emotional availability. You set goals for personal growth without understanding the limiting beliefs that will sabotage your efforts.

Real change—lasting change—begins with real clarity. And real clarity requires the courage to look at the whole picture, not just the parts we're comfortable examining.

THE POWER OF HONEST SELF-ASSESSMENT

Taking a comprehensive look at your life can feel like standing at the edge of discovery: intriguing, full of possibility. You might wonder, *What patterns will I finally see clearly? What connections have I been missing?* or, *What will this reveal about why some solutions worked while others didn't?*

These questions are intelligent responses to the opportunity that real assessment provides. And they deserve to be honored, not rushed.

Emma, a successful marketing executive, felt exactly this way one day as she sat at her laptop, cursor hovering over the REVEAL360—Purposehood WholeBeing Assessment link her friend had sent her. She found herself paused by a compelling question: "What might I discover about the whole picture?"

I know something's off, she told herself. *I'm exhausted, I'm snapping at people, and I can't figure out why I feel so empty even though I have everything I thought I wanted.* She'd tried journaling, meditation apps, and a dozen self-help books, and the idea of a comprehensive assessment felt like finally getting the missing piece.

Emma's curiosity makes perfect sense. Mapping your entire Whole-Being is different from focusing on just one area of struggle. When you're working on your career, you see one angle. When you're addressing a relationship issue, you see another piece. But when you're looking at everything—your sense of Purposehood, your relationships, your work, your community connections, your relationship with nature—you get to see how it all fits together. That comprehensive view can feel illuminating.

I've talked to many people who felt drawn to assessments. Some were excited to discover strengths they hadn't fully recognized. Others were curious about patterns they'd sensed but couldn't articulate. Still others wanted to understand why certain changes felt so difficult despite their best efforts. And the insights they gain are almost always more valuable than expected.

A WholeBeing assessment is designed to show you the fascinating complexity of who you are and where you're going. Think of it this way: When you go to the doctor for a complete physical, the tests aren't meant to shame you about your current health. They're meant to give you a complete picture of how your body is functioning. Some results might surprise you in positive ways. Others might reveal areas that could benefit from attention. But all of it serves the same purpose: helping you make informed decisions about your well-being.

The same is true for assessing your WholeBeing. Some areas of your life might be thriving in ways you hadn't fully recognized. Others might have room for growth you hadn't considered. None of it defines your worth or determines your future; it simply gives you the information you need to make empowered choices.

Moreover, comprehensive assessments like the REVEAL360 often reveal something fascinating: the patterns you've been sensing become crystal clear when mapped systematically. When you can see exactly how different areas connect—when you can locate specific dynamics within the broader context of your WholeBeing—what once felt overwhelming becomes workable.

What helped Emma move forward was something her friend told her: "This isn't about finding more problems. It's about finally understanding the connections you've been sensing all along."

That reframe sparked her interest. Instead of seeing the assessment as another evaluation, she began to see it as a way to understand the patterns that had been just outside her awareness.

Many people tell me that taking the assessment satisfied a curiosity they didn't even know they had. One client said, "I'd been wondering why certain areas of my life felt so connected, but I couldn't put my finger on it. When I could see the specific relationships between different areas, plus all the things that were actually working well, I realized I wasn't confused; I just needed the right map."

If you're feeling drawn to WholeBeing assessment, that interest is information worth following. Maybe you're ready for this level of clarity right now. Maybe you're curious about patterns you've been sensing. Maybe you want to understand why some changes have been easier than others.

And if you can embrace the curiosity, if you can welcome not knowing what you'll discover, if you can approach your own life with the same fascination you might bring to solving an interesting puzzle, then you're ready for something that could illuminate what truly matters. Because on the other side of that curiosity is something invaluable: the clarity to finally stop guessing about what you need and start knowing exactly where to focus your energy for maximum impact. Emma discovered this firsthand.

EMMA'S REVEAL360 JOURNEY

Emma hesitated for a moment, then clicked the REVEAL360 link. "I realized I was more excited about what I might discover than worried about staying in patterns I already knew," she later reflected.

Once she began the assessment, what intrigued her most was the framework the questions revealed. Instead of the typical personality questionnaire she'd expected, the assessment began with a simple but profound premise: "You are a WholeBeing, made up of interconnected parts, and your well-being depends on how all those parts are functioning together."

"I'd never thought about it that way," Emma said. "I'd been trying to fix my mood without considering my work stress, improve my relationships without addressing my exhaustion, find meaning without looking at how disconnected I'd become from everything that used to matter to me."

REVEAL360 didn't ask her to rate her happiness on a scale of 1-10 or categorize her personality type. Instead, it invited her to explore specific areas of her life: her relationship with herself, her family dynamics, her work environment, her community connections, and her relationship with nature.

For each area, it asked two simple questions: "Are you struggling or not struggling?" and "Are you seeking change or not seeking change?"

Emma had been expecting complex psychological analysis, but instead she found herself answering questions that felt like having honest conversations with herself about each area of her life; conversations she hadn't realized she needed.

"The questions helped me get specific about things I'd been keeping vague," she explained. "Instead of *I'm stressed about work*, I got to think about whether I was actually struggling with my job itself or with my co-workers, or with my clients or with how I was approaching my work. Each component invited its own honest exploration."

When she reached the questions about her work life, something stirred. As she answered, she realized her drive wasn't just healthy ambition. It'd begun to spill over, consuming energy that other parts of her life needed.

"I thought being ambitious was always good," she said. "I didn't realize that even strengths could become imbalanced when they're disconnected from everything else."

As Emma continued through the assessment, she began to recognize patterns she'd been sensing but couldn't name. Her emotional exhaustion was connected to her work obsession. Her relationship struggles were linked to her disconnection from nature. Her spiritual emptiness was related to her lack of meaningful community involvement.

"For the first time, I could see how everything was connected," she said. "My work stress wasn't an isolated problem. It was affecting my marriage, my friendships, my physical health, even my ability to enjoy simple things like being outside."

The assessment took less than thirty minutes, but by the time she submitted her responses, she felt like she'd had a conversation with herself that was years overdue. The questions helped her organize insights and feelings that had been forming without structure.

"I finally had language for what I'd been experiencing," she said. "Instead of feeling generally overwhelmed, I could see specific patterns and specific areas that were ready for attention."

But Emma's real clarity came when she saw her REVEAL360 results. For the first time, she had a clear map of her entire WholeBeing—her challenges and her strengths, her struggles and her growth, not isolated issues but an integrated picture of how it all connected.

What she discovered would change not just how she understood her current situation but how she approached every aspect of healing and growth going forward.

READING YOUR WHOLEBEING RESULTS

✖	◼	●	▲
Contraction	**Healing**	**Comfort**	**Growth**
Resignation (Negative)	**Dependency** (Negative)	**Complacency** (Negative)	**Excess** (Negative)
• Self - Emotional Self	• Family - Parents	• Family - Extended Family	• Work - Job
• Work - Coworkers		• Work - Shareholders	
• Communities - Associations		• Communities - Neighbors	
• Nature - Air			
• Nature - Animals			
• Nature - Plants			
• Nature - Earth (Land/Water)			
Endurance (Positive)	**Empowerment** (Positive)	**Contentment** (Positive)	**Ambition** (Positive)
• Self - Existential Self	• Self - Mental Self	• Self - Spiritual Self	• Self - Physical Self
	• Family - Partner (Husband)	• Family - Siblings	• Communities - Circles
	• Work - Customers	• Communities - Friends	• Nature - Universe/ Awe
	• Family - Children	• Communities - Acquaintances	
		• Work - Suppliers	

When Emma saw her assessment results, she felt like she was looking at herself through a new lens, one that brought everything into focus for the first time in years.

"I had no idea there was this much to explore," she said. "I mean, I knew my life was complex, but seeing it all organized like this, it was enlightening and energizing."

Although the framework organizing her results was simple, it was also comprehensive. Her entire life had been mapped across her Five Extensions of Being: Self, Family, Work, Communities, and Nature. Each extension contained five components, and each component had been placed in one of four zones based on her responses.

As Emma looked across the map of her life, a pattern emerged that explained why she had felt so scattered for so long. Some parts of her were pushing forward with energy, others were struggling just to hold on, and a few had quietly gone numb. She could see how her drive at work had begun to consume energy meant for relationships, how emotional exhaustion had narrowed her sense of belonging, and how years of living indoors and on screens had left her feeling ungrounded. Even within her closest relationships, some connections were actively being repaired while others had simply been left on autopilot—stable but no longer nourishing. For the first time, Emma wasn't looking at isolated problems. She was seeing how different parts of her life were moving at different speeds, pulling against one another, and creating the tension she'd been feeling.

What truly changed Emma's perspective was realizing that each part of her life was operating in a different kind of terrain:

The Contraction Zone: She was struggling but not seeking change. "I realized I wasn't trying to improve my connection to nature or my communities," she said. "I'd accepted the disconnection rather than working to change it."

The Healing Zone: She was struggling but actively seeking change. "My marriage was here, which actually felt hopeful. We were working on things and both committed to improvement."

The Comfort Zone: She wasn't struggling and wasn't seeking change. "My friendships were here, which was great—stable and nourishing, exactly where I wanted them."

The Growth Zone: She wasn't struggling and was actively seeking change. "My physical health and my work were here—I was performing well and pushing for more opportunities."

The deep insight came when Emma understood the positive and negative states within each zone. "I realized that even being in the 'good' zones wasn't always actually good. My work was in the Growth Zone, but in a negative state that was creating problems everywhere else. And some of my Comfort Zone relationships were complacent rather than truly content."

But the biggest insight was seeing how everything was connected. "My work excess was draining energy from my marriage. My emotional resignation was affecting my ability to connect with community. My disconnection from nature was contributing to my feeling ungrounded in every other area."

For the first time, Emma could see her life as an integrated system rather than a collection of separate problems. "I stopped feeling like I had to fix everything at once, because I could see that changing certain key patterns would have ripple effects throughout my whole system."

The assessment had given her something invaluable: a clear, comprehensive map of exactly where she stood across every dimension of her life. And it had shown her how those dimensions influenced each other, creating the patterns of struggle and growth that shaped her daily experience.

Now she understood that she'd been trying to adjust individual components without understanding how they fit into her larger system. With this new map, she could finally begin to make changes that would support her WholeBeing rather than creating new imbalances.

REVEAL360—YOUR WHOLEBEING NAVIGATOR

As Emma reflected on her results, she began to understand why this assessment felt fundamentally different from other assessments she'd taken.

"I've taken a lot of assessments over the years," Emma said. "Personality tests, strengths finders, career assessments. They all gave me interesting information, but nothing that actually helped me understand how to move forward. This one was different because it didn't try to categorize me; it helped me locate myself."

That distinction matters more than you might think. Most assessments are designed to put you into a category: you're this type of personality, that kind of communicator, this style of leader. The problem with categories is that they're static. They tell you what they think you are, but not where you're going or how to get there. REVEAL360 works differently. Like navigation technology, it shows you where you are and helps you navigate to where you want to go.

"The genius of it was that it met me exactly where I was without judgment," Emma said. "It didn't compare me to other people or tell me how I should be feeling. It just showed me the reality of my current situation so I could make informed decisions about where to focus my energy."

Unlike assessments that rely on what psychologists call the Barnum effect—where vague, general statements feel personally relevant—this assessment provides specific insights based on your responses about your actual life circumstances.

"Every piece of feedback felt personally relevant," Emma said. "It wasn't telling me about people like me; it was telling me about me, based on the specific patterns in my own life."

The assessment is built around a simple but profound insight: you can't navigate to a better place until you know exactly where you're starting from. And *exactly* means comprehensively, across all five extensions of your being, with an understanding of how each component is influencing the others.

What makes this approach particularly valuable is its dynamic framework. Instead of static categories, it maps you into zones that represent different stages of healing and growth. And it shows you the positive and negative states within each zone, giving you specific direction for where to focus your efforts.

"I loved that it didn't assume all struggle was bad or all comfort was good," Emma said. "It helped me understand that I could be in the Growth Zone but in a negative state—like my work situation—or in the Comfort Zone but in a positive state—like my friendships. That nuance made all the difference."

This distinction among zones and states allows for sophisticated understanding of your current situation. Being in the Growth Zone isn't automatically positive if you're in an excess state that's creating imbalance. Being in the Contraction Zone isn't automatically negative if you're in an endurance state that's building resilience.

Perhaps most important, the assessment is designed for regular recalibration. Your zones and states change as your life changes, as you grow, as circumstances shift, and the assessment becomes a resource for ongoing navigation, helping you stay aware of where you are and make course corrections as needed.

"I retook it three months later," Emma said, "and it was fascinating to see how my map had shifted. Some areas had improved, others had new challenges, and the overall pattern was completely different. It helped me see that growth isn't linear; it's dynamic and ongoing."

Regular check-ins help maintain awareness across your WholeBeing. Whether daily, weekly, or monthly, consistent self-assessment keeps you connected to your zones and states as they naturally shift.

When working with a therapist, coach, or counselor, having a clear map of your WholeBeing helps focus sessions on what matters most. Instead of spending time figuring out what to work on, you can dive directly into the areas that need attention while building on the areas that are thriving.

"It completely changed how I approached my coaching sessions," Emma said. "For the first time, we could see the patterns clearly and actually work with them."

The REVEAL360 process had given her language and structure for what had once felt like chaos. In less than thirty minutes, she'd uncovered insights that would shape months of growth.

But the real proof wasn't in the report. It was in what she did next.

⏸ PURPOSEHOOD PAUSE

Before taking any comprehensive assessment, honor your readiness.

Which areas of your life feel most stable right now? Which feel most uncertain?

What would it mean to see your whole life clearly, both struggles and strengths?

If you discovered exactly where you stand across all five extensions, what would you do with that clarity?

Remember: Assessment is information, not judgment. You're mapping.

TRY THIS ON YOUR OWN

Even though the formal REVEAL360—Purposehood WholeBeing Assessment makes it easier to follow the structure, you can build clarity anytime by asking yourself two simple questions for any area of your life.

Am I struggling here?

Am I seeking change here?

Use your answers to locate your zone:

- ☐ Struggling + Not Seeking Change → Contraction Zone → Then ask: Am I in *Resignation* or *Endurance?*

- ☐ Struggling + Seeking Change → Healing Zone → Then ask: Am I in *Dependency* or *Empowerment?*

- ☐ Not Struggling + Not Seeking Change → Comfort Zone → Then ask: Am I in *Complacency* or *Contentment?*

- ☐ Not Struggling + Seeking Change → Growth Zone → Then ask: Am I in *Excess* or *Ambition?*

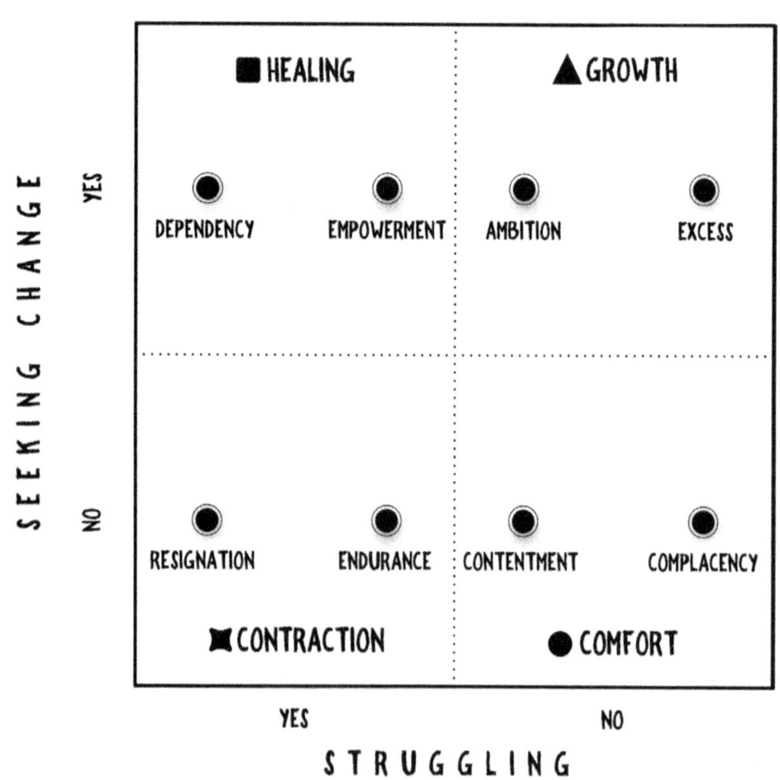

Each answer helps you build self-awareness. Over time, this simple reflection practice can become a powerful habit for navigating your life with skill and intention. You don't need to guess where you stand. You can ask, answer, and know.

EMMA'S TRANSFORMATION: SIX MONTHS LATER

Contraction	Healing	Comfort	Growth
Resignation (Negative)	**Dependency** (Negative)	**Complacency** (Negative)	**Excess** (Negative)
	• Family - Parents	• Work - Shareholders • Communities - Neighbors	• Work - Job
Endurance (Positive)	**Empowerment** (Positive)	**Contentment** (Positive)	**Ambition** (Positive)
• Self - Emotional Self	• Self - Existential Self • Communities - Associations • Self - Mental Self • Work - Customers • Family - Children	• Work - Coworkers • Family - Husband • Family - Extended Family • Self - Spiritual Self • Family - Siblings • Communities - Friends • Communities - Acquaintances • Work - Suppliers • Nature - Air • Nature - Animals • Nature - Plants • Nature - Earth (Land/Water)	• Work - Job • Self - Physical Self • Communities - Circles • Nature - Universe/ Awe

Six months after taking the REVEAL360 assessment, Emma found herself in a place she hadn't expected.

"The changes weren't dramatic," she said. "I didn't quit my job or reinvent my life. But everything felt different."

When she retook the assessment, the map of her WholeBeing had shifted in quiet but meaningful ways. Some areas hadn't changed zones at all, but they had changed states, and that made all the difference.

Her emotional life, once marked by resignation, had moved into endurance. "I stopped fighting my emotions," she said. "I started listening to them." That alone freed up energy she hadn't realized she'd been losing.

Her existential questions also evolved. What had once felt like stuckness turned into direction. "I wasn't asking what was wrong with my life anymore," she said. "I was asking what I wanted to build."

At work, her ambition remained—but without the excess that had been draining everything else. She set clearer boundaries, focused her energy, and paradoxically became more effective. "I didn't become less driven," she said. "I became more intentional."

What surprised her most wasn't any single improvement; it was how changes in one area supported changes in others. Feeling more grounded emotionally improved her relationships. Reducing work excess gave her space for connection. Reconnecting with nature helped her regulate stress across the board.

"For the first time," Emma said, "I could see how everything was connected. I didn't need to fix everything at once. I just needed to start in the right places."

The assessment hadn't solved her problems. But it had given her a way to navigate them—again and again—as life changed.

Your WholeBeing map is waiting for you, but before you explore your REVEAL360 assessment, you'll want to know how to read it. The next few chapters will help you do exactly that. You'll learn to recognize the terrain of each zone, understand what positive and negative states feel like, and build the skills to shift from where you are to where you want to be.

Emma's transformation didn't happen just because she took the assessment; it happened because she learned how to navigate with it. The same will be true for you. Think of the coming chapters as learning to use a compass before you begin a long journey. You could venture out with just the map but knowing how to use it is what keeps you on track and helps you build a life worth loving.

CHAPTER 7

THE CONTRACTION ZONE
WHEN LIFE SQUEEZES IN, REBOUND

There's a pressure that doesn't always arrive as crisis. Sometimes it builds slowly, like water rising around your ankles. Other times, it hits all at once: a diagnosis, a breakup, a death, a betrayal. Whether gradual or sudden, it marks the start of contraction. Life doesn't just pause; it starts to reverse. Possibility shrinks. Hope fades. You lose the sense that forward is even available.

Some seasons feel like collapse. The lights dim. The walls close in. Even breathing takes effort. But what if those moments weren't signs of failure, but invitations to begin again from the inside out?

The Contraction Zone shows up in many ways. You might look fine on the outside, still meeting deadlines and checking boxes. Or not. You might be in crisis—publicly unraveling, gripped by addiction, or buried in despair. Whether quiet or loud, visible or hidden, something essential has stalled within. Meaning becomes hard to reach. Even direction feels far away.

To navigate our path to healing and growth, we first need to recognize where we are and fully understand the terrain we're in.

Each of the next four chapters explores one of the well-being zones. But that doesn't mean your entire life is in that zone. Most of us live in several at once: contracted at work and healing in a relationship, comfortable in our community while growing spiritually. You'll probably recognize yourself in different parts of each. That's the point: our lives are lived across zones, not confined to just one. Understanding these zones helps you make sense of your REVEAL360—Purposehood WholeBeing Assessment not just intellectually, but as a lived experience.

We begin with the Contraction Zone not because it's the worst, but because it's where transformation most often begins. It's where struggle takes hold, but the will to change hasn't yet awakened. It's where meaning slips, and functioning replaces fulfillment.

The Contraction Zone isn't just difficulty; it's density. Like a muscle that contracts before it can expand or a seed that breaks open before it can sprout, this zone stores the pressure required for what's next. Yet it's one of the most misunderstood zones of well-being, often pathologized or pitied but rarely explored with the respect it deserves.

Like all zones, Contraction includes two distinct states:

Contraction – Purposehood = Resignation

Contraction + Purposehood = Endurance

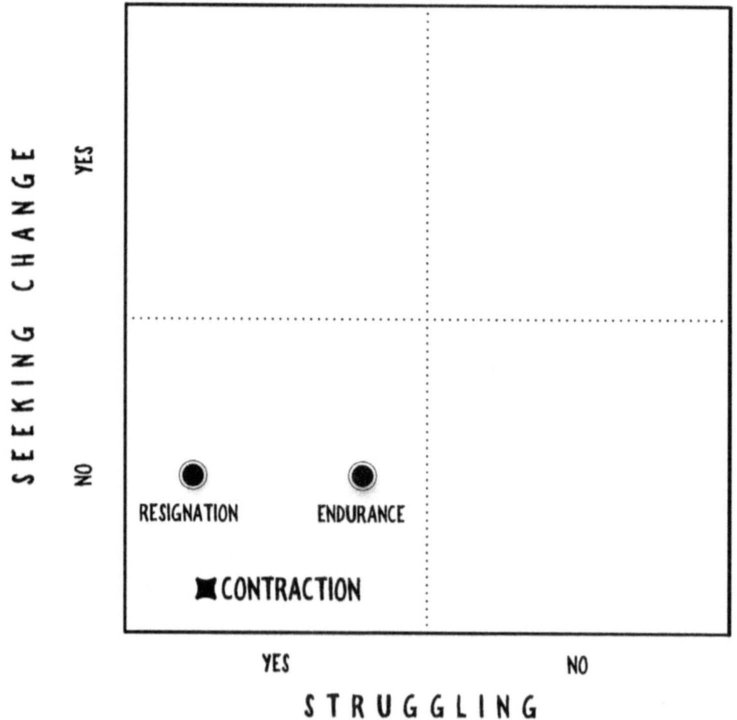

The goal of this zone is to rebound—to find the inner endurance needed to face misdirection and disorientation and begin the journey back to yourself.

This chapter won't offer solutions, not yet. It offers something deeper: recognition. A mirror. You may see yourself here. Or someone you love. Either way, knowing the terrain is the first act of navigation.

Let's begin where Sarah's story began: the moment when life squeezed in and she realized something had to change.

SARAH'S CONTRACTION ZONE DISCOVERY

The human resources director of a midsize tech company reached out because employee turnover was out of control. Her CEO, an old friend of mine, had recommended she talk to me.

"We've been losing about 18 percent of our employees a year for the past three years," Sarah said over Zoom, her tone clipped. "It's not just costing us time and money; it's making it impossible for the company to scale." She looked tired. Defensive. "I'm not sure how this became my problem, but my CEO said your assessment might help."

I asked if the CEO had explained why REVEAL360 would be useful.

"Not really," Sarah said. "She just said it might show employees where they want to make changes so we can offer support or make referrals."

"It's wonderful that your company wants to invest in its people," I said. "Do you know why they're leaving?"

"Mostly dissatisfaction. Based on exit interviews, the biggest reason is that they don't see a path to advancement. They start looking for one somewhere else. And until they find it, they're miserable."

"How productive are they in the meantime?"

She shrugged. "It depends. Most of them do the minimum."

What Sarah was describing wasn't just disengagement; it was resignation, a slow erosion of will. The difference between endurance and resignation is subtle but essential. Endurance is active. Resignation is passive. Struggling people are enduring. Suffering people are resigned.

I told her, "If employees can find meaning in their struggle, they'll be more productive until they find a new job. And some of them might even decide they want to stay."

Sarah frowned. "That makes sense, but I don't understand how an assessment can help people who are resigned find meaning."

"It can't," I said. "But it can help them pinpoint where to find it themselves. Becoming aware of where and how we're struggling gives us the opportunity to change our relationship to the problem. If the problem can't be fixed or the circumstances can't be changed, we can change our perspective."

She was quiet.

"In both cases," I added, "we can use the problem as an opportunity to learn, heal, or grow."

Sarah took a breath. "Okay. I want to take the assessment myself before we give it to employees."

When we met a few days later to review Sarah's REVEAL360 results, she wasn't happy that her job component was in the Contraction Zone.

"I love the people I work with, get along fine with our leadership, and have good relationships with our suppliers," she said, "but it's been a while since I've enjoyed the job."

"May I ask if you're looking to make a change in your situation?"

She sighed and shook her head. "When they hired me, I told myself I'd stay at least three years. It hasn't even been two."

"So how are you handling your disappointment with your job?"

"Wine." She laughed, but it didn't sound like her heart was in it.

"Based on your assessment and what you're sharing, you don't think you can make changes in your situation. Is that accurate?"

"Yes, but it's not like I haven't thought about options. I'd ask about making a lateral move, but the only department I can transfer to is Compliance and that sounds deadly. I wish I could change jobs, but unless a miracle happens, this is where I'll be for at least another year."

I explained that desiring change is a passive state. It's wishing for things to be different and maybe dabbling in random actions to alleviate suffering. Whereas truly seeking change means shifting from wishful thinking to deliberate action. We create a concrete plan for healing and start to execute it.

Sarah's assessment results showed what many employees were experiencing: Resignation in their work component. She was functioning effectively but had stopped believing meaningful change was possible. This is how misdirection and disorientation show up in the workplace, as quiet emotional withdrawal from possibility.

Sarah's story also reveals something deeper about the Contraction Zone: We can appear professionally capable while feeling existentially numb. We can meet every external expectation and still lose our inner compass.

When you review your own REVEAL360 results, notice where you might be showing up out of obligation rather than orientation, where function has replaced meaning and presence has turned into performance.

INSIDE THE CONTRACTION ZONE

Resignation and endurance can wear the same face. You get up. You meet your deadlines. You smile when needed. But inside, a part of you is still searching while another has quietly gone silent.

This is the strange terrain of the Contraction Zone. You may be surrounded by activity but feel emptied of meaning. You may be enduring a deep challenge or simply drifting without direction. In resignation, life feels like a script you no longer believe in, but you still act it out. In endurance, you're still in the struggle, but something in you refuses to let go of the "why."

The difference isn't in how loud the pain is but in whether the pain still feels like it has purpose. If you find yourself numbing, shrinking, or slowly surrendering to "this is just how it is now," you may be in resignation. If you're still breathing with intention, holding on to even a thread of belief that this matters, you may already be enduring.

Neither state is shameful. Both are deeply human. But only one keeps you connected to movement. And only movement, however subtle, however small, can lead to healing.

So ask yourself: *Is my stillness rooted in patience or in despair? Have I stopped hoping, or am I still holding something sacred, even if I can't name it yet? Am I functioning or quietly folding in on myself?*

You don't need to answer right away. Just let the question open something. Because even in the Contraction Zone, your life is still speaking, and when you listen closely, you may realize you haven't given up. You've just been waiting to be seen.

And now you are.

TWO STATES OF CONTRACTION

Not all struggle is the same. One person wrestles with life but keeps moving. Another feels like life has already decided the outcome and they've given up inside. That's the difference between the two states of the Contraction Zone:

Contraction – Purposehood = Resignation

Nothing will change.

Why bother?

This is just how it is now.

Contraction + Purposehood = Endurance

It's hard, but I'm still here.

I don't know how this ends, but I believe it matters.

This is not the end of my story.

The difference isn't always visible. From the outside, both people might look like they're functioning. But inside, one is still connected to meaning while the other has quietly let go.

Resignation is often subtle. It doesn't always scream or collapse. It simply simmers.

Endurance, on the other hand, is the quiet strength to carry on because something deeper still holds. It's fueled by Purposehood. It doesn't erase the pain, but it keeps the person moving through it with integrity, patience, and resolve.

WHY PEOPLE STAY IN CONTRACTION

People stay in the Contraction Zone for a variety of reasons, and understanding these patterns is crucial to recognizing your own experience.

Some find a strange comfort in the familiarity of their struggles. When you've been in pain for a long time, the pain becomes predictable. Change—even positive change—introduces uncertainty, and uncertainty can feel more threatening than familiar suffering.

Others become paralyzed by fear of the unknown. *What if I try to change and fail? What if I make things worse? What if I'm not strong enough?* These questions can feel overwhelming when you're already struggling.

Many lack the emotional, financial, or social resources to seek change. Real transformation requires energy, support, and often practical resources that may not be available.

But perhaps most commonly, people are tethered to the Contraction Zone because they don't know or refuse to believe they're in it. Denial is common because it can be hard to admit we're stuck or suffering. It's easier to say "I'm fine" or "This is just temporary" than to face the reality of where we are. But if we deny our reality, we can't devise an escape plan or identify the tools or help we need to change the situation or our mindset. Just like there's no answer to a question we don't ask, there's no solution to a challenge we don't recognize.

Awareness is the first step—not change, not action, just noticing. It's okay to not be okay. It's okay to feel stuck, to struggle, to feel over-whelmed. There's no shame in struggle. But the more honestly we name our state, the more clearly we can understand what it's asking of us. We don't have to escape it today, but we do have to acknowledge it, because change begins with seeing.

RESIGNATION—WHEN HOPE FADES

Resignation isn't dramatic. It's not a breakdown or a crisis. It's quieter than that and more dangerous.

It's the attitude that nothing's going to change, so why even try? The goals don't matter. The roles feel hollow. You're still moving through life, but there's no story underneath it anymore.

In resignation, effort feels pointless. Even if you wanted things to be different, it wouldn't make a difference. So you stop wanting. You lower your expectations until they disappear.

People in this state often look fine on the outside—they're still showing up to work, still handling obligations—but they've emotionally checked out. They're functioning without believing. This is the heart of existen-tial suffering in the Contraction Zone.

What creates this hollow functioning? It emerges when two deeper patterns converge: You've lost your guiding purpose—there's no "why" to orient your struggle—and you've lost your sense of when and where you are in your life. Time blurs. Goals dissolve. You forget what you were aiming for in the first place.

Together, misdirection and disorientation create a kind of psychic fog. You're not sure how you got here or how to move. So you don't.

Sometimes people stay here not because they've chosen to but because change truly isn't possible. You can't undo a loss. You can't reverse a diagnosis. You can't go back and relive a moment that's passed. Other times, people stay here because they don't believe change is possible or they no longer know how to find it.

To survive that kind of stuckness, it's natural to seek relief in distraction. Some people go numb. Some overwork. Some turn to substances or behaviors that provide temporary escape. Not all addictions are chemical. Some are emotional. Some are just the comfort of what's familiar.

It's not laziness or weakness. It's the erosion of meaning. And like erosion, it happens slowly, then all at once. That's why resignation is so dangerous: it looks like nothing is happening, but inside the anchor is gone.

This is where Sarah found herself when we first spoke—in the quiet erosion of belief that anything could change.

ENDURANCE—PURPOSEFUL PERSISTENCE

If resignation is the quiet collapse of meaning, endurance is the quiet commitment to hold on to it.

Endurance isn't about pushing through blindly or pretending everything is okay. It's about carrying what's hard with intention, with integrity, and with the belief that it still matters. It's continuing to show up even when the outcome is uncertain.

In our follow-up session, Sarah asked, "Can you give me some examples of how someone could find meaning while they're still stuck?"

I shared that we can often find meaning in the Contraction Zone in one of three ways: by recognizing how the struggle benefits us, by seeing how carrying on supports others or contributes to something we believe in, or by identifying possible positive outcomes.

Sometimes enduring a difficult job feels worthwhile if it helps provide for a family or supports a mission we care about. Sometimes enduring a difficult relationship reveals who we are or what we need to change. Even when we can't fix the problem immediately, we can learn from it, grow through it, and find meaning in what it shows us.

"He who has a why to live," Nietzsche said, "can bear almost any how."

This is the essence of endurance. It's the ability to withstand hardship with direction rather than indifference.

I told Sarah that if she did this, every struggle she encountered would enrich her journey by equipping her with the knowledge and resilience to navigate challenges more effectively. Each challenge would become part of her training, something she could fall back on when life presented new obstacles and fresh opportunities to use her hard-earned strength and wisdom.

Endurance isn't about staying stuck. It's about building the strength to move when the time is right. It's about understanding what this moment is here to teach. Every struggle carries a hidden message, something about who we are, what we value, or what needs to change. Endurance gives us the stillness and strength to listen.

In the Contraction Zone, patience isn't passive. It's self-compassion in action. It gives you time to breathe, to matter again, and to quietly gather strength.

People who are enduring aren't in denial. They face the truth. They aren't bypassing pain. They're engaging with it. They choose to wait, not passively but purposefully. If change is possible, they endure until it comes. If it's not, they endure in order to live meaningfully within it.

⏸ PURPOSEHOOD PAUSE

Take a moment to recognize, without judgment, where contraction might be present in your life.

- Which area of your life feels like you're going through the motions but have lost the deeper why?

- Can you sense the difference between endurance (still connected to meaning) and resignation (quietly given up)?

- What would it feel like to shift from "Nothing will change" to "This is hard, but I'm still here for a reason"?

Remember: Simply naming your state is the first step toward conscious navigation.

FINDING YOUR INNER ENDURANCE

Endurance doesn't boast. It doesn't ask for credit. Most of the time, it doesn't even feel like strength. It feels like getting out of bed when you'd rather not. Showing up when no one notices. Holding on when you're not sure why, except that something in you refuses to let go.

That something is Purposehood, the quiet current beneath your pain that orients toward meaning even when everything else feels stuck. You may not feel it clearly here, and that's okay. In the Contraction Zone, Purposehood doesn't shout; it whispers. It's fueled by direction, endurance, patience, mattering, and meaning—the Purposehood pillars that matter most in this zone.

You may not be able to change your circumstances yet. You may feel uncertain about your place in time, your role in the world, or what goals are worth pursuing. But Purposehood reminds you that you aren't your past. You aren't the title you've lost or the box you've been put in. You aren't even the version of yourself that's struggling right now. *You're the one still looking.* Still caring. Still willing to read these words and ask if something more is possible. That willingness isn't weakness; it's your strength in its most honest form.

You don't have to fix anything today. Just recognize that if you're still here, something is carrying you through.

IF YOU RECOGNIZE YOURSELF HERE

Maybe this chapter felt uncomfortably familiar. Maybe you saw your reflection in Sarah's story or in the silence between the words. If so, take a breath.

However you arrived here, this zone isn't your identity. And it's not forever.

What you're feeling is real. The heaviness, the pause, the sense of being lost—all of that is part of the terrain. You're not broken. You're just in contraction.

All four well-being zones offer opportunities and challenges, and none of them are inherently good or bad. But when we're in the Contraction Zone and we're able and ready, we naturally want to move toward healing. If we stay here for an extended period, we risk becoming prisoners of our own suffering. But don't force yourself forward. Remind yourself that even if you don't know how to move yet, even if nothing around you has changed, something within you has. You've named it. You've seen it. That's where transformation begins.

You don't need a plan yet. You just need to keep listening to what this zone is asking of you.

You've endured more than you know. And if you're still here, that means something. That quiet persistence, that refusal to completely surrender, is your Purposehood speaking. Even in the darkness, even in the squeeze, something in you still believes this matters.

In the next chapter, we'll explore what happens when the fog begins to lift, when struggle starts turning into intention, when the will to change, however faint, begins to return. But for now, let this be enough: You've looked inward. You've seen where you are. And you're still moving.

That's everything.

CHAPTER 8

THE HEALING ZONE
WHEN COURAGE MEETS CHANGE, RECOVER

Struggling is hard. But struggling while seeking change, that's a different kind of strength entirely.

Welcome to the Healing Zone, the space where courage lives.

This isn't the courage of heroes or grand gestures. It's the quiet courage of someone who's stopped pretending everything is fine. The courage to admit that something hurts and that you want it to be different. The courage to seek change even when you don't know what that change will look like.

The Healing Zone is where recovery begins. You've already paused in the Contraction Zone to gather strength, and now you're ready to actively seek change.

You might arrive here after a major loss, a health diagnosis, the ending of a relationship, or a career derailment. Or you might find yourself here after a quieter awakening—the gradual realization that the life you're living isn't aligned with who you're becoming. Wherever it starts, the Healing Zone represents one of the most hopeful places in human experience. It's where pain transforms from something that happens to you into something you actively engage with. It's where you stop being a victim of your circumstances and start becoming the author of your recovery.

Like all zones, this one contains two distinct states:

Healing – Purposehood = Dependency

Healing + Purposehood = Empowerment

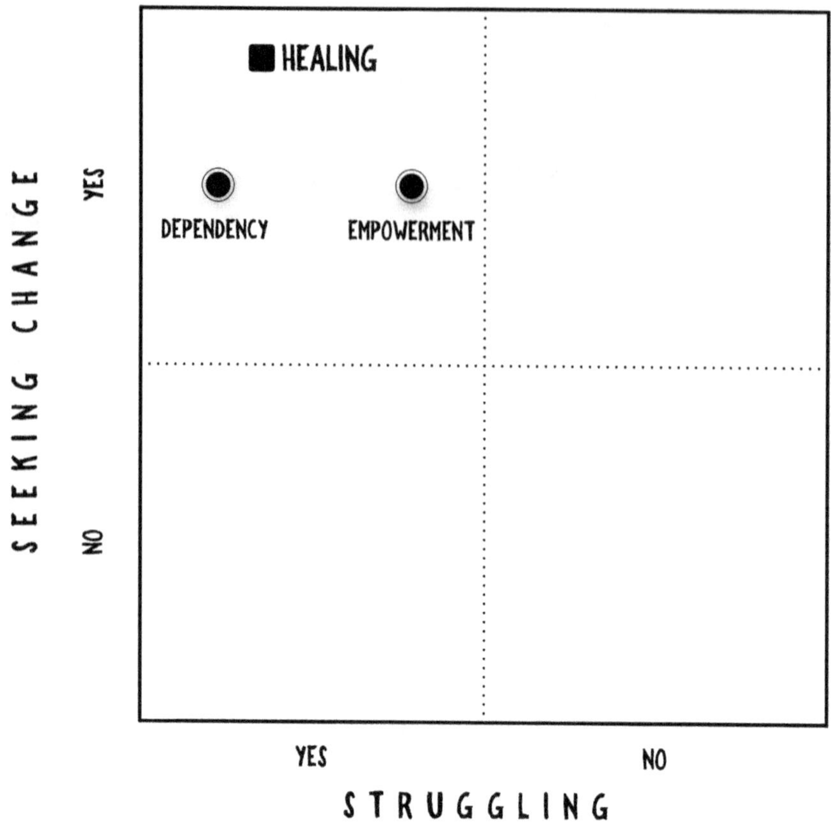

The goal of the Healing Zone is to recover—to rebuild a stable sense of empowerment after the collapse of identity, trust, or meaning.

In this zone, suffering most often arises from misdirection (losing your deeper purpose) and limiting beliefs (the quiet voices that whisper you're not ready, not capable, or not strong enough to lead your own healing). But even in dependency, you're already moving. Even when you're relying on others, you're still seeking. The very fact that you're in the Healing Zone means that something powerful has awakened in you: the belief that change is possible.

This chapter won't offer solutions—those come later. It offers something more foundational: recognition of the terrain, understanding of what you might be feeling, and validation that wherever you are in this zone, you're already on a path toward something better.

Let's begin with stories of people who found their way from dependency to empowerment by learning to partner with their pain.

STORIES FROM THE HEALING ZONE

CARLOS—WHEN HEALING STALLS

Carlos, the founder of a successful real estate company, asked to meet at a quiet café near his office. He'd recently completed the REVEAL360— Purposehood WholeBeing Assessment and said it had brought some things into focus; things he hadn't made space to look at.

What stood out most was his partner component. The results weren't surprising, but they were sobering. "I've been divorced for two years," he said. "But apparently my healing didn't get the memo." He smiled as he said it, but there was something heavy underneath. "I want to get my head back in the game, but I'm not feeling it. Honestly, I've been thinking about selling the company." The reasons he mentioned were vague, and he didn't talk about wanting to pursue something else.

"Have you thought about what you want to do next?" I asked.

"Every day," he replied, swirling his coffee. "But I keep coming up empty."

As Carlos filled in the details, I learned that he wanted to heal from the divorce and move forward, but he wasn't taking full ownership of making that happen. He was taking stimulants to get through the day and sleeping pills to get through the night. He talked to his therapist almost weekly, but he wasn't following her recommendations. What concerned me most was his lack of self-efficacy—his confidence in his ability to take the actions needed to heal.

"I can't help how I feel," he said. "Some things are out of your control."

Carlos didn't call it dependency. He just knew he didn't want to keep saying yes when everything in him said no. But the way out seemed distant and unclear.

When Carlos's wife moved out, the shock and emotional pain led him into the Contraction Zone, initially in a state of resignation. Although he managed to endure and rebound, entering the Healing Zone, he didn't believe he could overcome his pain without a lot of outside help.

"I've been in therapy," he added. "It helps—some days more than others. I'm working on it, but I still feel stuck. Like I've taken apart the machine but don't know how to put it back together."

Carlos wasn't avoiding the pain. He was in it. He was showing up. He wanted change. But according to his assessment results and his own reflection, he was still in the negative state of the zone: dependency. It wasn't that he didn't care. It was that he was still waiting for something—or someone—to fix it.

"I've read the books," he said. "I'm doing the breathing. I know I need to move forward. But it still feels like something outside me has to happen first. Like I'll feel better when... something shifts."

ANDREEA—CHOOSING EMPOWERMENT

In 2020, Andreea's life was full in all the best ways. She was a thriving entrepreneur, celebrated author, and devoted mother of two. She'd built a consulting practice that allowed her to travel, speak internationally, and make a meaningful impact while maintaining flexibility for her family.

What began as a strange pain on one side of her face quickly escalated. Then came the diagnosis that halted her life: a benign brain tumor.

"It wasn't just the health scare," she said when we spoke months later. "I realized I'd been running on momentum instead of meaning. The illness forced me to stop, and when I stopped, I had to face how disconnected I'd become from what actually mattered."

Andreea recognized that multiple components of her life were in the Healing Zone, and unlike Carlos, she was clearly in its positive state: empowerment.

"I could've waited for doctors to fix me or for my energy to come back," she said. "And I did do some of that at first. But I realized healing was something I had to take part in, not just something that would happen to me."

Andreea's healing journey wasn't about denying the reality of her diagnosis or pretending positive thinking would cure everything. It was about recognizing what remained within her control and taking ownership of those areas.

Before her diagnosis, Andreea had been making choices based on momentum and obligation, always asking *What do I have to do?* But during her healing journey, her questions began to change: *What brings me joy?* and *How can I bring joy to others?*

She simplified her business, deepened her relationships, and started writing again—not for publication or profit but for the pure pleasure of putting words together. She spent more intentional time with her children as a way of being present with what mattered most.

"I stopped trying to get back to who I was before," she said. "I started getting curious about who I was becoming."

Her choices became simpler: Will this bring joy? Will it bring joy to others? And little by little, she came back to herself.

Today, Andreea's life is still full—but differently. It's calibrated by meaning, not momentum. Her story isn't about conquering illness. It's about choosing to live—honestly, gently, with gratitude—even when the outcome remains uncertain.

What made the difference? Andreea understood that healing belonged to her. She could ask for help, follow medical guidance, and lean on support, but she never outsourced her agency.

INSIDE THE HEALING ZONE

Carlos was still waiting. Andreea had already chosen.

Neither of them had all the answers. Both of them were hurting. But their postures toward healing were fundamentally different. Carlos still believed something outside him needed to change before he could feel whole again. Andreea believed that healing could begin even if external circumstances remained uncertain.

That's the heart of the Healing Zone. You're not resigned—you're reaching. But how you reach makes all the difference.

When healing depends entirely on others, you stay tethered to outcomes you don't control. When healing includes your own belief in your worth, your meaning, and your direction, something fundamental shifts. You stop trying to be fixed. You start showing up as someone who matters, even before you're better.

If you recognize yourself in this zone, notice:

Do you feel like a patient in your own life, or a participant?

Are you waiting for permission to heal, or are you already giving it to yourself?

When you think about getting better, do you picture others doing the work, or do you see yourself as part of the solution?

You don't have to heal alone. Empowerment means you understand that healing is something you do, not something that happens to you. It means you can ask for help while still being the author of your recovery.

The zone itself is neutral, neither good nor bad. Being in the Healing Zone simply means you're already engaged with change, which is remarkable. And where you are within the zone shows you what kind of support and approach will serve you best.

Dependency isn't failure. It's information. And information, when recognized, can become transformation.

⏸ PURPOSEHOOD PAUSE

Close your eyes and think of an area of your life where you're struggling but actively seeking change.

- What does dependency feel like in your body when you think about this challenge?

- What would empowerment feel like instead—in your thoughts, emotions, and actions?

- If you knew you were the primary author of your healing, what's one small step you could take today?

Remember: Moving from dependency to empowerment isn't about having all the answers—it's about trusting your capacity to find them.

TWO STATES OF HEALING

Not all healing journeys look the same. Some people lean into the process with hope and agency. Others seek relief but remain quietly convinced that the answers lie somewhere outside themselves. That's the difference between the two states of the Healing Zone:

Healing – Purposehood = Dependency

I hope this works.

Tell me what to do.

I need someone to fix me.

Healing + Purposehood = Empowerment

I'm learning to trust myself.

I may need help, but this healing belongs to me.

I'm not there yet, but I know I'm on my way.

The external actions might look identical—both people might attend therapy, read books, follow treatment plans, and seek support—but the energy underneath is completely different.

Dependency doesn't mean you're not trying. It often looks like tremendous effort. You're taking the medication, showing up to appointments, doing the practices. But something in you still feels like a passenger in your own recovery.

Empowerment doesn't mean that you're healed or that you have all the answers. It means you know that healing belongs to you—that you're the primary agent in your own transformation, even when you need help along the way.

WHY PEOPLE STAY IN HEALING

It's one thing to recognize you're struggling and want change. It's another to know how and when to actually move forward. Many linger here because healing reshapes identity—and letting go of who you were is often harder than holding on to pain you've learned to live with.

Some become dependent on the very systems or people helping them heal. When someone else has been holding space, offering tools, or showing the way, it can feel frightening to imagine going it alone. Reclaiming full agency comes with some risk.

Others get stuck in the identity of healing. After long periods of pain or confusion, finally being in a space of support can feel like a relief. "I'm healing" becomes a safe story to tell ourselves, one that validates effort and progress, even if we're not yet ready to transform that healing into action.

Many carry lingering limiting beliefs. Deep scars—emotional, cultural, or psychological—don't dissolve just because we want them to. We might be learning new truths, but the old voices still whisper: "You're not strong enough." "You always mess it up." "You'll never be whole." And so we pause.

Some are waiting for ideal conditions. They want more confidence, more clarity, more energy—something they believe they need to have before stepping into empowerment. But healing isn't linear. It's rarely tidy or complete. And waiting to feel ready can itself become a trap.

Sometimes people simply don't know how to integrate what they've learned. They have insights but no map for applying them. The bridge from awareness to action hasn't been built yet.

Lingering in the Healing Zone means you're still gathering strength, but the moment we become aware of our reasons for lingering, we start building that bridge. That awareness—gently, honestly—marks the beginning of empowerment.

DEPENDENCY—SEEKING WITHOUT OWNING

Dependency can disguise itself as dedication. That's what makes it so hard to recognize.

You're engaged. You're trying. You're following guidance. But deep down, you may still believe that your healing depends on something— or someone—to rescue you.

This state often forms in the aftermath of overwhelm or trauma. You may have tried therapy, support groups, even lifestyle changes, and yet still felt stuck. When effort doesn't lead to relief, discouragement sets in. Slowly, a subtle shift happens: you stop trusting your own role in the process. You start waiting instead of leading. That's the quiet seed of dependency. You're still engaged and still hoping but no longer claiming your healing as your own.

Sometimes we're in dependency because we're physically ill or have a diagnosed condition that requires medical intervention. That's appropriate and necessary. But even in those situations, we can choose to be active participants in our healing rather than passive recipients of care.

The hallmarks of dependency in healing are:

Believing others hold the key to your recovery

Feeling helpless when external support isn't available

Measuring progress by what others do for you rather than what you do for yourself

Waiting for permission to feel better

Outsourcing hope to professionals, medication, or circumstances

Dependency is rooted in misdirection and limiting beliefs. You've started the healing journey, but you don't yet trust your own capacity to lead it. The limiting beliefs whisper: "You're not strong enough," "You don't know enough," "You need to be fixed by someone who understands better."

But here's the truth that dependency obscures: Even in professional care, even with medication, even with the best support systems, healing ultimately happens within you. Others can guide, support, and provide tools, but the healing itself is an internal process that only you can engage.

Carlos exemplified this pattern. He was doing many of the right things—therapy, reflection, trying to process his emotions—but he was still waiting for the healing to happen to him rather than recognizing his role as its primary author.

EMPOWERMENT—OWNING YOUR JOURNEY

Empowerment in the Healing Zone means you understand that healing is collaborative, between you and your support systems, you and your treatments, you and your own inner wisdom.

Empowerment is rooted in direction, patience, mattering, and meaning—the Purposehood pillars that transform healing from something you endure into something you actively engage.

When you're empowered in healing:

You ask for help from a place of strength, not desperation

You follow guidance while staying connected to your own inner knowing

You measure progress by your growing capacity, not just external outcomes

You see setbacks as information, not failure

You understand that healing is a relationship you build, not a destination you reach

Andreea demonstrated empowerment beautifully. She didn't deny her diagnosis or refuse professional care. Instead, she took ownership of what remained within her control—her choices, her focus, her daily practices, her relationships with joy and meaning.

The shift from dependency to empowerment often begins with a simple recognition: I am not broken. I am healing. And I have more power in this process than I realized.

This doesn't happen overnight. Empowerment in healing is built through small acts of agency—choosing to follow treatment, practicing self-compassion by speaking to yourself with care instead of criticism, and showing up even when you don't feel like it. Each empowered choice builds evidence: You are not helpless. You are not just a victim of circumstances. You are an active participant in your own recovery, and your participation matters more than you know.

BUILDING YOUR HEALING CAPACITY

Despite its challenges, the Healing Zone offers something extraordinary: the opportunity to rebuild your relationship with yourself from the ground up.

When life pulls us into struggle, when we're forced to acknowledge that something needs to change, we're also given a rare gift: the chance to examine everything. What's working? What isn't? What do we want to keep? What are we ready to release?

And gently, another question begins to surface—one that healing makes possible but never rushes: *Who are we becoming next?*

This zone teaches us that we're more resilient than we knew. It shows us that pain doesn't have to equal powerlessness. It reveals that seeking help is a form of strength, not weakness, when it's motivated by empowerment rather than desperation.

Most important, the Healing Zone teaches us that transformation is possible, the kind that integrates our experiences into wisdom, our pain into compassion, and our struggles into strength.

Both Carlos and Andreea entered this zone through difficulty. What they discovered—and what you may begin to notice—is that healing isn't about going back to who you were. It's about learning to live from where you are now, with greater honesty, care, and courage.

IF YOU RECOGNIZE YOURSELF HERE

If any part of your life lives in the Healing Zone right now, take a breath. You're exactly where rebuilding happens.

Maybe you're still working through limiting beliefs about your capacity to heal. Maybe you're afraid to move forward without guarantees. Maybe you're learning that healing isn't a finish line—it's a relationship you build with yourself day by day. That's not only okay, it's exactly right.

You don't have to be fully empowered today. You don't need to have all the answers. Just know this: You're allowed to trust yourself. You're allowed to begin, even before you feel ready. Your desire to heal isn't weakness; it's strength. It's your system recognizing that healing is possible and reaching toward it.

The Healing Zone is where the deeper part of you starts to speak again. It's where you remember you're not just someone who survived something hard; you're someone who's capable of transforming that hardship into wisdom.

Whether you're in dependency or empowerment, you're already healing. The fact that you're seeking change, that you want something different, that you haven't given up—that's healing in motion.

This zone will teach you things you can't learn anywhere else. That you're stronger than you knew. That healing happens in layers, not lines. That asking for help is brave. That owning your recovery is even braver.

All four zones of well-being offer opportunities and challenges, and this zone's gift is profound. It shows you that you're recovering *and* remembering who you are. And when you remember who you are, you'll discover something beautiful: you're evolving.

In the next chapter, we'll explore what happens when healing settles into something steadier—the Comfort Zone, where peace becomes possible and rest becomes a foundation for what comes next. But for now, let this be enough: You've stopped waiting for permission and begun to trust your own capacity for healing. And you're discovering that transformation is something you actively create.

Recovery becomes remembering, reclaiming who you've always been beneath what was broken.

CHAPTER 9

THE COMFORT ZONE
WHEN PEACE BECOMES A QUESTION, REST

You've been through struggle. You've sought change. And now you've landed somewhere more peaceful.

Welcome to the Comfort Zone, the space most of us spend our lives trying to reach.

This chapter is about the zone where peace becomes possible, where stability feels real, and where the urgent pressures of life finally seem to ease. It's also about the subtle tension that can arise when that peace becomes too comfortable, when rest drifts into something that feels less like restoration and more like retreat.

The Comfort Zone is a necessary and powerful part of well-being, a foundation for growth, but like every zone, it contains complexity. It holds two distinct possibilities:

Comfort – Purposehood = Complacency

Comfort + Purposehood = Contentment

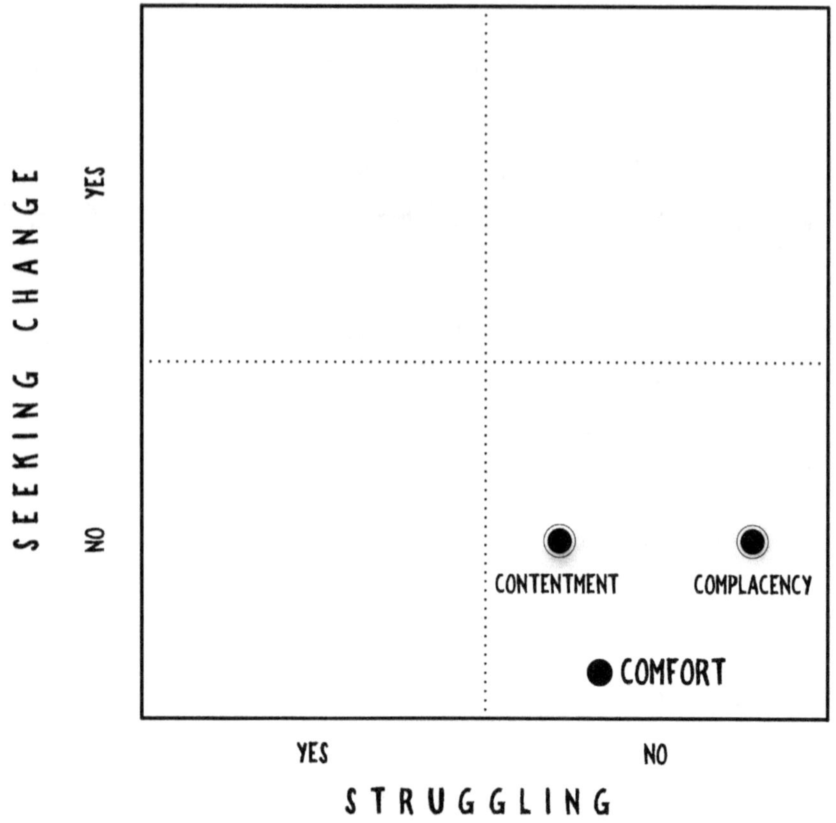

The goal of the Comfort Zone is to rest—to restore stability without slipping into stagnation and to deepen your sense of gratitude, connection, and contentment.

Here you're not in crisis. You're not actively seeking change. You've stabilized. You're safe. And that's something to honor. After seasons of contraction or healing, arriving in comfort can feel like the reward you've been working toward.

But there are questions this zone asks us: Is this rest serving your wholeness, or is it slowly dimming your light? Are you anchored here with intention, or have you drifted here without noticing? Suffering in this zone often arises from misdirection and stagnation. You may have lost touch with your deeper purpose, and the absence of challenge may have allowed growth to slow or stop entirely.

This chapter isn't here to pull you out of the Comfort Zone. It's here to help you understand what kind of comfort you're experiencing and whether it's still serving the life you want to create. The zone itself is neutral; the question is your relationship to it.

Let's begin with a story that might feel familiar, not because it's dramatic but because it's common in ways we often overlook.

LINDA'S COMFORT ZONE CHALLENGE

Linda wasn't struggling. That was the problem.

"Linda says she feels comfortable with her current success but doesn't feel motivated to take on new challenges or set more ambitious goals," Anton said when we connected for our regular meeting.

Anton was a certified Purposehood Engineer and experienced therapist who'd recently started coaching the vice president of a consulting company. Her recent self-assessment showed that multiple components of her life were in the Comfort Zone. That in itself wasn't concerning. The Comfort Zone is a necessary and welcome part of life, and so is the contentment it can offer. The problems set in when we get *too* comfortable there.

"She said she thought everything was fine until she was getting ready for her annual review with the company's board," Anton said. "Then she realized she wasn't feeling motivated about making new plans or setting new goals."

He explained that after this realization, Linda reviewed the goals she set for the company during the previous two years and noticed they weren't nearly as innovative as the ones she'd set a few years earlier. "That was a wake-up call for her," Anton said. "She knows she has to do something to improve things, but she's comfortable with her success and said she can't get motivated to make changes."

She had a stable career, strong relationships with leadership and suppliers, a supportive team, and consistent results. On paper, it was exactly the kind of professional success most people strive for. But when Anton dug deeper, Linda kept using one word to describe her experience: *fine.*

Her work was fine. Her relationships with colleagues were fine. Her performance reviews were fine. But when he asked what felt alive in her work lately—what energized her, inspired her, or stretched her—she paused.

"I used to have big ideas for this company," she said. "I used to stay late because I was excited about projects. Now I just... manage things. I guess that's enough."

She wasn't sad. She wasn't overwhelmed. She wasn't angry. She was simply idling, like a song that had lost its melody but kept playing.

When Anton reviewed Linda's patterns with me, it became clear she was experiencing the Comfort Zone's negative state: complacency. She wasn't in distress, but she wasn't deeply engaged either. Her professional life had slipped into a kind of autopilot—familiar, stable, but lacking the vitality that had once characterized her work.

"It's like her career is in cruise control," Anton said. "She's not accelerating or changing lanes. Just maintaining."

There was no crisis to resolve, no breakdown to address, but there was also no hunger, no direction, no stretch. That's the subtle challenge of complacency—not where things are actively bad, but where nothing is pulling you toward what's possible. When Anton and I looked over Linda's patterns, it was clear she was drifting—not struggling but no longer lit up. She was in the Comfort Zone's shadow state: nothing was asking her to stretch.

"The goal isn't to wake her up with pressure," Anton said. "It's to help her hear what's quietly calling."

Over the next few months, Linda didn't overhaul her role or chase some big new goal. Instead, she began noticing where her work still stirred her, where it felt hollow, where aliveness flickered beneath the routine. She paid more attention to her days. She asked better questions. And slowly, the way she inhabited her work shifted—not her position, not her plans, but the way she showed up each day.

When Anton and I reconnected months later, he had an update. "She's not trying to become someone else," Anton told me. "She's finally recognizing the version of herself that's been waiting inside the stillness."

INSIDE THE COMFORT ZONE

The Comfort Zone rarely arrives with fanfare. It doesn't announce itself with crisis or celebration. It settles in quietly, often disguised as maturity, wisdom, or well-earned peace. And in many ways, it is all those things. But when comfort stops being intentional and starts being automatic, something subtle but significant begins to shift.

You're no longer resting—you're stalling. You're no longer content—you're complacent. You're not stuck because life is difficult. You're stuck because nothing is demanding that you move.

That's why the Comfort Zone can be so easy to settle into indefinitely. There's no obvious reason to leave. No crisis forcing change. No external pressure creating urgency. But if you pay attention, you might notice the signs:

Your days start to blur into predictable patterns

Your ambitions quietly shrink to match your routines

Your language softens—"I guess," "It's fine," "Maybe someday"

The distance grows between the life you're living and the life that still wants to emerge

Contentment is alive. It's full of presence, gratitude, and quiet alignment with what matters. Complacency is the absence of tension, but also the absence of growth. One nourishes your wholeness. The other slowly numbs your edge.

That's the paradox of this zone: Rest is necessary for sustainable well-being, but without direction, rest can become retreat. Without purpose, peace can become plateau.

If you feel a quiet dullness rather than peaceful clarity, if your routines keep you safe but not inspired, if your comfort comes at the cost of aliveness, then you need to ask: What in you still wants to move?

TWO STATES OF COMFORT

The Comfort Zone, like every zone of well-being, has two states: one that restores, and one that quietly diminishes.

Comfort – Purposehood = Complacency

Why mess with a good thing?

This is fine; I don't need more.

Change is risky. I'd rather stay where I am.

Comfort + Purposehood = Contentment

I'm at peace but open to what's next.

I'm grateful for now and curious about more.

I'm resting, not resisting.

On the surface both states can look remarkably similar: a steady routine, a manageable life, the absence of major conflict or distress. But beneath that surface they feel entirely different.

Complacency is what happens when comfort becomes unconscious. You're no longer reaching, not because you're fulfilled but because you've quietly stopped listening to what's possible. It arises from misdirection and stagnation: you've lost your guiding purpose and closed yourself off to growth.

Contentment, on the other hand, is deliberate stillness. Rest with awareness. Alignment without urgency. In this state, you're not pushing toward something, but you're not drifting either. You're anchored in what matters.

The difference is intention. Contentment is full of meaning. Complacency has let meaning fade.

Both can wear the mask of peace. Only one is truly nourishing.

⏸ PURPOSEHOOD PAUSE

Take a moment to honestly assess your relationship with comfort.

- Which area of your life feels most settled right now?

- In that area, are you experiencing contentment (peaceful but open) or complacency (settled but stagnant)?

- What would "conscious comfort" look like—rest that restores rather than retreats?

- If you imagined bringing more aliveness to your most comfortable routines, what would shift?

- Are you staying here because it's right or because it's easy?

Close your eyes and feel the difference between peaceful stillness and numbing stagnation in your body. Let comfort be your cradle, not your cage.

WHY PEOPLE STAY IN COMFORT

The Comfort Zone is, by design, a place that feels good to inhabit. Unlike zones where internal tension eventually creates motivation for change, the Comfort Zone can feel so pleasant that people remain there for years without recognizing they've stopped growing.

Some find deep satisfaction in predictability and control. After periods of uncertainty or challenge, the ability to know what each day will bring can feel profoundly healing. The routines become sacred, the stability becomes precious, and any disruption feels threatening rather than exciting.

Others become attached to the identity of "having arrived." When you've worked hard to achieve comfort—financial security, stable relationships, professional recognition—leaving that comfort can feel like ingratitude or foolishness. "Why would I risk what I've built?" becomes the guiding question.

Many simply don't realize that comfort without an openness to growth can become its own form of limitation. They mistake the absence of problems for the presence of fulfillment.

Some people linger because they fear that seeking more means they're ungrateful for what they have. There's a cultural narrative that says wanting more when you're already comfortable is selfish or greedy. But there's a difference between wanting more stuff and wanting more aliveness, more contribution, more growth.

Others stay because they've conflated comfort with completion. They believe that if they're not struggling, they must be done growing. But well-being isn't a destination; it's a dynamic process that requires ongoing attention and intention.

And sometimes people stay for an even simpler reason: they can't see what lies beyond the Comfort Zone. Without a clear vision of possibility, staying comfortable feels safer than stepping forward.

Whatever the reason for lingering, it's important that we recognize it. When we understand our reasons for staying, we can decide whether those reasons still serve us or whether it might be time to explore what else is possible.

COMPLACENCY—WHEN GROWTH STALLS

Complacency doesn't look like failure. That's what makes it so insidious. From the outside, people in complacency often appear to be successful, stable, and well-adjusted. They're meeting their obligations, maintaining their relationships, and avoiding major problems. But inside, something has gone quiet.

Complacency is the state of functioning without flourishing. It's going through the motions while the deeper currents of purpose and growth have slowed to a trickle. You're not suffering in an obvious way, but you're also not truly alive to your possibilities.

The hallmarks of complacency are:

Routines that feel more like ruts than rhythms

Goals that have shrunk to match current comfort levels

Resistance to opportunities that would require stretching

A subtle but persistent sense that something's missing

Defending current circumstances rather than exploring alternatives

Misdirection and stagnation work together to open the door to complacency. Misdirection means you've lost connection to your Purposehood—the why that once gave your choices meaning and direction. Without that guiding star, decisions become based on comfort and convenience rather than alignment and growth. Stagnation means you've stopped challenging yourself in meaningful ways. The absence of growth doesn't feel urgent because there's no crisis, but eventually your capacity for handling complexity, embracing change, and engaging with life's challenges begins to atrophy. A kind of existential sleepiness sets in. You're awake enough to function but not awake enough to truly engage with what's possible.

Linda's experience was a perfect example. She wasn't failing at her job; she was succeeding within increasingly narrow boundaries. Her goals had become modest, her expectations had adjusted downward, and her sense of what was possible had quietly contracted to match her current reality.

The danger of complacency is that it feels fine, and "fine" can become a prison as confining as any crisis, just more comfortable. But the Comfort Zone holds another possibility; one that looks similar from the outside but feels entirely different from within.

CONTENTMENT—INTENTIONAL PRESENCE

If complacency is unconscious comfort, contentment is comfort with awareness. It's the ability to rest without retreating, to be satisfied without becoming stagnant, to enjoy what you have while remaining open to what's emerging. It means you're growing from a place of stability rather than desperation. You're not pushing yourself toward the next achievement because you're trying to escape dissatisfaction—you're choosing your direction from a place of wholeness.

The hallmarks of contentment are:

Deep appreciation for what you've created and experienced

Openness to new possibilities without urgency or desperation

Routines that nourish rather than constrain

The ability to be fully present with current circumstances

Openness to growth without attachment to specific outcomes

Contentment is anchored in the Purposehood pillars that matter most in this zone: direction, gratitude, connection, and meaning. Even in stillness, you remain oriented toward what matters. Even in rest, you stay connected to the larger currents of your life.

DANIEL'S CONTENTMENT JOURNEY

Anton shared another story from his coaching practice that illustrated contentment beautifully.

Daniel was a senior executive at a global logistics company whose assessment showed most of his life components in the Comfort Zone, but unlike Linda, he wasn't drifting. He was deliberately still.

"He told me, 'This is the first time in twenty years I don't feel like I'm chasing something,'" Anton said. "'I've reached a plateau, and for once I want to sit on it and breathe.'"

At first Anton was concerned, but as their sessions unfolded, it became clear that Daniel wasn't in complacency. He was in contentment. He celebrated his achievements. He rested intentionally. He traveled slowly. He made time to reconnect regularly with mentors. He also made it a habit to review his WholeBeing map every month, asking himself whether his comfort still aligned with his evolving Purposehood. And in one session he shared a planning document with five columns—one for each extension of WholeBeing—with a single question at the top: "What kind of growth do I want to plant from here?"

That's what contentment looks like in practice. Not checking out, not stopping, but designing with clarity from a place of alignment.

"He's not stuck," Anton said with a smile. "He's anchored."

This is the distinction that matters: Complacency drifts, contentment chooses. Both can look like peace from the outside, but only contentment maintains agency within that peace.

NAVIGATING COMFORT CONSCIOUSLY

What carries you through the Comfort Zone isn't force or urgency. It's awareness, ongoing attention to whether your comfort is serving your growth or replacing it. You don't need to fix anything in this zone, but you do need to stay awake.

This zone rewards and deceives at the same time. It offers genuine rest and restoration—gifts that are essential for sustainable well-being. But if you're not paying attention, it can slowly dim the very light that makes rest worthwhile.

That's where Purposehood becomes essential, not as pressure to do more but as orientation toward what matters. Purposehood in the Comfort Zone might sound like: *I know why I'm here. This pause is part of my path. Resting doesn't mean I've stopped being open to growth. I'm grateful for this peace, and I'm listening for what wants to emerge.* The key Purposehood pillars in this zone don't push you out of comfort. They help you inhabit comfort consciously.

You don't need to force a plan for what comes next. In the Comfort Zone, the work is to rest without drifting, to restore yourself without retreating. This is the season to celebrate what's steady, to practice gratitude for what's here, and to listen for whether your comfort is nourishing renewal or quietly dimming your growth.

IF YOU RECOGNIZE YOURSELF HERE

If any part of your life is living in the Comfort Zone, pause here and ask: *Is this comfort still nourishing me? Or is it quietly dimming my light?*

You're allowed to rest. You're allowed to be content. And you're allowed to listen for what's next. This exploration doesn't require dramatic action. It doesn't mean you have to leave your job, end your relationship, or upend your life. It means paying attention to the subtle currents beneath your comfort.

Are you anchored here with intention, or have you drifted here without choosing? Is your peace full of presence, or has it become a kind of pleasant numbness? When you imagine the person you're becoming, does your current comfort support that vision or constrain it?

The Comfort Zone's gift is that it gives you the stability to explore these questions without panic or urgency. You can take your time. You can be thoughtful. You can make conscious choices about how long to stay and what kind of comfort serves you best.

This zone offers the profound gifts of teaching you that peace is possible, showing you that you can create stability, and providing the foundation from which all other growth becomes sustainable. But like every zone, it asks something of you in return: Stay conscious. Stay connected to what matters. Stay open to what wants to emerge.

You don't need to launch into action—just listen to your comfort, to your contentment, and to the quiet voice that knows whether this rest is restoring you or constraining you. Never passive, contentment is the stillness that prepares you for whatever movement wants to come next. And if you're really paying attention, you'll know when that time arrives.

If the Comfort Zone is your cradle of renewal, the Growth Zone is your edge of emergence. One restores, the other reawakens. And when your comfort becomes saturated with readiness, you'll feel it: that quiet pull toward expansion.

CHAPTER 10

THE GROWTH ZONE
WHEN GROWTH OUTPACES MEANING, RISE

You're creating something extraordinary. Building. Expanding. Discovering capacities you didn't know you had.

There's electricity in your days, the kind that comes from stretching beyond familiar boundaries and watching possibility become reality. You're not just surviving anymore; you're designing, contributing, becoming.

This is what you've been working toward: the sweet spot where vision meets momentum, where your efforts compound into something greater than their parts.

Welcome to the Growth Zone, the space where human potential unfolds.

This chapter explores the most dynamic territory of human experience—where rising becomes both your greatest possibility and your subtlest risk.

You're driven. Focused. Energetic. You're thriving. But sometimes, even at the peak of expansion, something can feel off—stretched thin, unsettled in ways that are hard to name.

The Growth Zone is where most of us want to spend our time. It's dynamic, energizing, and full of the satisfaction that comes from developing our capabilities and creating impact. It's where we stretch beyond our current boundaries and discover what we're truly capable of becoming.

But as you can probably predict by now, it's not that simple. Like the other zones, the Growth Zone is nuanced, with two distinct states:

Growth – Purposehood = Excess

Growth + Purposehood = Ambition

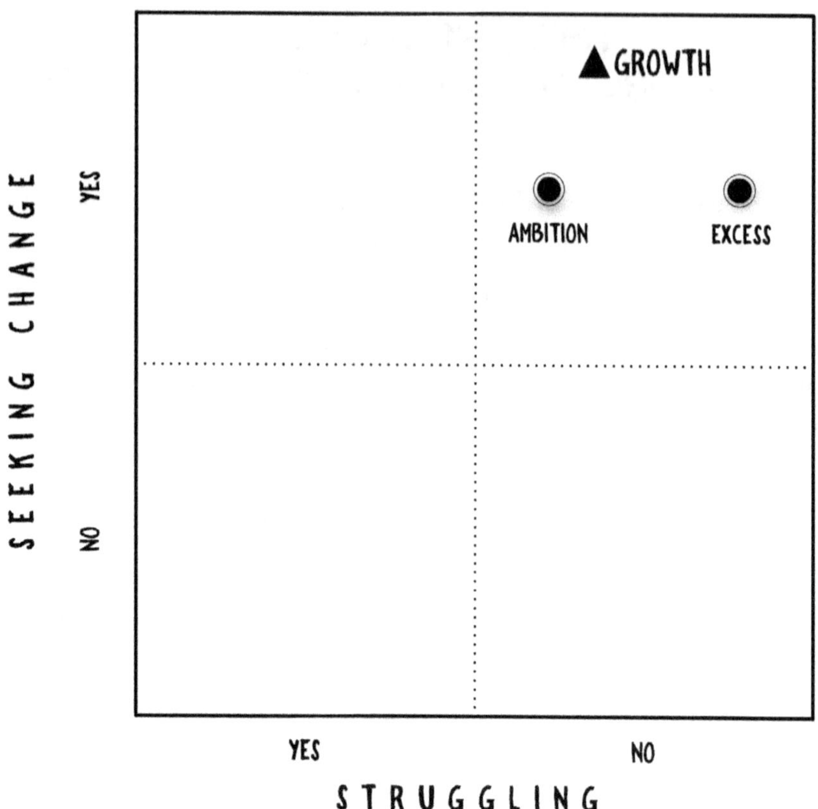

The goal of the Growth Zone is to rise—to expand with purpose, align ambition with meaning, and guard against excess by staying rooted in your sense of Purposehood.

This chapter is about the art of conscious expansion—how to harness the incredible energy of growth while maintaining the deeper connections that make achievement meaningful.

Not all growth serves the same destination. Some growth flows from authentic calling, expanding your capacity to contribute and create.

Other growth becomes reactive, compulsive, driven by internal pressure rather than purposeful direction. In this zone, the challenge often comes from misdirection and craving. You're moving fast, but toward what? You're achieving more but feeling less connected to why it matters.

This is what makes the Growth Zone both exhilarating and complex: the same energy that can elevate your life can also scatter it if it's not guided by something deeper than momentum alone. The very qualities that fuel your expansion can also redirect it. The drive that creates breakthrough can become the force that pulls you away from what matters most. Success itself can become seductive enough to make you forget why you wanted it in the first place. Like any powerful force, growth requires conscious direction to ensure that it serves your wholeness rather than consuming it.

When growth is rooted in Purposehood—when ambition serves something larger than itself—it becomes a calling and a conscious evolution in service of meaning. You don't need to slow down your growth or shrink your ambitions, but you'll benefit from asking: Is your growth guided by Purposehood, or is it pulling you away from what you value most?

Let's begin with stories from people who've navigated this territory and discovered the difference between growth that serves and growth that consumes.

STORIES FROM THE GROWTH ZONE

YPO LEADERS ON GROWTH CHALLENGES

During the first session of the Purposehood Engineering training for YPO members and their forum groups—a peer-learning expansion circle of fellow business leaders—the room was buzzing with energy. These were founders, presidents, and leaders of sizable businesses—people who had built significant organizations and were committed to continual improvement, not just in business but across all areas of life.

John, the founder of several international companies, was especially enthusiastic. His focus was razor-sharp, and it was clear he was committed to growth. His recent assessment results showed that many of his life's components were in the Growth Zone, giving him an ideal opportunity to expand beyond his current achievements.

As I began explaining the Growth Zone, John raised his hand. "How can I really capitalize on this Growth Zone? I'm always looking for ways to improve, but I want to make sure I'm growing in the right direction, not just spinning my wheels."

Alia, a tech entrepreneur, leaned in, nodding. "I'm wondering the same thing. There's always pressure to grow and push forward, but how do we know if we're overdoing it?"

Ravi, who'd built a successful consulting firm, added his perspective: "I've seen people, myself included, burn out from pushing too hard. How do we keep that balance between ambition and overexertion?"

This opened the floor to a rich discussion, with members sharing their experiences of growth and the challenges that came with it.

"Let's take a deeper look at what can happen when growth becomes unbalanced," I said. "While the Growth Zone is a place of vibrant expansion and potential, when we push too hard without proper anchoring, excess can create problems that undermine the very growth we're pursuing."

Ravi raised his hand again. "How's that possible if we're already growing?"

"Great question," I said. "Let me give you some examples of how this typically unfolds."

HOW EXCESS CREATES IMBALANCE

Overworking and Burnout

"Think about the initial phase of growth," I said to the group. "We set ambitious goals and work diligently to achieve them. This phase often brings tremendous satisfaction and momentum."

John nodded. "That's exactly what happened when I launched my second company. The energy was incredible."

"But what happens when we become so engrossed in our goals that we start overworking, neglecting rest, and pushing our bodies and minds beyond healthy limits?"

Alia winced. "Physical and mental exhaustion."

"Exactly. That exhaustion—what we call burnout—depletes the very energy and creativity that fuel sustainable growth. You end up having to stop and recover, often for months."

Neglect of Relationships

"Here's another pattern I see frequently," I said. "Personal and professional relationships initially provide support, inspiration, and opportunities for growth. Strong connections often fuel further progress."

Ravi leaned forward. "But when you become excessively focused on personal ambitions..."

"You start neglecting those relationships," I finished. "You spend less time with loved ones, become emotionally unavailable, prioritize work over social connections. The resulting isolation and conflict drain your energy and can destabilize the very foundation that supported your growth."

Obsessive Goal Pursuit

"The mental and emotional strain from relentless pursuit can create anxiety, depression, and a loss of perspective that undermines both performance and satisfaction," I explained.

John shifted in his seat. "I think I've experienced some of that. The pressure to constantly achieve more."

Crisis and Collapse

"Sometimes we face major crises—business failures, health scares, market collapses, or personal losses," I said. "When leaders who've been in relentless growth mode suddenly encounter these challenges, they can find themselves completely derailed, questioning everything they've been working toward."

Alia nodded. "I've seen that. It's like all that drive just... disappears."

"That's where we return to Purposehood," I said. "When we operate from Purposehood, aligning our growth with deeper meaning, we prevent ourselves from veering into excess."

ELENA—SUCCESS WITHOUT SATISFACTION

After the intensive two-and-a-half-hour session, I received a follow-up message from Elena, a marketing company president who'd attended with her YPO forum. She wanted to discuss her assessment results privately.

When we met the following week, she was direct about her situation.

"My life looks like success," she said. "Youngest president in my company's history. Leading international expansion. Board seats. Speaking engagements. On paper, I'm exactly who the world says we should become." She paused. "And I'm exhausted."

Elena's REVEAL360—Purposehood WholeBeing Assessment results had shown a clear pattern: multiple components in the Growth Zone but several tipping into its negative state—excess.

Elena wasn't falling apart. She was simply out of alignment. Her calendar was full, her goals were ambitious, and her energy was relentless, but something fundamental was missing.

"I wake up at 5 a.m. for workouts, have back-to-back meetings until 8 p.m., then work on presentations until midnight," she said. "I'm achieving everything I thought I wanted, but I can't remember the last time I felt satisfied."

Elena was recognizing the signs of excess: misdirection and craving. She was moving fast but had lost connection to why the movement mattered. She was achieving more but feeling less fulfilled.

"I keep thinking that the next acquisition, the next deal, the next industry recognition will make me feel complete," she said. "But it never does. There's always something more to chase. My life feels like it's running without me."

This is excess in action: growth that's become compulsive rather than conscious, driven by an internal craving for more rather than by a connection to deeper purpose and wholeness across all extensions of being.

Elena's story illustrates how success itself can become a trap when it's not anchored in deeper meaning. The very achievements that appear to validate growth can become evidence that we're accumulating rather than evolving, gaining more without becoming more.

INSIDE THE GROWTH ZONE

John was energized by the challenge of optimizing his growth. Elena was exhausted by the relentlessness of hers.

Both were in the same zone. Both were achieving significant results. But their relationships to growth were fundamentally different.

John was asking, *How can I grow more effectively?* Elena was wondering, *Why doesn't this growth feel like enough?*

That difference reveals the heart of this zone: You can be expanding rapidly and still feel misaligned. You can be achieving more than ever and still sense that something essential is missing.

The Growth Zone asks a question that can't be answered with more activity: What is this growth in service of?

When growth becomes unmoored from existential purpose, it can feel like:

Running faster on a treadmill that's going nowhere

Accumulating achievements that don't add up to fulfillment

Expanding your capacity while contracting your joy

Being successful in ways that don't feel meaningful

When growth is anchored in Purposehood, it feels like:

Stretching toward something sacred

Building capacity in service of what matters

Expanding in ways that include rather than exclude other parts of your life

Becoming more of who you're meant to be

If you recognize yourself in this zone, notice:

Are you growing toward something or away from something?

Does your expansion feel sustainable, or are you running on fumes?

Are you becoming more integrated or more fragmented?

When you imagine slowing down, does it feel like rest or like failure?

The zone itself is neutral—neither good nor bad. Being in the Growth Zone means you're engaged with expansion and possibility, a state that can be both powerful and revealing. Where you are within the zone simply shows you what kind of growth is most aligned with your well-being.

TWO STATES OF GROWTH

Not all growth serves the same master. Some growth is conscious, sustainable, and deeply satisfying. Other growth becomes compulsive, exhausting, and somehow empty despite external success. That's the difference between the two states of the Growth Zone:

Growth – Purposehood = Excess

I have to keep going or I'll fall behind.

Success is everything, even if I'm burning out.

If I slow down, I'll lose everything I've built.

Growth + Purposehood = Ambition

I want to grow but not at the cost of myself or my relationships.

My drive is aligned with my values.

I'm expanding with purpose, not just pressure.

The external activities might look identical—both people might be working long hours, setting big goals, and achieving impressive results—but the internal experience is completely different.

Excess is growth that's lost its grounding in meaning. It's driven by craving—for more recognition, more achievement, more control, more validation. The growth becomes compulsive rather than conscious.

Ambition is growth that serves something bigger than itself. It's driven by calling rather than craving, by purpose rather than pressure. The growth feels integrated rather than fragmented.

WHY PEOPLE STAY IN GROWTH

The Growth Zone can become surprisingly addictive, precisely because it feels so positive and productive. Unlike zones where discomfort eventually motivates change, the Growth Zone can feel so energizing that people remain there long past the point when it stops serving their sense of balance.

Some become intoxicated by the "growth high": the biochemical rush of achievement, the social validation of success, and the sense of momentum can create a kind of addiction. The fear of losing that high keeps them pushing forward even when other areas of life begin to suffer.

Others confuse activity with progress. They mistake being busy for being productive, movement for advancement. The sheer volume of growth-related activity can feel like evidence of success even when the growth lacks direction or sustainability.

Many are driven by comparative growth, measuring themselves against others rather than against their own values and purposes. Social media, professional networks, and cultural messages can create pressure to grow faster, bigger, and more visibly than feels authentic or sustainable.

Some linger because they fear that slowing down means giving up. They've internalized the truth that "if you're not growing, you're contracting," but they've mistaken constant external expansion for growth. The idea of intentional pausing or strategic consolidation feels like stagnation rather than a necessary part of the growth cycle.

Others stay because they don't know how to integrate what they've achieved. They've accumulated skills, resources, and opportunities but haven't developed the capacity to synthesize them into sustainable systems. So they keep adding more instead of deepening what they have.

Perhaps most commonly, people linger in growth because they're using expansion to avoid other emotional work. Growth can feel safer than healing, more socially acceptable than rest, more controllable than the uncertainty of other zones. The constant forward motion can become a way to outrun internal questions or unresolved issues.

When we recognize why we linger, we ensure that our growth serves our wholeness rather than fragmenting it. The invitation isn't to stop but to grow with grace—to let Purposehood, not momentum, lead the way.

EXCESS—WHEN GROWTH CONSUMES

Excess doesn't look like failure from the outside. People in excess are often highly successful, respected, and achieving impressive results. They're the ones others look to as examples of what's possible. But inside, something essential has been sacrificed on the altar of expansion.

Excess is growth without integration, expansion without sustainability, achievement without fulfillment. It's the state of constantly doing more while feeling less connected to why any of it matters.

The hallmarks of excess are:

Chronic feelings of "not enough" despite external success

Difficulty enjoying achievements because you're already focused on the next goal

Physical, emotional, or relational strain from unsustainable pace

Growth in one area, neglect in others

Workaholism, strained relationships, compromised health

A sense that slowing down would mean losing momentum or falling behind

Excess mainly arises from misdirection and craving. As we've learned, misdirection means you've lost connection to your deeper purpose, and without that guiding star, growth becomes about attaining more for the sake of more rather than expansion in service of something meaningful. Craving is the compulsive need for more—more achievement, more recognition, more control, more validation. It's growth driven by internal emptiness rather than by fullness seeking expression.

Together, these create a distorted mindset about success—the belief that you must constantly prove your worth through achievement rather than grow from inherent worth.

Elena clearly held this belief. She was extraordinarily successful by any external measure, but her growth had become compulsive rather than conscious. Each achievement created pressure for the next one rather than satisfaction with the current one.

The danger of excess isn't that it produces poor results—it's that it produces great results at an unsustainable cost. And eventually, that cost catches up with us, often leading to the very contraction that the excess was trying to prevent.

AMBITION—PURPOSEFUL GROWTH

If excess is unconscious growth, ambition is growth with awareness and intention. It's the ability to expand sustainably, achieve meaningfully, and develop capacity in service of something larger than personal gratification. It means your growth is guided by purpose rather than driven by craving, anchored in values rather than driven by comparison, integrated across your whole life rather than concentrated in one area.

The hallmarks of ambition:

Clear connection between your growth activities and your deeper purpose

Sustainable pace that honors your whole system, not just your productivity

Integration of achievements into wisdom rather than just accumulation

Growth that enhances rather than competes with other areas of life

The ability to pause, reflect, and choose direction rather than just react to opportunities

Ambition is anchored in the Purposehood pillars that matter most in this zone: direction, gratitude, connection, and meaning. These pillars ensure that growth serves wholeness rather than fragmenting it.

John demonstrated healthy ambition beautifully. His questions weren't about how to achieve more, but about how to ensure that his growth was aligned and sustainable. He wanted to capitalize on his Growth Zone positioning without losing himself in the process.

When you're in healthy ambition:

You grow from strength rather than from emptiness

Your achievements feel satisfying rather than just stimulating

You can enjoy success without immediately needing the next success

Your growth enhances your relationships rather than threatening them

You expand in ways that feel integrated with who you're becoming

The shift from excess to ambition often begins with a simple question: What is this growth in service of? When you can answer that question with something deeper than "more," you've found your way back to Purposehood.

CHANNELING GROWTH WITH PURPOSEHOOD

What carries you through the Growth Zone is clarity about why you're growing and who you're becoming through the growth. This zone tests your relationship to existential purpose more than any other.

It's easy to stay connected to meaning when you're struggling and need hope or when you're healing and need direction, but success makes it tempting to ride the momentum rather than stay conscious of the direction. And that's where Purposehood becomes essential, not as a brake on your growth but as a compass for it. The key Purposehood pillars in this zone ensure that your growth builds something that's sustainable rather than just impressive.

Purposehood in the Growth Zone might sound like: *I know why this matters. This expansion serves something larger than me. I can grow without losing myself. My ambition includes my wholeness.*

You don't need to apologize for your ambition or scale back your dreams. You just need to make sure that your dreams are truly yours and that achieving them will make you more of who you're meant to be, not less.

⏸ PURPOSEHOOD PAUSE

Think of an area where you're growing or achieving

Does this growth energize or exhaust you?

Are you expanding toward something meaningful or away from something uncomfortable?

What would "enough" look like in this area?

When you imagine slowing down, do you feel relief or anxiety?

Note: Growth guided by purpose feels different in your body than growth driven by craving.

IF YOU RECOGNIZE YOURSELF HERE

If any part of your life is living in the Growth Zone right now, pause for a moment of honest reflection.

You're not doing too much simply because you're ambitious. You're not in danger just because you're moving fast. Growth isn't the enemy. But ask yourself: Is this still growth—or has it become craving?

If you feel stretched, driven, even overwhelmed—without knowing exactly why—you may be tipping into excess. If so, it's time to reorient, to remember your why, your Purposehood.

When you align your growth with meaning, choose what truly matters, and pace yourself from within, you're living in the state of ambition. Hold it gently. Honor it. Stay close to it.

The Growth Zone is powerful. When navigated with awareness, it becomes a catalyst for success, significance, and the purposeful expansion of who you're meant to become.

This zone's gift is to reveal capacities you didn't know you had and prove that you can be an active agent of transforming your life into the life you want. And what it asks in return is that you stay conscious, stay connected to what matters, and stay integrated.

Alignment is what growth requires. When you discover this truth, your expansion becomes a gift not just to yourself but to everyone your life touches.

This completes our journey through the four zones of well-being. You've explored contraction and healing, comfort and growth. You've seen how each zone contains both challenges and opportunities and how your relationship to Purposehood determines which experience you have. Take a moment to appreciate that clarity.

When you're ready, we'll explore how to work skillfully with these zones, how to support yourself in moving between them consciously, and how to build the capacity for navigating all of life's terrain with wisdom and grace. But for now, let this be enough: You've mapped the territory of your experience. You understand where you are and what each location offers. You've developed the most essential skill for well-being: the ability to clearly see where you are, without judgment, and with deep appreciation for the journey itself.

The question that will guide everything that follows isn't whether you can change but how consciously you can navigate the changes that are already unfolding, how skillfully you can support yourself through every zone, how intentionally you can design a life that honors both your humanity and your highest aspirations.

182

already unfolding, how skillfully you can support yourself through every zone, how intentionally you can design a life that honors both your humanity and your highest aspirations.

CHAPTER 11

SUPPORT
THE ART FRAMEWORK

A few days after completing her REVEAL360—Purposehood WholeBeing Assessment, Sarah (the HR director we met earlier in the Contraction Zone) sat in her office alone, reviewing the results one more time.

She understood the zones and could clearly identify with the state of each of her components. Her job component was in the Contraction Zone with resignation. Her emotional self was also struggling and not seeking change. Many other components were in positive states, but she wasn't yet sure how to build on them.

For the first time in a long while, she had clarity. She understood where she was and what needed attention. The assessment hadn't just given her information; it had given her language. Her WholeBeing was no longer a tangled ball of stress and instinct; it was a mapped landscape of zones and states, each inviting a different kind of response.

But understanding the map and knowing which direction to take next were two different things.

"It's like I finally see it," she said to me on a follow-up video call. "I know where the problems are, and that they're mine to work on. I just don't know where to go next, or how to stay on track when life pushes back."

Sarah had run into one of the most common challenges in the transformation process: the gap between assessment and action. She wasn't confused or unmotivated—she was engaged. But what she lacked was structure. She needed a way to move forward intentionally, without slipping back into old patterns. She needed support. Not encouragement or vague advice but systematic support. A clear way to act on what she'd already discovered without trying to fix everything at once.

This is where the third step of the EASE process becomes essential. Once you've engaged with your desire to change and assessed your WholeBeing across the zones and states, you need systematic support and guidance to turn insight into sustainable transformation.

In the Purposehood Method for Existential Health, you stay at the center of your own healing and growth. Support is not there to take the wheel; it strengthens your capacity to steer. It equips you to move through life with clarity. What you receive is direction: a compass that helps you navigate your mapped WholeBeing intentionally, choosing the resources that truly match your zone and state rather than reacting to whatever feels urgent in the moment.

Sarah didn't need to overhaul her entire life. She just needed to know how to shift from resignation and emotional strain to emotional strength, and she needed a framework she could later share with the employees who were struggling too.

RETHINKING WHAT SUPPORT MEANS

"I've tried therapy, coaching, self-help—they helped with specific issues, but I still felt scattered," Sarah said. "They all promised to help, but most of them just made me feel like I was failing when I couldn't keep up with their systems."

Sarah's hesitation about support wasn't uncommon. In fact, it revealed something important about why many people struggle with transformation: they've learned to distrust the very idea of support.

For many who've done inner work, the term support feels loaded. It might feel:

Prescriptive: someone telling you what to do without understanding your unique situation or readiness level

Overwhelming: too many tools, steps, or practices that add pressure rather than provide relief

Temporary: helpful during sessions or while reading but hard to sustain in real life

One-size-fits-all: generic advice that didn't match your specific circumstances, relationships, or constraints

Dependency-creating: systems that made you feel capable only when following someone else's guidance

If any of that resonates, your hesitation makes perfect sense. Your resistance is intelligent self-protection based on experience. Rather than honoring how transformation actually works from the inside out, most approaches to support are built on external strategies. Real support doesn't push—it aligns. It works with your readiness and your resistance, not against them. It honors your WholeBeing rather than treating you as a problem to be solved.

A unique strength of The Purposehood Method for Existential Health is that it guides multiple components of your WholeBeing—each in different zones and states—and shows, with simplicity, what to do with that complexity. That's what Sarah needed. Her desire for change was clear, and her REVEAL360 assessment results showed her exactly where she stood. Now she needed systematic support that honored her readiness without overwhelming her. So I introduced her to the ART framework.

THE ART FRAMEWORK

Think of ART—*Attain, Retain, Train*—like tending a fire. *Attain* is striking the spark, a fragile but vital beginning. *Retain* is feeding it with care, so it grows steady and strong. *Train* is learning how to keep it burning through wind and rain so the warmth lasts even when the world grows cold.

The ART framework is the heart of the support step in the EASE process. It's the structured method we use to turn insight into a plan and then make that movement sustainable across time, setbacks, and changing life conditions.

Each phase of ART answers a specific need in the transformation process:

Attain: What's the first meaningful shift I can make to move from a negative state to a positive one before leaving my zone?

Retain: How do I stabilize that shift, reinforce it, and make it part of my new normal?

Train: How do I build the capacity to sustain positive states and return to them whenever life tests me?

Together, these steps form a repeatable framework you can apply to any component of your WholeBeing, whether it's your existential health, physical well-being, your emotional landscape, your family dynamics, your work challenges, or your relationship with nature.

At its essence, ART is beautifully simple: Attain what needs shifting. Retain what's working. Train to make it last.

You don't need to master every zone or component at once. Start with just one—Attain one shift. Retain one gain. Train in one practice.

UNIVERSAL FRAMEWORK, PERSONAL APPLICATION

The ART framework is universal in structure but uniquely personal in application. Two components may both be in the Healing Zone and yet require completely different interventions. One might need emotional empowerment, the other work-related clarity. The zone is shared, but the expression is unique to each component.

Your assessment results will reveal a mosaic of states across your WholeBeing. Some components may be stuck in resignation or complacency, while others may be healing or thriving. That's why ART is strategic. You apply the right step to the right state.

Here's how the three steps of ART apply to your WholeBeing components:

If a component is in a negative state of resignation, dependency, complacency, or excess, your plan begins with *Attain*: shifting it toward its positive counterpart within that same zone.

If a component is already in a positive state of endurance, empowerment, contentment, or ambition, your plan focuses on *Retain*: reinforcing those gains and protecting your progress.

Over time, you'll *Train*: building the capacity to navigate challenges with the deeper knowledge and practices aligned with each zone.

This becomes your compass for healing and growth. But keep in mind that ART works best when kept simple. Choose one component that feels ready for attention. Then attain one shift, retain one gain, and train in one practice. Everything else can wait, because the ultimate goal is to sustain all your components on the path of ease: remaining in positive states across zones, even as life changes.

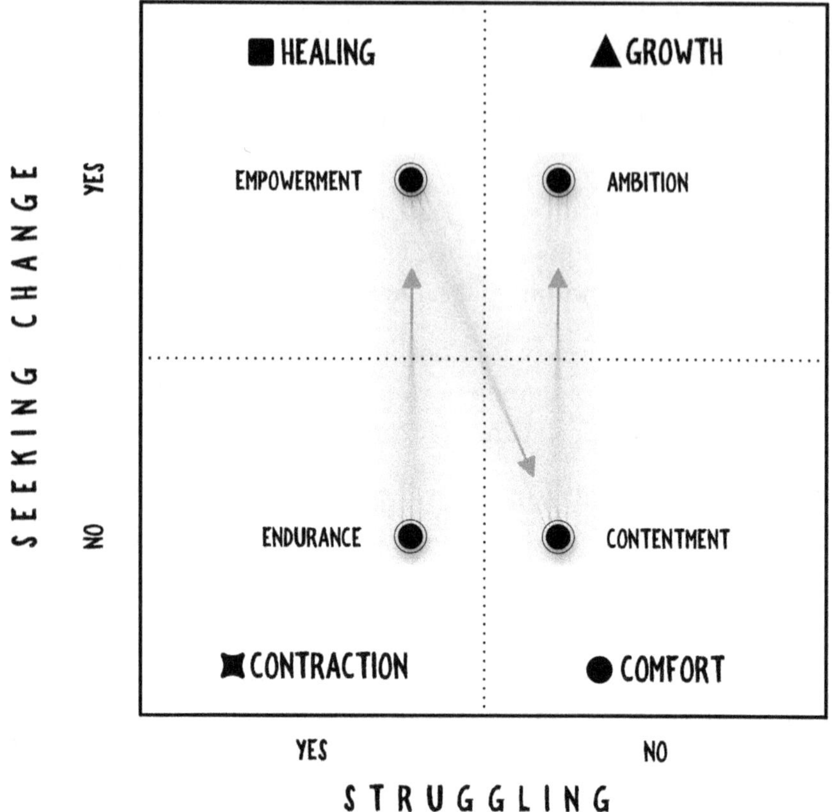

ATTAIN—SHIFTING TO POSITIVE STATES

Because every change starts with one internal shift

The first step in the ART framework is simple to understand and deceptively powerful in practice: Attain.

Attain means making a meaningful internal shift from a negative state to a positive state within the same zone of well-being. It's about finding a foothold where you are and shifting one component of your Whole-Being from stuck to flowing, from constriction to movement, from withdrawal to engagement.

When we're in a negative state, especially for a long time, it can feel like we're trapped in quicksand. Every effort is exhausting. We may start to believe that change isn't possible or that it requires something huge, dramatic, or externally imposed. *Attain* breaks that illusion. It helps you find your first steppingstone—just enough stability to stop sinking, just enough movement to remind you that change is possible.

Attain says: You don't need to escape your life. You need to shift within it.

Making this shift matters because:

It breaks the downward spiral. Without intervention, negative states reinforce themselves. *Attain* interrupts that pattern.

It builds confidence and personal agency. A successful shift, even a small one, restores your sense of possibility.

It creates the foundation for deeper change. We can't retain anything if we haven't first moved toward a positive state.

Attain requires finding the change your system is existentially ready for. Your assessment results revealed which components of your WholeBeing are in negative states and *Attain* invites you to choose one and begin an existential shift, a meaningful movement from inner misalignment to alignment. The shift may be subtle, but it should be felt. It should be powerful enough that your internal experience of that component begins to transform, not just functionally but in terms of identity, direction, and meaning.

Attain means shifting from a negative state to a positive one within the same zone. Here's what that looks like across the four zones:

Contraction Zone—Attain Endurance

Move from resignation: *Nothing will change* to endurance: *It's hard, but I'm still here for a reason.*

Healing Zone—Attain Empowerment

Move from dependency: *Someone else needs to fix this for me* to empowerment: *I'm learning to trust my own capacity.*

Comfort Zone—Attain Contentment

Move from complacency: *Why mess with a good thing?* to contentment: *I'm at peace but open to what's next.*

Growth Zone—Attain Ambition

Move from excess: *I have to keep going or I'll fall behind* to ambition: *I want to grow, but not at the cost of my wholeness.*

The power of *Attain* lies in its directionality, not its magnitude. A micro-existential shift is enough if it changes your state. For example, the shift might sound like this: "I don't need to solve this today. I just need to shift how I relate to it." Most transformation efforts fail because they leap too far too fast. *Attain* respects the step you're ready to take now.

RETAIN—STRENGTHENING POSITIVE STATES

Because progress stays only when you give it roots

Attain is the spark. *Retain* is the flame-keeper, the deliberate practice that makes shifts sustainable.

Just like with *Attain,* your REVEAL360 results will show you which components are already in positive states. *Retain* is your way of reinforcing those states immediately instead of waiting until something slips. It's also what you'll apply after making an *Attain* shift to hold the new state steady. Either way, *Retain* is active, precise, and essential to sustaining your path forward, whether you're stabilizing new growth or nurturing existing strengths.

Once you've shifted a component of your WholeBeing into a positive state, the work isn't over; it's just beginning. In Purposehood, *Retain* means anchoring an existential shift long enough for it to become part of who you are, practicing it until it reshapes your identity.

Without retention, even profound breakthroughs like reconnecting with meaning, reclaiming agency, or restoring mattering can fade under life's pressures. We regress when the inner architecture hasn't been reinforced. *Retain* is about deliberately sustaining the internal and external conditions that made the existential shift possible and then deepening them.

Retain:

- Prevents regression to the original negative state (e.g., endurance sliding back into resignation)

- Deepens the positive state so it becomes less fragile and more embodied

- Supports upward movement along the ease path (e.g., endurance → empowerment → contentment → ambition)

Retain is existential integration, the process of turning insight into identity and turning positive state into a stable platform for Purpose-hood-centered growth. Most people underestimate this phase, believing that once a breakthrough happens, it should "stick." But in reality, our old defaults are deeply ingrained—emotionally, relationally, neurologically, even culturally.

A person who rebuilds their confidence must actively nurture it, not just intellectually, but in their body. Notice how confidence feels different in your chest when it's genuine rather than performed. *Retain* means paying attention to that felt sense, creating the conditions that let real confidence settle into your nervous system.

RETAIN STRATEGIES BY ZONE

Each zone has a corresponding positive state to retain. Retaining that state keeps your WholeBeing from slipping and supports your next evolution.

Contraction Zone—Retain Endurance

Maintain structure and simple routines. Remind yourself why you're still showing up. Anchor yourself with small meaningful wins.

Healing Zone—Retain Empowerment

Keep choosing agency. Reinforce new beliefs. Celebrate progress. Stay connected to environments that support autonomy.

Comfort Zone—Retain Contentment

Practice gratitude. Savor the ordinary. Don't confuse peace with passivity. Stay meaningfully engaged without forcing more.

Growth Zone—Retain Ambition

Stay grounded in values. Use intentional practices like reflections or "Nondays"—a weekly soul spa day away from distractions to reset and ensure that your drive remains aligned with your Purposehood.

This isn't about holding on tightly; it's about cultivating conditions. Retention lives in the background rhythms: meaningful rituals, nourishing environments, and regular check-ins that help you notice when your state is deepening or slipping.

TRAIN—BUILDING LONG-TERM CAPACITY

Because under stress, you fall back on what you've practiced

Train is what makes Attain and Retain sustainable. It's how positive states endure across time. The logic beneath it is simple:

Zone – Purposehood = Negative State

Zone + Purposehood = Positive State

Zones will shift. Life will test you. Components will move. Whether you remain on the path of ease depends on whether Purposehood is present when pressure arrives. Training is how you ensure that presence.

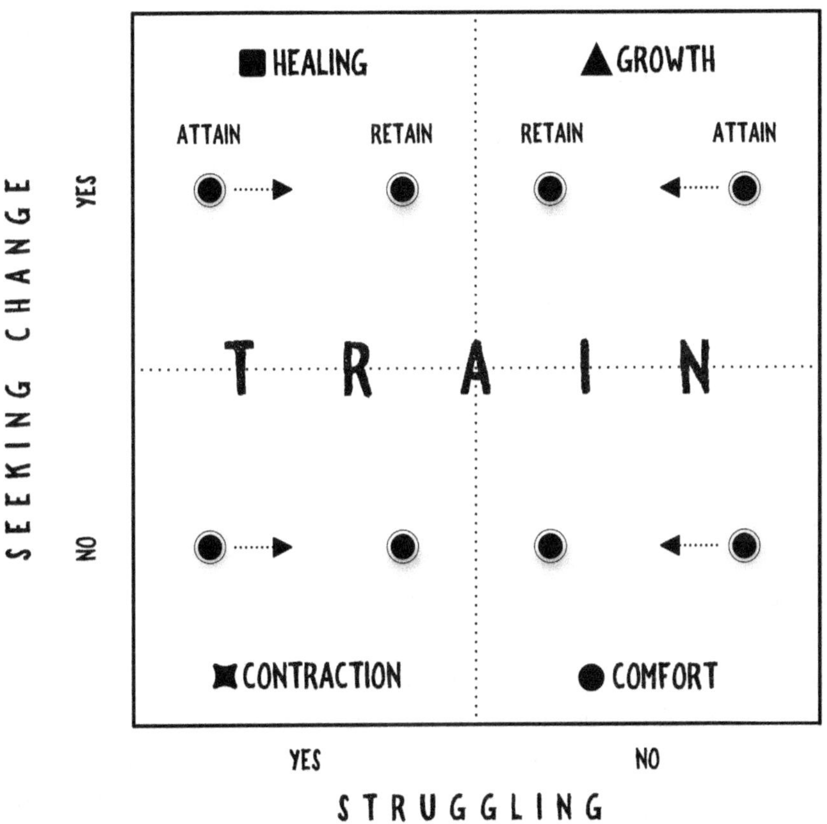

Without training, even your strongest shifts erode. Motivation fades. Old patterns resurface. Comfort drifts into complacency. Growth slides into excess. Contraction hardens into resignation. Healing slips back into dependency. Progress becomes fragile, dependent on mood and circumstance. With training, Purposehood doesn't disappear when life becomes unpredictable. It becomes embodied.

Once you've made a shift, life will inevitably test you—through crisis, temptation, distraction, or the quiet unraveling of habit. When it does, what will you fall back on?

Years ago, at a YPO event in San Diego, a Navy SEAL elite trainer said something I've never forgotten: "When my SEALs come under attack, I don't want them to rise to the challenge; I want them to fall back on their training." The same truth holds across every extension of your WholeBeing. Under pressure, we fall back on our conditioning. Training ensures that what you fall back on is Purposehood.

In Purposehood, training is existential readiness. It's ongoing preparation that keeps your WholeBeing positively anchored across all zones. It complements any clinical, psychological, or specialized support you may receive by strengthening the foundation beneath it—direction, meaning, and alignment. You're not just working on yourself; you're building a structure that holds you when life becomes chaotic.

Each zone carries a predictable source of existential suffering, and each requires its own disciplined training. ART provides the logic of support; Purposehood Engineering provides the structured training system through which that support is practiced over time. In the Contraction Zone, you train to Rebound, overcoming disorientation with direction and endurance. In the Healing Zone, you train to Recover, replacing limiting beliefs with empowering ones. In the Comfort Zone, you train to Rest without drifting into stagnation. In the Growth Zone, you train to Rise, guarding ambition from cravings and excess. Beneath them all, you train to Realize, remaining rooted in your Purposehood Guiding Star—a clear declaration of the one thing you most deeply want for yourself and the one contribution you choose to make to the world. This grounding is continuous. You don't train only when you fall. You train so falling becomes less likely.

Training builds the capacity to move components consciously across zones while keeping them in positive states. It makes Attain repeatable and Retain durable. It builds the foundation of existential health from which healing and growth become sustainable rather than accidental.

This training unfolds through three reinforcing forces. Knowledge clarifies your patterns and sharpens awareness so you can recognize misdirection before it deepens, stagnation before it hardens, craving before it controls. Practice embeds insight into habit; repeated alignment turns intention into reflex, and what once required effort becomes embodied. Teamwork ensures that growth isn't solitary. Through community, expansion circles, or trusted partnerships, accountability strengthens discipline and support stabilizes progress.

Over time, something deeper begins to happen. Training stops being a defensive strategy. It becomes mastery.

STRATEGIC ORCHESTRATION— FROM TRAINING TO MASTERY

When Purposehood is practiced consistently, you stop reacting to life component by component. You begin orchestrating it. You're no longer trying to push every extension into Growth at once. You understand that stability in a positive state matters more than constant expansion. You don't need every component in the Growth Zone; you need every component in a positive state.

Sometimes that means Ambition. Sometimes it means Contentment. Sometimes it requires Empowerment. Sometimes it calls for Endurance. This is the dynamic design of WholeBeing stability in motion.

Life unfolds in seasons, and when every extension is pushed into expansion simultaneously, fragmentation is inevitable. Mastery recognizes that growth must rotate. One extension may stretch forward while others remain deliberately stabilized. Work may accelerate while family rests in steady contentment. Relationships may require renewed ambition while professional life holds its position. This isn't retreat; it's disciplined positioning.

There are moments when a component can't immediately expand or heal. A health limitation, financial constraint, or relational complexity may require time. Training allows you to hold that component in Endurance rather than Resignation. You remain steady without collapsing meaning.

Instead of reacting impulsively, you assess consciously: what needs Growth? What needs Stabilization? What requires Healing? What must simply be endured with patience? The reference point for every shift remains your Purposehood Guiding Star.

Without training, shifts happen unconsciously. With training, you notice early signals—tension, withdrawal, subtle loss of meaning—and reposition deliberately before negative states solidify.

Mastery is also relational. Because your extensions are interconnected, repositioning requires transparency. Expectations are aligned. Energy shifts are communicated. Collaboration replaces resistance.

For example, if you have been investing significant Ambition in your Family extension, rebuilding connection, strengthening bonds, and being intentionally present, while your Work extension has been resting in steady Contentment, there may come a season when work requires renewed expansion. Orchestration then means communicating clearly at home that your professional Ambition is about to increase. Together, you agree on expectations, time boundaries, and support structures so that Work can move into Ambition while Family remains stable in positive Contentment. The shift is coordinated, not reactive, and aligned with shared Purposehood.

Over time, this disciplined orchestration produces coherence. Not the ease of comfort, but the ease of alignment. You're no longer dependent on mood, momentum, or circumstance. You're capable of guiding your twenty-five components across the zones while keeping them in positive states.

That is existential mastery. And it's built through training.

WHY ART WORKS

Most self-help or coaching systems follow a familiar arc: awareness →
action → results. But this arc often breaks down for four reasons:

Mismatched interventions: You're given advice that doesn't match your
state. Someone in emotional resignation can't use the same tools as
someone in overdrive.

Surface-level fixes: Many approaches target symptoms like stress or
procrastination without addressing the deeper existential causes underneath.

Fragile structures: Motivation fades quickly without a framework to
hold change in place.

Shallow integration: Even when breakthroughs happen, they rarely stick
unless reinforced over time and internalized—not just as new habits but
as shifts in identity.

ART works because it integrates what most approaches leave fragmented. It resolves each of these four breakdowns with precision:

Precision matching: ART uses your REVEAL360 results to align the right
support with your actual state, whether you need to attain or retain. For
example, a couple might be facing the same disconnection, but he's
approaching it from resignation in the Contraction Zone while she's
engaging from empowerment in the Healing Zone. The challenge is
shared, but the starting points and interventions are unique.

Root-level focus: Instead of managing surface symptoms, ART addresses
deeper existential drivers—misdirection, limiting beliefs, cravings—
that shape your patterns.

Structural support: Its phased approach provides scaffolding that sustains change even when motivation fades.

Identity integration: ART anchors transformation at the identity level,
making shifts lasting rather than temporary.

EASE gives you the process, REVEAL360 gives you the map, and ART gives you the compass—together forming an integrated navigation system designed specifically for existential health. Transformation requires a precise key to unlock the door you've been pushing against; this is that key.

(II) PURPOSEHOOD PAUSE

Think of a pattern you've been trying to change for months or years:

- What zone is this component of your life in?

- What small shift could you make to attain a positive state?

- How could you retain that shift without overwhelming yourself?

- What would training for resilience in this area involve?

Honest answers matter more than perfect ones.

CHOOSING YOUR STARTING POINT

You don't need to apply ART to every component at once. After you've mapped your WholeBeing, the first decision is choosing where to begin. If some components are in crisis, those take priority. Others may be calling quietly for growth or support. Start where the need feels most important or where you feel most ready to act.

If a component feels too heavy, that's information. Resistance might mean it's not the right time. You can shift your focus to another area, even something small, where movement is possible. Or instead of trying to attain a new state, you might choose to retain what's already working and build strength there. This process is about making wise supported moves, one component at a time.

SARAH'S ART JOURNEY

You first met Sarah in Chapter 7, when her job component was stuck in resignation. Applying ART, her first challenge was to shift toward endurance within the Contraction Zone—changing how she related to her work.

"I realized I'd been telling myself, 'I can't change anything here, so why bother trying?'" she said. "That's classic resignation—no agency."

Her *Attain* shift came through a simple but profound practice. Every morning, before checking email or diving into crisis management, she spent ten minutes writing down one specific way she could add value that day, to people as well as tasks.

"I stopped thinking of my job as just HR tasks. I started seeing it as an opportunity to impact people, even in small ways."

This internal shift (from "nothing I do matters" to "I can still make a difference") moved her from resignation to endurance. Same job, same challenges, but now she was actively engaged rather than emotionally withdrawn.

Attaining endurance was just the beginning. Sarah needed to retain this shift, especially when company pressures intensified.

She created a Purposehood intervention:

Morning anchor: Her ten-minute value reflection became nonnegotiable. She prepared her notepad the night before, placing it by her coffee maker. On chaotic mornings, she'd do it mentally during her commute.

Weekly purpose check: Every Friday, she reviewed: *Where did I add value this week? Where did I miss opportunities? What's possible next week?*

Resilience partnerships: She found a few colleagues who were also interested in bringing more purpose to their work. They met monthly to share wins, challenges, and accountability.

"I had to practice seeing my work differently," Sarah said. "When budget cuts hit and we had to lay off good people, my old pattern was resignation. Instead I asked myself, 'How can I help the remaining employees find more meaning in their bigger roles?'"

Sarah understood that sustaining her endurance required more than good intentions. She needed to train for the inevitable challenges that would test her progress. She began by training in Realize, crafting a personal Purposehood Guiding Star statement that linked her deepest selfish and altruistic desires. She also wrote one for her role: "I want to feel energized and fulfilled in my daily work because I want to contribute to a world where people bring positive energy home to their families and communities instead of exhaustion and frustration."

From there, her training focused on Rebound: she practiced maintaining endurance in progressively tougher situations—first in one-on-one conversations, then in team meetings, and eventually in high-stakes leadership discussions about layoffs and restructuring. She also visualized staying purposeful amid specific pressures such as angry employees, budget cuts, and leadership demands to 'just fix the numbers,' and built quick-return protocols for when resignation crept back, often reconnecting with her morning practice or calling her accountability partners.

"The training was crucial," she said. "I wanted to make sure I remembered my Purposehood under pressure so I could live it, not just talk about it."

Five months into her ART practice, Sarah's transformation was evident—both in her own experience and in the organization around her. Her job satisfaction had increased dramatically. Where once she dreaded Monday mornings, she now felt genuinely energized by work challenges rather than drained by them. Colleagues began seeking her input more frequently, and her influence in leadership meetings grew as others noticed her grounded presence during difficult conversations.

The organizational changes were equally striking. Employee engagement rose 12 percent, while turnover dropped from 18 to 14 percent in areas where she implemented Purposehood-focused initiatives. When she successfully introduced REVEAL360 assessments for interested employees, it created a ripple effect of self-awareness that spread naturally through informal conversations and team dynamics.

"The only reason I could guide others was because I'd lived it. When I taught moving from resignation to endurance, I told my own story so they knew it wasn't just theory."

WHEN ART MEETS RESISTANCE

Even the most aligned implementation will meet resistance. This just means your extensions are speaking.

Throughout the EASE process, you've learned to view resistance as information. Within ART, resistance helps you adjust with precision rather than force.

Zone mismatches

Signal: Actions feel impossible or exhausting.

Adjustment: Match your approach to your actual zone, not where you think you "should" be.

Readiness gaps

Signal: You can see the positive state but can't seem to access it.

Adjustment: Step back to where you have solid ground and build from there.

WholeBeing conflicts

Signal: Actions work in one area but create problems in another.

Adjustment: Find approaches that support all your extensions, not just one component.

System limitations

Signal: Your changes work at home but fail at work, or vice versa.

Adjustment: Recognize when personal change has reached the limits of your environment.

When resistance shows up in implementation, approach it with curiosity rather than force. Ask yourself what it might be protecting and what it could be trying to tell you.

Stay committed to healing and growth while adjusting your approach. Resistance doesn't mean you should stop—it signals the need to recalibrate.

Learn to tell the difference between resistance that protects your boundaries and resistance that quietly limits you. This discernment becomes a practice in itself: knowing when a boundary needs respect, and when growth is asking you to stretch beyond it.

There's something profound that happens when you stop trying to fix yourself and start learning how to move with yourself. When resistance is no longer treated as the enemy of growth but as information about readiness and safety, transformation becomes sustainable.

ART isn't just a tool—it's a compass you can return to in any moment. The real transformation comes when that compass is no longer something you consult, but something you live.

CHAPTER 12

ENACT
TURNING PLANS INTO LASTING CHANGE

You've now engaged genuinely with your desire for healing and growth. You've assessed your WholeBeing with clarity, mapping exactly where you are across all twenty-five components. You've built systematic support through the ART framework—you know when to shift states, maintain progress, and prepare for what's ahead.

The question is no longer what you know but what you do with what you know.

We've all felt the momentum of insight. A powerful realization hits during a quiet morning. A moment of clarity emerges from a difficult conversation. A plan forms that feels alive with possibility. In those moments, change seems inevitable. You can see exactly who you want to become and how to get there.

But then Monday arrives. The meeting runs long. The kids need attention. Life gets real—and somehow you're back in familiar patterns.

This isn't because you don't care. It's not because you lack willpower or forgot what matters. The greatest challenge in transformation isn't deciding to change—it's becoming the person who follows through.

Here's what most people miss: Follow-through doesn't fail because of weak discipline. It fails because we're trying to impose new behaviors on an identity that hasn't yet evolved. When our actions aren't matched to who we're becoming, even our best plans can backfire.

This chapter is about building the system that lets you live your Purposehood daily—not once, not ideally, but continuously.

WHAT MAKES ENACTMENT DIFFERENT

Sarah discovered this the hard way. After her breakthrough with the ART framework, she felt invincible. She'd just read a book about "starting your day like a CEO," so she created an ambitious plan: 5 a.m. wake-up, meditation, journaling, exercise, smoothie, plus evening family check-ins and weekly zone assessments. She followed it religiously for three weeks.

Then her mother got sick, work became chaotic, and her "perfect system" collapsed overnight. On day three of trying to maintain her CEO routine while managing the crisis, she hit "snooze," skipped breakfast, and cried in the shower.

"I thought I was broken again," she told me. "All that momentum just collapsed. I started blaming myself, thinking maybe I was never the kind of person who could really change. I thought I was just lazy."

But looking at her recent REVEAL360 map, she realized she was still in Contraction across several components. Her plan wasn't just ambitious; it was completely misaligned with her actual capacity during crisis.

That's when the fog lifted. Instead of abandoning change altogether, she began her day differently. She scrapped the CEO routine and started with something her system could actually handle. Every morning, as she naturally woke, she'd quietly speak her Purposehood Guiding Star statement as a gentle reminder of her deeper life intention and direction. Then she'd drink a glass of water and stretch for two to three minutes.

"I realized I was pushing myself to become someone I wasn't yet. What I needed wasn't discipline, it was compassion and recalibration."

Unlike traditional implementation approaches, enactment recognizes that your current zone determines what kind of action will actually work for you right now. Each zone calls for a different way of enacting change. What works in one zone can backfire in another, which is why enactment must be zone-aware rather than one-size-fits-all:

- Contraction Zone: Traditional advice says, "Start small and build momentum," but if you're experiencing resignation, pushing for momentum might deepen your disconnection.

- Healing Zone: The same "start small" advice might miss what you actually need: empowering actions that rebuild self-trust.

- Comfort Zone: Playing it too safe can maintain the very complacency you're ready to outgrow.

- Growth Zone: Overdoing can re-create the excess patterns you're trying to balance.

True enactment honors your readiness and your zone. It works with your WholeBeing, not against it. When you understand how to implement change through zone-aware action, the experience itself transforms. What felt like discipline becomes natural expression. What required willpower becomes aligned flow. What demanded constant motivation becomes sustainable practice.

This transformation happens through three dynamics that work at both practical and readiness levels: Do It. Habitually. Together. Each dynamic is simple enough to remember but deep enough to support profound change.

DO IT—ZONE-AWARE ACTION

The moment you commit to change, you have to act. Not tomorrow. Not next week. Now.

But "Do it" doesn't mean what most people think it means. In EASE, action is strategic experimentation. Every time you act, you're testing what works for your current zone and readiness level. You're learning how to move through your WholeBeing with existential intelligence and ease.

That simple morning routine didn't just stick, it gave Sarah hope. "I needed to prove I could still choose something for myself," she said. "That tiny act reminded me I wasn't powerless."

She also began pausing throughout her day. Whenever she felt overwhelmed—which was often during her mother's illness—she'd stop whatever she was doing, take three slow breaths, and smile with gratitude for simply taking charge of that moment. Five times a day, this brief Purposehood practice created space between her stress and her reactions.

"Those tiny pauses saved my sanity," she told me. "I was learning to respond instead of react."

During her mother's treatment, she instituted "expansion moments," taking five minutes to silently extend wishes for healing and peace to her mother, her family, herself, the other families in the waiting room, the medical staff, and her co-workers. Besides calming her anxiety, this expansion practice, one of the core Purposehood daily practices, connected her to something larger during this difficult period in her life.

ACTION STRATEGIES BY ZONE

Every zone has its own rhythm for effective action:

Contraction Zone

Focus: Reorient with your Purposehood Guiding Star

Try this: Read your Purposehood Guiding Star statement and identify one small action that moves you toward it.

Why it works: When you're resigned or overwhelmed, reconnecting with your deeper direction restores meaning and guides your next step.

Healing Zone

Focus: Build empowerment and break dependency patterns

Try this: Speak one boundary. Write down one truth. Say no to something small.

Why it works: Limiting beliefs weaken when challenged through action. Each small act of self-advocacy builds evidence of agency and strengthens empowerment.

Comfort Zone

Focus: Spark curiosity and prevent stagnation

Try this: Try a new routine. Journal with a fresh prompt. Reach out to someone new.

Why it works: Comfort can become complacency. Small experiments reignite growth without threatening security.

Growth Zone

Focus: Maintain balance and prevent excess

Try this: Take a digital detox. Spend time in nature. Practice saying no to misaligned opportunities.

Why it works: High achievers need grounding practices to prevent burnout and maintain sustainable progress.

STARTING WHERE YOU ARE

The key is starting where your system feels ready to shift, not where you think you "should" be. Sarah began with her "evening balance check." After dinner cleanup, she'd take one minute to reflect: Had her day been mainly focused on caring for others or herself? Then she'd set a gentle intention for the next day to balance whatever was missing.

This simple Purposehood daily practice created a clear intention for her next day.

QUICK ACTION ASSESSMENT

Before taking any action, ask yourself:

What zone am I in for this area of my life? (Check your REVEAL360 results)

What does my zone need right now? (Use the guide above)

What would ease—not force—look like?

How will I know this is working? (*What will feel different?*)

Remember: Implementation isn't about perfect execution. It's about intelligent experimentation that honors your readiness and builds sustainable momentum. As you heal and grow, retake your REVEAL360 assessment at least every three months to ensure that your actions match your current zones, not where you were months ago.

HABITUALLY—WHOLEBEING INTEGRATION

Taking action once creates a moment. Taking action habitually creates a life. A single action can spark change, but it's what you do again and again that begins to shape who you are.

When a practice becomes rhythm and rhythm becomes expression, identity is no longer something you're building, it's something you're living. Most habit advice focuses on repetition, but in The Purposehood Method for Existential Health, habit is about integration across your WholeBeing. When your actions resonate through your body, emotions, thoughts, spirit, and relationships, they stop feeling like chores and start feeling like homecoming.

Sarah realized that her Purposehood practices could work together. Her morning affirmation naturally led to her pause practice during stressful moments. Her evening balance reflection created a bridge to the next day's intention. And three times during her day, she'd find a window for focused attention—sometimes gazing at a tree during her mother's medical appointments, sometimes focusing on her breath while coffee brewed, sometimes simply watching her daughter play.

"I wasn't adding more to-dos. I was learning to live more intentionally with what I was already doing."

When her eight-year-old started asking for a pause too, Sarah knew integration was happening across her WholeBeing.

That's the signal of integration: when you move from "I have to…" to "This feels like taking care of myself and all my extensions."

THREE ELEMENTS OF INTEGRATION

1. START ZONE-APPROPRIATE (HONORING CURRENT READINESS)

Not: *I'll meditate for an hour every morning.*

Instead, match the practice to your zone's needs. For example:

Contraction: One conscious breath after brushing teeth

Healing: Five minutes of self-compassion journaling

Comfort: Gentle morning movement while coffee brews

Growth: Brief intention-setting before checking devices

2. ANCHOR TO EXISTING PATTERNS (BUILDING ON ESTABLISHED RHYTHMS)

Connect new practices to something you already do naturally:

After I drink my morning coffee, I'll check in with my body.

After I close my laptop, I'll take three conscious breaths.

After dinner cleanup, I will reflect on the day's gifts.

This isn't just practical—it's extension design. You're building new expressions onto established patterns across your WholeBeing.

3. TRACK EXTENSION SHIFTS (WITNESSING INTEGRATION)

Instead of counting streaks, notice WholeBeing changes:

I found myself naturally wanting to move my body.

I felt more patient with my family this week.

Work conflicts felt less overwhelming.

I had more energy for friends.

WHEN HABITS DON'T STICK

If you keep "forgetting": The habit may not match your natural rhythm or current zone. Try different times, approaches, or zone-specific alternatives. Ask yourself: What would actually work for where I am right now?

If it feels like work: You may be imposing someone else's version or wrong-zone strategies. Simplify until it feels like self-care, not self-discipline. Remember: Integration should feel supportive, not hard.

If others resist your changes: Your growth may be disrupting familiar family or work systems. Focus on your own consistency rather than their approval. Note: Their discomfort often reflects their own resistance to change, not a flaw in your growth.

EASE AS DAILY PRACTICE

These daily practices aren't separate from your EASE cycle—they become how you naturally live it:

Your morning check-in becomes how you *Engage* with each day.

Your evening reflection becomes how you *Assess* what needs attention.

Your weekly zone review becomes how you *Support* your continuous growth.

Your aligned actions become how you *Enact* sustainable change.

When practices feel effortless, when they arise from readiness rather than discipline, when they support your whole system rather than fragmenting it, that's when you know implementation has become integration.

⏸ PURPOSEHOOD PAUSE

Take a moment to feel where you are right now.

Which zone feels most active in your life today—Contraction, Healing, Comfort, or Growth?

What is one habit your WholeBeing is ready to live?

If you could anchor one meaningful practice to something you already do daily, what would that look like?

What would it feel like to act purposefully from exactly where you are?

Let these questions settle without forcing answers. Your readiness will speak when it's ready.

TOGETHER—EXTENDING YOUR IMPACT

No one transforms alone. We've been taught that change is a private battle, that we should get our act together and then share the results, but transformation happens in relationship. We become who we are through connection with others.

Your healing or growth is directly influenced by the people and environment around you. And to sustain lasting change, you need to be intentional about who you surround yourself with.

Most transformation efforts treat change as a solo journey when it's actually a community practice. The most sustainable transformation happens through three intentional relationship circles.

THREE LAYERS OF SUPPORT

To sustain change, you need to shift how you engage with three types of connections:

Create Distance from Draining Dynamics. Some relationships consistently pull you back into old patterns. You need to set boundaries that protect your healing and growth. Eliminate or at least limit time with those who dismiss, mock, or resist your transformation.

Lean into Compassionate Supporters. These are the people in your life—family, friends, colleagues—who may not use the same language or tools, but they respect your journey, uplift your growth, and stand by you with genuine care.

Build Your Purposehood Expansion Circle. This is your intentional growth circle, a carefully selected group of eight to ten people committed to healing, growth, and Purposehood. Modeled after YPO forums—long regarded as the most valuable experience in that elite leadership network—expansion circles offer structured, confidential, purpose-driven engagement. Unlike casual friendships, these circles exist for shared support.

BUILDING YOUR PURPOSEHOOD
EXPANSION CIRCLE

No matter how strong your initial commitment to change, life will test you. Challenges will arise, motivation will wane, and distractions will threaten your progress. Your Purposehood Expansion Circle serves three critical functions:

Expanding your awareness: helping you see blind spots and challenge limiting beliefs

Ensuring follow-through: keeping you accountable to your commitments

Providing wisdom: offering diverse perspectives and real-life experiences to navigate challenges

A strong Purposehood community is the difference between short-term effort and lifelong change. Expansion circles meet monthly in a structured format that includes:

Opening with Purposehood Guiding Star statements

Individual updates across all five extensions

Everyone shares their challenges, and the group selects two urgent ones to explore in depth

Closing with gratitude and compassion

The emphasis is on total confidentiality, candid sharing, and collective growth through shared experience.

BUILDING YOUR SUPPORT COMMUNITY

You don't have to figure this out alone. There are many ways to begin, depending on what feels possible right now:

Start small: Find one accountability partner or begin growth conversations with friends or family.

Expand gradually: Create a virtual circle with people in different locations or invite a small group (eight to ten) to meet informally and set shared intentions.

Anchor in Purposehood: Use The Purposehood Method for Existential Health as your shared language and commit to regular monthly meetings.

Join existing communities: Look for Purposehood groups in your area, bring the method to an existing group of friends or colleagues, or participate in online circles.

Go wider: Attend workshops, connect with aligned organizations, or join an existing Purposehood Expansion Circle.

Lead by example: Start your own transformation community or simply model the change in daily life—sharing a pause practice at work or inviting a friend into your evening reflection.

YOUR TRANSFORMATION RIPPLES OUTWARD

When transformation is genuine, it extends naturally. Your family experiences your increased presence. Your workplace feels the impact of your grounded responses. Your community benefits from your sincere engagement. Even your relationship with nature deepens—you find yourself more aware of seasons, more grateful for simple moments outdoors, more connected to the rhythms that sustain all life.

By committing to transformation supported by others who understand the journey, together you create not just personal change but collective healing and growth that ripples outward to touch every system you're part of.

You've now walked through the full Purposehood Method for Existential Health. Transformation is no longer just a possibility—it's something you've practiced step by step. You already carry what you need. Congratulations!

The seven inner shifts that follow distill your entire journey into seven simple affirmations for living it fully.

PART III

INTEGRATION AND EXPANSION

CHAPTER 13

SEVEN SHIFTS FOR A LIFE WORTH LOVING

This chapter distills your entire journey into seven shifts, existential reorientations that create optimal existential health. Through these shifts, each day becomes a return to conscious living.

THE SEVEN SHIFTS FOR A LIFE WORTH LOVING

You've made these shifts. Now it's time to live them.

Each one reflects a fundamental reorientation in how you see, support, and sustain your existence. Together, they form your daily compass—a way to revisit, repeat, and reinforce the transformations that made healing and growth possible.

SHIFT 1. FROM FRAGMENTS TO WHOLEBEING

Stop fixing pieces. Start conducting your symphony.

The shift: recognizing yourself as an integrated system across all Extensions of Being—Self, Family, Work, Communities, and Nature—rather than isolated problems to be solved separately.

The science: Integration beats fragmentation. Multi-behavior interventions consistently outperform single-focus approaches, producing stronger improvements in physical and psychological outcomes. (Comprehensive Meta-analysis, 2024)

SHIFT 2. FROM SURFACE FIXES TO ROOTHEALING

Stop managing symptoms. Start transforming sources.

The shift: addressing the five sources of existential suffering—misdirection, disorientation, limiting beliefs, stagnation, and cravings—at their core to restore existential health rather than just treating their surface manifestations.

The science: Root-focused healing sustains longer. Treatments that address underlying causes, rather than surface symptoms, produce more enduring change. (Clinical Psychology & Trauma-informed Reviews, 2021–2024)

SHIFT 3. FROM DEPENDENCY TO LEADERSHIP

Stop waiting for directions. Start authoring your transformation.

The shift: moving from "Who will fix this for me?" to "How do I create the conditions to lead my healing and growth?" Leadership means building systems that make self-direction easier than self-abandonment.

The science: Self-leadership strengthens resilience. Structured self-leadership strategies significantly boost well-being and reduce emotional exhaustion. (Sjöblom et al., 2022, Journal of Leadership & Organizational Studies)

SHIFT 4. FROM AVOIDANCE TO ENGAGEMENT

Stop hiding from difficulty. Start showing up fully.

The shift: bringing genuine openness, trust, and commitment to your growth rather than superficial participation or chronic avoidance.

The science: Engagement eclipses avoidance. Approach-oriented coping strategies are linked to higher resilience, emotional regulation, and well-being. (Journal of Behavioral Medicine, 2023)

SHIFT 5. FROM CONFUSION TO ASSESSMENT

Stop guessing where you are. Start mapping your zones with precision.

The shift: using zone and state awareness to understand your current position across all components of your WholeBeing and respond accordingly.

The science: Clarity conquers confusion. Regular self-monitoring and high-quality feedback significantly increase learning, accurate self-perception, and professional performance. (Annual Review of Organizational Psychology & Organizational Behavior, 2025)

SHIFT 6. FROM EFFORT TO SUPPORT

Stop trying harder. Start giving yourself the right support.

The shift: matching support with the state of your component—Attain in negatives, Retain in positives, and always Train for resilience.

The science: Support makes it last. Daily supportive practices—such as intention-setting, micro-habits, and structured routines—produce measurable neural and behavioral change over time. (Neuroscience & Habit-Formation Research, 2011–2024)

SHIFT 7. FROM PLANNING TO ENACTMENT

Stop thinking about transformation. Start living it daily.

The shift: implementing change through zone-aware action guided by three dynamics: Do it. Habitually. Together.

The science: Action with others sustains transformation. Strong social relationships increase survival likelihood by about 50%, supporting better long-term health and reduced mortality risk. (PLOS Medicine, 2010)

THE SEVEN DAILY REALIGNMENTS

Daily maintenance creates lifelong transformation. Sustainability is about return, having daily orientations that help you find your way back to alignment when life inevitably knocks you off course.

Every morning, ground yourself in these seven shifts—not just as reminders but as simple affirmations, daily check-ins with your Whole-Being:

I stay whole. *I honor all five extensions—nothing is left out.*

I see deeply. *I look beneath the surface to what truly matters.*

I lead. *I respond with rhythm, not urgency.*

I show up. *I meet life with presence, not resistance.*

I know my zone. *I sense where I stand and act accordingly.*

I move artfully. *I attain, retain, and train with ease.*

I do what matters. *I enact my Purposehood through daily action.*

At the end of the day, maybe just before bed, briefly revisit these seven realignments. Where did you honor them? Where did you forget? What does tomorrow's growth require?

This is how you maintain a life worth loving—not by achieving it once but by choosing it again every day.

LIVING THE SEVEN SHIFTS AS YOUR WAY OF BEING

The seven shifts evolve as you do. Each shift deepens over time, moving from conscious application to natural embodiment to lived identity. You're not just learning new techniques, you're becoming someone for whom these orientations feel increasingly natural.

To make this practical, it can help to see how the seven shifts often unfold over time. Think of the following not as rigid timelines, but as milestones many people experience as they move from practicing the shifts to embodying them:

MONTH 1: CONSCIOUS ORIENTATION.

I need to remember to see myself as a WholeBeing.

Let me check: Am I addressing the root or just the symptom?

What shift do I need to make here?

MONTH 6: EMBODIED AWARENESS.

You naturally sense when you're fragmenting and automatically return to wholeness.

You intuitively recognize surface fixes and organically seek deeper sources.

You feel the shifts happening in your body before your mind names them.

MONTH 12: LIVING IDENTITY.

WholeBeing awareness feels like your natural state of consciousness.

RootHealing becomes how you instinctively approach any challenge.

These shifts aren't something you do; they're expressions of who you are.

These time frames reflect common patterns I've observed, though individual progression varies based on starting point and consistency of practice. What matters isn't the calendar—it's the gradual weaving of the seven shifts into the fabric of your being.

Integration Indicators

You know the seven shifts are becoming your way of being when:

WholeBeing awareness feels more natural than fragmentary problem-solving.

You automatically ask What's the source? rather than How do I fix this symptom?

Self-leadership arises naturally, even in difficult moments.

Genuine engagement flows spontaneously rather than requiring conscious effort.

Zone awareness emerges from intuitive body knowledge rather than mental calculation.

Supporting yourself systematically feels like natural self-care rather than external pressure.

Enacting change expresses your true self rather than forced discipline, and including others happens organically rather than from obligation.

This is the difference between learning existential shifts and living them, between applying principles and embodying wisdom.

You're no longer the same person who began this journey. When you opened this book, you were someone seeking to recover and rise. You had struggles to address, patterns to understand, zones to navigate. You needed a method, a framework, a systematic way forward. Now, something fundamental has shifted.

You understand your WholeBeing and how all five extensions work in concert. You can identify the root sources of suffering and address them systematically. You've mastered the EASE process and learned to navigate all four zones with wisdom. You've integrated these seven shifts into a daily orientation of conscious living.

You're no longer just someone who heals and grows. You're someone ready to engineer transformation.

This distinction is subtle but profound. Healing and growth teach you to move skillfully with what life presents. Engineering invites you to design what life can become.

You've earned your foundation. Now you stand at the threshold of creation where structure meets purpose and wisdom becomes design. Welcome to the next chapter in your journey: Purposehood Life Engineering.

CHAPTER 14

PURPOSEHOOD LIFE ENGINEERING
THE BLUEPRINT OF YOUR LIFE

Imagine if when you were growing up, you were handed a blueprint for a life worth loving. Not a rigid plan that ignored your uniqueness but a flexible framework that taught you how to design meaning into every day, build resilience through any challenge, and sustain joy that no crisis could steal.

What if you'd learned from an early age how to align with your Purposehood, use setbacks as fuel for growth, release limiting beliefs that don't serve you, and rest and recharge in ways that make you stronger and more inspired? Imagine being shown how to navigate the inner landscapes of your own emotions and desires, build relationships grounded in mutual respect and shared growth, and recognize your vital connection with nature as a source of well-being.

That blueprint was written into your operating system at birth. And slowly, it was replaced. Survival instructions took its place. Social expectations. Fear-based thinking. The laws of the jungle: chase desires, run from fears, compete rather than co-create, react rather than respond.

You were taught to identify with labels rather than your essence—family identity, nationality, religion, ethnicity, social status. These became invisible chains, systematically obscuring the most important truth about yourself.

But here's a truth they couldn't take away: You were born to become a creator.

YOUR EXISTENTIAL INTELLIGENCE

In the late 1960s, Dr. George Land, a researcher known for his work on creativity and innovation, became interested in how creative capacity develops and changes over time. In work often associated with NASA—then operating at the edge of human possibility during the space race—Land observed that only a small fraction of adults demonstrated exceptionally high levels of creative problem-solving.

Curious about where creativity originates, Land explored how children performed on similar creativity assessments. In widely cited presentations and writings, he reported that very young children demonstrated remarkably high levels of imaginative and divergent thinking, with far fewer adults showing the same capacity later in life. Across repeated observations, this pattern appeared remarkably consistent: as people aged, creative expression often narrowed rather than expanded.

We seem to begin life with an extraordinary imaginative capacity—one of evolution's greatest gifts—yet social conditioning, fear of failure, and rigid systems often constrain how freely we continue to use it.

What Land's work points to is not a loss of intelligence, but a loss of permission. Children are born with a natural ability to imagine, explore, and create meaning without self-censorship. And imagination is the raw material of meaning. You weren't just born creative—you were born a world-builder, a meaning-maker, a Purposehood Engineer.

When did you first ask, *Why am I here?* Maybe you were seven, staring at stars and wondering what it all meant. Maybe it hit you at seventeen during heartbreak that felt world-ending. Or maybe it emerged during a career crisis, a loss, or one of those 3 a.m. moments when life suddenly felt both precious and puzzling.

That question—that deep, persistent wondering about your place and purpose—is evidence of something profoundly right: you're functioning exactly as you were designed to. You're a meaning-making creature.

More than that, you were born to be an engineer of that meaning. That capacity has a name—existential intelligence.

Existential intelligence is the wisdom of asking meaningful questions and then meaningfully questioning the answers. It invites us to test their roots, their implications, and their alignment with lived experience. It's not merely the ability to think deeply but the willingness to do so continuously. It's the uniquely human capacity to stand before the vast unknowns of life—questions of identity, meaning, death, time, freedom, purpose—and engage them with curiosity, courage, and humility.

Existential intelligence isn't measured by certainty but by the quality of inquiry. It seeks to expand awareness. It thrives in paradox, wrestles with complexity, and embraces the evolving nature of truth.

To live with existential intelligence is to live in a dynamic dance between wonder and wisdom, where every answer opens the door to a deeper question and every question brings us closer to the essence of our Purposehood.

This intelligence allows us to:

- Recognize patterns and seek meaning in experience

- Create stories that help us navigate uncertainty

- Build internal frameworks for understanding our place in the world

- Engineer our own sense of direction and purpose

This isn't a privilege reserved for philosophers or mystics. It's standard human equipment. The same capacity that helped our ancestors find meaning in life and death now helps us navigate careers, crises, and change.

My daughter, who taught kindergarteners at an inner-city school in Baltimore, once shared a moment that has stayed with me. One of her five-year-old students, Jackson, asked her out of the blue, "Ms. Charani, I know we come from heaven, and when we die, we go back to heaven—but why are we on this Earth?"

Caught off guard, she answered honestly, "I don't know, Jackson. Why do you think we're on this Earth?"

Jackson paused, looked at her, and said, "To play, and be teached." Then he ran off to play.

When I later shared this story with Howard Gardner, the Harvard professor of education who introduced the theory of multiple intelligences, he reflected that most children ask existential questions, but that existential intelligence begins to show itself when those questions are returned to, explored, and lived over time—sometimes through words, sometimes through imagination, sometimes through play. That distinction matters. What we often lose as we grow older is not the capacity for meaning, but the permission to keep asking the questions that once came so naturally.

⏸ PURPOSEHOOD PAUSE

When did you last ask yourself a question that really mattered?

Not: *How do I get through this week?* or *How do I fix this problem?* But the deeper questions: *What am I here to create? How do I want to show up in the world? What legacy am I building with my daily choices?*

Take a moment now. What's one meaningful question about your life that you've been avoiding?

Notice how asking it feels different from solving immediate problems. This is your existential intelligence awakening, your natural capacity to engineer meaning rather than just manage circumstances.

That questioning mind? That's not restlessness. That's your design.

THE EDEN WE WERE BORN INTO

Think about the children you've known, really known—before the world told them who they should be, before they learned to doubt their instincts, before they absorbed limiting beliefs about their capabilities. They lived with natural Purposehood. They didn't need to search for meaning because they embodied it. They approached each day with curiosity, created freely without self-judgment, and moved through the world with an inherent sense that they mattered. They experienced a sense of happiness, success, and fulfillment every day of their lives.

This wasn't blind optimism. It was existential health in its purest form.

Every child is born into what we might call Inner Eden, a state where direction feels natural and emerging, never forced or prescribed. In this state, creativity flows without internal resistance, like water finding its course. Connection happens spontaneously—with other children, with the wonder of discovery, with the joy that arises simply from being alive. Meaning isn't something they search for; it's created in real time through their engagement with life itself. Purposehood isn't something to find—it's something they live, moment by moment, breath by breath.

You lived this way once because you were designed to. That design hasn't disappeared; the same potential still lives within you, waiting to be reclaimed.

WHAT HAPPENED TO OUR NATURAL GIFTS

If we're born as meaning-making engineers, why do so many of us feel lost, stuck, or disconnected from Purposehood? The answer isn't that we lost our capacity. It's that we learned to distrust it.

Through well-meaning but misguided influences—labels that limited us, cultural messages that contradicted our inner knowing, educational systems that prioritized conformity over creativity—we began to believe that meaning came from outside ourselves. We started looking for permission to be who we already were.

Slowly, we migrated from Inner Eden into what feels like a jungle, a confusing landscape where purpose becomes something we have to earn or discover rather than simply reclaim. Once effortless, creativity now requires overcoming resistance. Connection, which once emerged spontaneously, now demands effort and strategy. Most devastating, meaning begins to feel scarce rather than abundant, something to hoard rather than create.

But the jungle isn't your natural habitat. It's where you've learned to survive, not where you're designed to thrive. Your Inner Eden—your natural capacity to create meaning and engineer your life—is still there, waiting to be remembered.

ENGINEERING AS YOUR BIRTHRIGHT

Your capacity to engineer a life that reflects your deepest values and highest aspirations worked when you were five and everything felt possible. It worked when you were fifteen and could envision futures that adults called unrealistic. It's working now, even if you've learned not to listen to it.

Purposehood Life Engineering is the structure and support for what you're already designed to do: create a life worth loving, in ways that matter to you, with people and Purposehood that bring out your best self.

You don't need permission to begin this work. You don't need credentials or preparation. You only need to remember what was true about you before the world convinced you otherwise: You've always been an engineer of meaning, a Purposehood Engineer. The only question is: Will you trust yourself enough to reclaim it?

WHY ENGINEERING?

Existence is engineered, not improvised. The universe follows discernible principles—systematic, intentional, and elegant. That's a matter of fact, not faith. Galaxies spiral with mathematical precision. Cells replicate through chemical choreography. Trees stretch toward light with optimized design. Rivers don't wander aimlessly; they carve persistent paths. Even your heartbeat is governed by patterns that balance pressure and flow.

Every system in existence behaves like an engineer, constantly optimizing and refining. Living organisms evolve to adapt and improve, striving for efficiency in growth, survival, and reproduction. When engineers optimize a design for sustainability, they have a lot in common with ecosystems that maintain balance. At its core, existence is a system of continuous improvement. And within this precise cosmos, you exist as both creation and creator. You're endowed with limitless creativity, infinite desires, and directional choice. Your potential role in existence isn't less than that of any other creator.

Engineering is a principle of life. So why should the human quest for meaning be any different? If the cosmos builds, adapts, and sustains with precision, why wouldn't your life require the same care and intentionality? Why drift, react, or merely cope when you were born with the capacity to design, build, and sustain a life that reflects your deepest purpose?

To engineer something means to apply wisdom to structure, to shape reality with awareness of how systems function, adapt, and evolve. It means you're working with what's true, what works, and what aligns. That's why we call it Purposehood Life Engineering. This is about creation, not improvement. It's not about fixing what's wrong but building what's true. It's not about waiting for meaning to appear but shaping it day by day. It's not about reacting to life but becoming a co-architect with it.

You're not here to passively discover your life's purpose like buried treasure. You're here to build it into being, across all extensions of your WholeBeing.

BEYOND SELF-HELP TO LIFE DESIGN

Self-help often asks, *What's wrong with me, and how can I fix it?* Purposehood Engineering asks, *What matters most to me, and how can I build a life that reflects it—sustainably, systemically, soulfully?*

Engineers understand what all great creators do:

- Clarity of vision isn't enough—you have to translate it into design

- Good intentions aren't enough—you have to build in integrity

- Change isn't enough—it has to be sustainable, adaptable, and holistic

When you start to engineer your life rather than simply react to it, everything shifts. You move from asking, *How do I cope with this?* to asking, *How do I design a life where even challenge has meaning?* From *What's wrong with me?* to *What am I now ready to create?* From surviving your circumstances to engineering a life that reflects your essence, your rhythm, and your Purposehood.

LIVING AS A PURPOSEHOOD ENGINEER

Something profound changes when you begin to engineer your life rather than live out assigned scripts. Sometimes the change comes in a flash of clarity, and other times it unfolds like the slow, sure turning of a season. One day you realize that the quality of your existence has fundamentally changed. You're no longer just carried along by life. You're consciously creating it.

NAVIGATING YOUR INNER WORLD

A Purposehood Engineer relates to their inner world differently. They don't run from difficult emotions or chase pleasant ones; they treat the entire emotional spectrum as information about alignment.

When anxiety arises, they don't immediately try to eliminate it. They pause, listen, and ask, What is this telling me about my current direction? Is this the anxiety of growth or misalignment? They've learned that anxiety about expansion feels different from anxiety about betraying their true nature.

When happiness, success, or fulfillment bubbles up, they don't grasp at it or analyze it. They let it flow through, recognizing it as evidence of alignment, a signal that they're moving in harmony with their Purposehood Guiding Star.

They've developed existential intimacy with themselves, a quality of attention that's both gentle and precise. They know the difference between the resistance that signals wisdom and the resistance that signals fear. They can feel when they're forcing and when they're building with natural momentum.

Most importantly, they've stopped treating struggles as evidence of failure. Every challenge becomes an opportunity to strengthen the very pillars they're building their life on. Setbacks don't derail them; they inform the next iteration of their design.

YOUR RELATIONSHIP WITH TIME

A Purposehood Engineer understands that life moves in spiral cycles, not lines. They don't expect themselves to be in constant growth mode or fear seasons of rest or even contraction.

When they're in a generative season, they build with focus and intention. When life calls for recovery, they take the time to heal without guilt. When circumstances demand adaptation, they redesign without attachment to how things used to be.

They've learned to recognize the difference between productive action and busy work. Their days have rhythm rather than frantic urgency. They can be fully present with what's in front of them because they trust the larger structure they're creating.

Time becomes their ally, not their enemy. Instead of feeling like they're running out of it, they feel like they're dancing with it, aware of its passage but not anxious about its speed.

THE QUALITY OF DAILY LIVING

Watch a Purposehood Engineer move through an ordinary Tuesday and you'll notice something different. There's an underlying sense of coherence in how they approach everything, from drinking morning coffee to handling an unexpected crisis at work.

They don't compartmentalize their values—they live them integrated. The same care they bring to designing their life's direction shows up in how they listen to their partner, how they respond to their children, and how they engage with their work.

Their decision-making has a quality of ease because they have a clear framework for evaluating difficult choices. When opportunities arise, they don't agonize endlessly—they check alignment with their Guiding Star and move forward with confidence.

They've learned to distinguish between effort and strain. They work hard when the situation calls for it, but from a place of alignment rather than desperation. Their energy feels renewable because it's connected to Purposehood rather than drained by resistance.

TRANSFORMING YOUR FIVE EXTENSIONS

FAMILY EXTENSION TRANSFORMATION

A Purposehood Engineer doesn't try to fix their family—they become someone around whom existential health naturally emerges.

Their children feel the difference. Instead of experiencing a parent who's constantly stressed, reactive, or absent, they encounter someone who's genuinely here, calm, clear, and available. The engineer has learned to meet their children's big emotions without getting hijacked by their own, creating a safe space for honest expression.

Their partnership deepens. Their spouse or partner stops feeling like they need to manage the engineer's moods or walk on eggshells around their ambitions. Instead, they experience someone who's committed to growth as a way of showing up more fully within their relationship.

Family dynamics shift from reactive patterns to responsive choice. Instead of the same arguments playing out with predictable intensity, conversations happen from a place of curiosity and care. The engineer has learned to distinguish between their triggers and their values, responding based on the latter.

Holiday gatherings become easier. Extended family members might not understand the change, but they feel it—less tension, fewer power struggles, more genuine connection. The engineer no longer needs family members to change in order to feel okay. They can love from their center instead of through their wounds.

WORK EXTENSION TRANSFORMATION

The relationship between a Purposehood Engineer and their work undergoes a fundamental transformation. Work stops being something they only do to earn money or gain status and becomes a venue for expressing their Purposehood.

This doesn't necessarily mean they change jobs, though some do. More often, it means they bring a completely different quality of presence to what they're already doing. They find ways to align their role with their values, or they begin designing a transition that honors both their practical needs and their true calling.

Their colleagues notice the shift. The engineer stops participating in office drama because of a genuine disinterest in dynamics that don't serve growth. They become known for their reliability, their creativity, and their ability to stay calm under pressure.

Existential leadership—the ability to navigate all business challenges with ease while awakening the potentiality of those they lead—emerges naturally. They don't grab for power or position; they simply become someone others turn to for clarity and wisdom. Their decision-making is grounded in principles rather than politics, and their vision extends beyond quarterly earnings to sustainable impact.

They set boundaries that hold. Instead of burning out from overcommitment or checking out because of under-engagement, they find the sustainable pace that allows them to contribute meaningfully without sacrificing their other extensions of being.

COMMUNITIES EXTENSION TRANSFORMATION

The transformation is often visible in how a Purposehood Engineer relates to their broader community.

They stop being invisible neighbors and become people others genuinely know through genuine engagement with what they care about. They might organize a community garden or simply become the neighbor who remembers names and notices when someone needs help.

Their participation becomes purposeful rather than obligatory. They engage with activities that genuinely align with their values and interests, bringing energy to community efforts.

They begin to see social issues as opportunities to apply their unique gifts. They may not change entire systems, but they can make a meaningful difference in individual lives, mentoring one young person, supporting one struggling family, or contributing to one local initiative that aligns with their values.

Their presence alone begins to shift community dynamics. Groups they're part of become more collaborative, more creative, and more inclusive because they embody a way of being that invites the best from others.

NATURE EXTENSION TRANSFORMATION

The Purposehood Engineer remembers they're not separate from nature; they're nature becoming conscious of itself.

Their relationship with the natural world becomes intentional. They might start with something simple—daily walks without devices, weekends spent gardening, regular time by water. What matters isn't the specific activity but the quality of attention they bring to it.

They begin to notice cycles and align their life design with these natural patterns. Their consumer choices reflect their values, their concern for the systems that sustain all life.

They become teachers through modeling. Children especially notice how they interact with living things, gently, respectfully, with wonder intact.

Existential Leadership through Life Engineering

A Purposehood Engineer's transformation creates permission for others to transform. They don't have to convince anyone or sell anyone on personal growth. People simply notice that something is different and they want to know why. The engineer becomes a living example of what's possible when someone commits to designing a life that reflects their deepest values.

Other parents see their calm presence with children and begin questioning their own reactive patterns. Colleagues witness their clear decision-making and start examining their own relationship with integrity. Friends observe their genuine contentment and wonder if life might be more than just surviving until the weekend.

And the ripple effects extend far beyond what can be seen. A conversation an engineer has with their teenage daughter influences how she treats her classmates. A decision they make at work shifts company culture in ways that affect families they'll never meet. Their vote, their purchases, their simple presence in community gatherings all become expressions of their engineered life.

They become what the world needs more of—someone who's learned to live on purpose, who's healed their relationship with struggle, who's remembered that they're here to contribute something beautiful to the whole.

SIGNS YOU'RE A PURPOSEHOOD ENGINEER

You experience more rhythm than urgency in your days

Your choices increasingly reflect your values

Struggles feel like design feedback, not failures

You're more interested in alignment than approval

Your sense of time has shifted from scarcity to reverence

THE FIVE CORE TRAINING MODULES

The five core training modules of Purposehood Engineering offer life-long skills for healing and growth, awakening existential intelligence, strengthening existential health, and cultivating existential leadership along the way.

Together, they equip your WholeBeing to navigate any zone, respond to any challenge, and live forward from your Purposehood. Each module builds essential skills, naturally preparing you for life's evolving demands.

REALIZE—THE FOUNDATION OF ALL HEALING AND GROWTH

Goal: to establish direction by reconnecting to your existential purpose and clarifying what truly matters

Helps with: misdirection—the confusion that comes from living according to borrowed definitions of success, meaning, or identity

Every meaningful life begins with direction. The Realize module focuses on discovering your Purposehood Guiding Star, not as a fixed destination but as a coherent direction that pulls you toward meaning.

It's about distinguishing what you were told to want from what your existential intelligence is trying to remember. It's about learning to organize your life around values that feel native to your soul.

This involves identifying your unique gifts, clarifying your deepest values, and crafting a personal Purposehood Statement that serves as your navigational Guiding Star. This work invites you to recognize when you're living from borrowed dreams versus existential direction and develop the courage to make choices aligned with your true nature.

This module builds the skill that makes all other healing and growth possible—without clear direction, even the most sophisticated techniques become mere busywork.

REBOUND—NAVIGATING THE CONTRACTION ZONE WITH ENDURANCE

Goal: to regain orientation and agency in the face of resignation or overwhelm, rebuilding the energy to engage

Helps with: disorientation—the sense of losing your way when life shifts faster than you can adapt

The Rebound module is a preparation for what life inevitably brings: rupture, loss, transition, and uncertainty. It provides the skills to regain footing without having to start over, to honor what broke without losing what matters.

It's about learning to drive through the fog with endurance, treating life as a journey where you focus on the road ahead while using the rearview mirror only for perspective, not to dwell on what's behind you.

This module centers on three essential reorientations that address disorientation and build endurance:

Time Orientation: The skill to balance your focus between a positive future vision (your destination), mindful present awareness (your current road conditions), and insightful past reflection (lessons from your rearview mirror) without getting stuck in regret or overwhelm.

Role Orientation: The choice to act as a Creator—someone who gains for themselves and their extensions without causing harm to others. This differs from being a Consumer (focused only on personal gain), Martyr (giving at personal expense), or Destroyer (pursuing personal and group gain at the cost of harming others).

Goal Orientation: The realignment of your goals with your Purposehood Guiding Star, ensuring your actions and aspirations serve your deeper purpose rather than just reacting to circumstances or pursuing disconnected objectives.

Through these three reorientations, the specific type of endurance needed to navigate the Contraction Zone and move from resignation to purposeful forward motion is cultivated.

RECOVER—CULTIVATING EMPOWERMENT IN THE HEALING ZONE

Goal: to replace limiting beliefs with empowering ones and take ownership of your healing journey

Helps with: limiting beliefs—the internal stories that say, "You can't," "You shouldn't," or "You're not ready."

These beliefs were inherited, absorbed, internalized through wounds, systems, and silence. The Recover module develops the skills to examine what you never gave conscious permission to hold and offers tools to release it.

It's about clearing the ground like preparing a field choked with weeds and then planting empowering beliefs and nourishing them through the Five Streams of Potentiality.

The Five Streams of Potentiality are interconnected areas that support your healing: Beliefs (replacing limiting beliefs with empowering ones), Mindfulness (cultivating present-moment awareness, intentions, and gratitude), Giving (practicing intentional acts of kindness to self and others), Wellness (caring for your body through nourishment, movement, and rest), and Belonging (building supportive relationships and community connections). These streams work together like tributaries feeding a river, each one strengthening your capacity for transformation.

This work involves techniques for identifying unconscious limiting beliefs, processes for safely releasing what no longer serves you, and systematic approaches for installing empowering alternatives. It cultivates the ability to distinguish between helpful caution and paralyzing fear, while fostering the self-compassion needed for deep healing work.

REST—EXPANDING CONTENTMENT IN THE COMFORT ZONE

Goal: to protect contentment without slipping into complacency, allowing space for renewal and reflection

Helps with: stagnation—the invisible burnout caused by chronic doing without conscious being

In a culture addicted to striving, the Rest module reclaims the sacred role of reflection and replenishment. It builds the skills to pause without guilt, celebrate without fear, and restore without collapse.

This work invites you to tune in to the different kinds of rest your WholeBeing needs: somatic rest (physical recovery), emotional rest (processing feelings), mental rest (quieting overthinking), and spiritual rest (connecting to something greater than yourself). This module reveals rest not as the absence of activity, but as the foundation of creative strength and sustainable growth.

It develops the skills to recognize the difference between healthy satisfaction and stagnant complacency. It cultivates practices for celebrating achievements without losing momentum, savoring positive states without clinging to them, and using periods of stability as launching pads for conscious growth rather than unconscious drift.

Rest also includes developing gratitude practices, reflection techniques, and the art of strategic pausing—knowing when to push forward and when to allow integration.

RISE—SUSTAINING AMBITION IN THE GROWTH ZONE

Goal: to channel ambition consciously, aligning expansion with purpose to prevent excess and ensure integration

Helps with: cravings—the restless drive for more that disconnects you from meaning

Ambition isn't the enemy. Misaligned ambition is. The Rise module builds the skills to distinguish between ego-fueled striving and purpose-fueled expansion. It shows how to grow without tipping into excess, and how to evolve without losing your center.

This module centers on transforming your relationship with desire itself. Instead of being driven by the Pyramid of Desires—where you chase basic needs hoping eventually to find meaning—you learn to flip this into a Pyramid of Values.

In the conventional Pyramid of Desires, you start at the bottom trying to satisfy basic cravings (security, status, comfort) hoping to eventually reach meaning at the top. Most people get stuck endlessly pursuing these basic desires and never reach their purpose. The Pyramid of Values flips this: you start with your existential purpose as the foundation and let that guide how you approach all your other desires. This way, even your basic needs become expressions of your deeper purpose rather than distractions from it.

The work invites you to harness ambition like a wild horse: powerful and beautiful when guided by direction but destructive when left unchecked by your Purposehood. This work includes exercises for distinguishing between genuine growth impulses and compulsive cravings, techniques for setting goals that serve your evolution rather than your ego, and practices for maintaining your center while expanding your reach.

The Rise module ensures that your ambition becomes a force for conscious evolution, both personal and collective, rather than unconscious consumption.

INTEGRATING THE FIVE MODULES

Once you've worked with all five modules, they become a dynamic toolkit. You'll move among them in waves as life requires:

Realize when misdirection creates an existential vacuum.

Rebound when disorientation collapses into resignation.

Recover when limiting beliefs harden into dependency.

Rest when stagnation settles into complacency.

Rise when cravings pull growth into excess.

A skilled practitioner learns to feel which skill is needed in the moment, like a seasoned builder who's mastered all the tools and can choose the right one for each phase of construction.

This is your blueprint. Not a curriculum, but a return to what has always been within you.

If you've read this far, you've already begun remembering that you're a meaning-making being by design. These modules are simply the structure that helps you build with clarity and ease.

The future belongs to those who engineer meaning, not just efficiency.

And meaning was never meant to stay personal. It was always meant to shape systems.

PART IV

BEYOND THE SELF

CHAPTER 15

THE UNIVERSALITY OF THE PURPOSEHOOD METHOD
FROM PERSONAL TO SYSTEMS CHANGE

Eight months after completing her EASE journey, Emma, the marketing executive you met in Chapter 6 who learned to navigate work excess and emotional resignation through WholeBeing mapping, felt caught between two lives. At home during her morning routine—meditation, Purposehood reflection, clear intention-setting—she experienced the alignment and centeredness she'd worked so hard to cultivate. But just outside her door, that sense of ease was quickly tested.

Her neighborhood, once a comforting backdrop to her healing, had become a quiet source of tension. Late-night noise from a neighbor's gatherings disrupted her sleep. A new homeowner had installed security cameras pointed toward multiple houses, sparking suspicion and discomfort. Shared spaces became battlegrounds for grievances over minor issues like unreturned tools and trash bin placement. What had once felt like a community was becoming a cluster of disconnected households tiptoeing around conflict.

Emma had changed. She'd moved from emotional resignation to resilient endurance, from overwork to balanced ambition, from disconnection to daily grounding. Her relationships had deepened, and her inner clarity had grown. But the system around her—this street of neighbors and unspoken assumptions—remained stuck in patterns of avoidance, blame, and isolation that mirrored her old self.

One evening, after a tense neighborhood association meeting full of complaints but no follow-through, Emma walked home with a quiet realization: *I've transformed, but my community hasn't. If the same stuck patterns are playing out here, maybe the same principles that helped me heal can help this neighborhood.* And she decided to try to find out.

Your transformation doesn't happen in isolation. Every breakthrough you've made, every zone you've navigated, every limiting belief you've dissolved—it all happens within systems that either support or resist your growth. The same principles that guided your healing and growth can transform any living system.

RECOGNIZING SYSTEM PATTERNS

Meanwhile, John, the CEO we met in the Growth Zone, had learned to integrate his work success with family presence and spiritual practice, and now he began noticing something remarkable during his company's strategic planning sessions.

"It felt like watching my own journey play out at the company level. Earlier this year, our exec team was acting just like I used to—chasing growth and missing purpose, creating success that felt hollow. We were in the Growth Zone's negative state of excess, just like I'd been."

John could now see that his company's "expansion at any cost" mentality was organizational craving, the same pattern that had once consumed his personal life. Their reactive decision-making was systemic disorientation. Their reluctance to question fundamental assumptions was collective limiting beliefs.

"The revelation was stunning," John said. "Organizations are living systems. They experience the same sources of suffering and the same capacity for healing that individuals do."

Carlos, who had moved from dependency in the Healing Zone to empowerment after his divorce, noticed similar patterns in his family extension. Even though he'd developed emotional resilience and clarity about his direction, family gatherings still triggered the old dynamics of avoidance, unspoken resentments, and surface-level connection.

"My family was operating from the Comfort Zone's negative state: complacency," Carlos said. "We'd all settled into familiar roles and patterns that felt safe but weren't actually nourishing anyone. We were going through the motions of family connection without real intimacy or desire for growth."

SYSTEMS ARE WHOLEBEINGS TOO

Emma, John, and Carlos discovered that communities, organizations, and families are living systems with their own capacity for health or dysfunction, growth or stagnation, alignment or misalignment.

Every system has its own form of Purposehood, its deeper reason for existing beyond just managing daily operations. John's company existed to create innovative solutions that genuinely improve people's lives but had drifted into maximize shareholder value through any viable product. Carlos's family had once been grounded in supporting each member's intended growth while maintaining loving connection but had devolved into avoiding conflict and maintaining appearances.

When systems lose connection to their Purposehood, they experience suffering stemming from the same five sources that individuals do:

Misdirection: organizations with inspiring mission statements that don't guide actual decisions, families with no shared sense of what they're building together beyond managing logistics

Disorientation: teams where past conflicts contaminate present conversations, communities stuck re-litigating old grievances instead of addressing current opportunities

Limiting beliefs: "We've always done it this way." "Our family doesn't talk about difficult topics." "Change initiatives never work here." "That's not how this industry functions."

Stagnation: the comfortable dysfunction that feels safer than the vulnerability of not knowing whether change efforts will succeed

Cravings: addictive organizational patterns—growth without purpose, control for its own sake, external validation that never satisfies the deeper need for meaningful contribution

But when systems align with their Purposehood, they strengthen the same ten pillars of existential health that individuals cultivate: clear direction, endurance through challenges, empowered participation, sustainable contentment, purposeful ambition, patience with natural timing, gratitude for what's working and who's working, meaningful connections, a sense of mattering, and deeper meaning.

FIVE EXTENSIONS IN ORGANIZATIONS

System Domain	Personal Extension	Shared Focus
Vision and strategy	Self	Direction, identity
Culture and people	Family	Relationships, belonging
Operations and work	Work	Contribution, achievement
Stakeholders	Community	Connection, impact
Environment	Nature	Sustainability, grounding

The same five extensions that make up your WholeBeing also exist in the systems you belong to. When healed or aligned, they reflect and reinforce each other.

ONE METHOD, INFINITE APPLICATIONS

As with individuals, transformation of systems begins by identifying the components of the system's WholeBeing and uncovering root causes and then applying the EASE process to guide change. Whether you're working with a couple, a family, a team, an organization, or a community, the fundamental principles remain consistent.

Purposehood Engineering for systems applies EASE at any scale:

Engage: Is the system genuinely ready for transformation? Do stakeholders want genuine change, or are they committed to maintaining current patterns with minor modifications?

Assess: What zone is the system operating from? Which aspects are thriving and which are struggling? What are the root sources of misalignment with the system's Purposehood?

Support: How do we help the system to initially move from negative states to positive states within their current zone? What structures and practices will reinforce new patterns of alignment?

Enact: How do we make changes sustainable? What habits, roles, and agreements will support ongoing alignment with the system's Purposehood?

APPLICATIONS ACROSS SYSTEM TYPES

The universal principles become practical when applied to specific types of living systems. Here are examples of how EASE transforms the systems where you already have influence:

Intimate Systems: Couples and Families

Carlos worked with a Purposehood engineer to help his family move from comfortable dysfunction to purposeful connection. Instead of individual intervention for each family member, they approached the family itself as the client.

"We started by engaging with everyone's readiness," Carlos explained. "Not everyone was equally motivated for change, and that was okay. We worked with the actual level of commitment we had rather than the level we wished we had."

The assessment revealed that different family relationships were in different zones. Carlos and his ex-wife's co-parenting relationship was in the Healing Zone with empowerment; they were actively working to create healthy patterns for their children. His relationship with his teenage daughter was in the Contraction Zone with resignation, as both had given up on meaningful connection. His relationship with his parents was in the Comfort Zone with complacency—stable but superficial.

"Instead of trying to fix everything at once, we focused on moving each relationship from its negative state to its positive state within the same zone," Carlos said. "My relationship with my daughter moved from resignation to endurance—we weren't close yet, but we stopped avoiding each other and started having real conversations about the divorce and her feelings."

The family created a shared Purposehood Guiding Star: "We want to be a family where everyone feels safe to be themselves and where conflicts become opportunities for understanding and growth, because we want to create a model of love and resilience that strengthens our extended family and friends."

Not long after, family gatherings transformed from tense obligations into genuine opportunities for connection. The conflicts hadn't all disappeared, but the family had developed systematic ways to address challenges that supported their shared purpose.

Professional Systems: Teams and Organizations

John applied Purposehood Engineering principles to transform his company culture. "We realized our organization was experiencing the same growth excess I'd struggled with personally: pursuing every opportunity without clear connection to deeper purpose."

The organizational assessment revealed that different departments were operating from different zones. Sales was in the Growth Zone with excess, hitting targets but burning people out. Customer service was in the Healing Zone with dependency, constantly reacting to problems rather than preventing them. Product development was in the Comfort Zone with complacency, maintaining adequate performance without pushing creative boundaries.

"The shift came when we developed our organizational Purposehood Guiding Star together," John said. "We moved from 'maximize market share through innovative products' to 'building a thriving, sustainable business where our team members can do their best work and grow as human beings, because we want to create solutions that genuinely improve people's daily lives and contribute to a better world.'"

This clarity transformed decision-making across the organization. New projects were evaluated not just on revenue potential but also on alignment with Purposehood. Hiring decisions took cultural fit with their values into account. Performance reviews encompassed *how* results were achieved.

"Employee engagement increased dramatically because people felt connected to meaningful work," John said. "Customer satisfaction improved because we were solving real problems rather than just selling products. And paradoxically, revenue grew because our clarity attracted both customers and employees who shared our values."

YPO Forum Systems Transformation

John's success with his organization inspired him to bring Purposehood Engineering to his YPO forum, which had fallen into the Comfort Zone's pattern of complacency. "We'd been meeting for three years, but our conversations had become predictable," he said. "We were showing up out of habit rather than excitement."

When the forum engaged a Purposehood engineer, they discovered that their system was experiencing the same stagnation patterns that families and organizations face. "It was fascinating to see that a peer learning group could have its own WholeBeing," said Ravi, another forum member. "We had all the components—trust, commitment, shared experiences—but we'd lost our collective sense of purpose."

The systematic assessment revealed that while the forum had strong relational foundations, its learning and developmental momentum had stalled. Members were sharing updates but not challenging each other. They were maintaining connection but not fostering transformation.

"Applying EASE to our forum was like giving it a complete health checkup," said Alia, the tech entrepreneur in the group. "We realized we'd been operating like a social club when we could be functioning as a transformation laboratory."

The forum members worked together to create their collective Purposehood Guiding Star: "We want to grow together as leaders and challenge each other to reach our highest potential, because we want to create positive impact in our businesses, communities, and the world beyond this room." This wasn't just a mission statement—it became the framework for redesigning their entire meeting structure.

The results spoke for themselves. "Our meetings went from comfortable catchups to genuine existential leadership development sessions," John said. "We started bringing real challenges, offering constructive feedback, and holding each other accountable for growth across all five extensions of our lives."

The ripple effects extended far beyond the forum. Members began applying the same systematic approach to their own organizations and families. "When you experience Purposehood Engineering in a small group, you understand how it can work anywhere," Ravi said. "It's given me a whole new lens for seeing challenges in my company."

Their peers began reaching out to learn about their approach to deeper engagement. "We went from being a nice support group to being a genuine force for systemic change in each other's lives and organizations," Alia said.

Community Systems: Neighborhoods and Civic Groups

Going forward, Emma didn't wait for a title or permission. When challenges surfaced in her neighborhood, she saw an opportunity to apply the same principles that had changed her life. She invited a few neighbors over for tea and honest conversation and suggested an open circle where anyone could share what was working, what was frustrating, and what they wished could change. To her surprise, nearly a dozen people showed up.

"We used the same EASE process," Emma said. "First we engaged with people's actual readiness for change rather than assuming everyone wanted the same level of involvement. Some people genuinely preferred just being informed about neighborhood issues. Others were hungry for collaborative action but didn't know how to move beyond discussion."

The assessment revealed that the community had strong connections—people cared about each other—but weak systems for collective action. Emma helped them redesign their approach to honor both needs: a community circle for those who wanted to stay informed and contribute ideas and an action team for those ready to implement specific projects.

"We applied the same principles of moving from negative to positive states," Emma said. "Instead of trying to force everyone into action mode, we helped the action team move from discussion-based engagement to implementation-based collaboration while supporting the community circle in becoming a more effective space for neighborhood connection and input."

Their first project, a neighborhood tool-sharing program, built confidence and skills for larger initiatives. Over time, they implemented a community garden, a monthly repair café, and an emergency preparedness network. More important, the neighborhood developed practical capacity for identifying shared challenges and creating collaborative solutions.

"We didn't fix everything," Emma said, "but we started living like neighbors again. We had language for where we were and tools to move forward. It turns out, even a street of strangers can become a WholeBeing."

(II) PURPOSEHOOD PAUSE

Think of a system you're part of that feels stuck—your family, team, or community.

- What zone might this system be operating from?

- How does your personal alignment influence this system's health?

- What would moving this system from its negative state to a positive state look like?

- Who else in this system might be ready for conscious change?

You can't force systems to heal or grow, but your embodied transformation becomes an invitation for collective possibility.

YOUR ROLE IN SYSTEMS CHANGE

You know how to distinguish between surface symptoms and root causes. You can recognize the difference between negative and positive states within each zone. You understand how systematic assessment leads to targeted intervention and sustainable change. These capacities transfer directly to systems work. When you can see that your workplace team is trapped in dependency patterns—constantly seeking external solutions rather than developing internal capacity—you understand why another reorganization won't address the underlying challenges. When you recognize your family operating from a point of complacency—comfortable with familiar dysfunction rather than risking the vulnerability of change—you can imagine what would support movement toward more purposeful engagement.

The ripple effect is profound: When systems align with Purposehood, they become sources of healing rather than stress. Families operating from shared Purposehood raise children who carry existential intelligence into their future relationships. Organizations aligned with meaningful mission attract people who bring those values into their communities. Communities with collaborative capacity become laboratories for positive social change.

You don't need to become a professional Purposehood engineer to participate in this work. There are natural levels of engagement:

Observer: recognizing systems patterns around you, using your understanding of EASE to make sense of family dynamics, workplace culture, and community challenges

Participant: applying Purposehood principles within your existing roles—asking questions that help groups recognize their own patterns, responding to conflicts with curiosity instead of reactivity, contributing to discussions in ways that build rather than just critique

Engineer: developing specialized skills to guide systematic transformation through training in Purposehood Engineering principles

Each level serves the larger healing. The conscious observer helps systems recognize their patterns. The purposeful participant creates space for healthier dynamics to emerge. The skilled engineer provides systematic guidance for transformation processes.

WHY EVERY SYSTEM NEEDS AN ENGINEER

While not everyone needs to become a Purposehood Engineer, every family, organization, and community benefits immensely from having at least one trained member who understands these principles. Just as families benefit from having someone with first aid training and organizations thrive when they have skilled facilitators, systems flourish when they include someone who can recognize patterns, guide conversations toward alignment, and help navigate challenges through a Purposehood lens. One person with these skills can transform the health and effectiveness of an entire system, turning reactive families into responsive ones, shifting organizational culture from dysfunction to purpose-driven collaboration, and helping communities move from stagnation to meaningful collective action.

SCALING THE METHOD

Whether working with a couple struggling with communication, a family navigating teenage challenges, a team trapped in crisis management, or an organization seeking alignment between values and practices, the framework remains consistent:

Universal principles: All systems experience the same fundamental patterns of suffering and healing.

Scalable assessment: The same diagnostic framework applies whether mapping individual or organizational well-being.

Targeted intervention: Moving systems from negative to positive states requires the same systematic approach.

Sustainable integration: Lasting change happens through structures and practices that reinforce alignment with Purposehood.

This universality means that every step you've taken in your own healing and growth has quietly prepared you for something larger. When you learn to move one life from misdirection to meaning, you gain insight into how entire systems do the same. Personal transformation becomes transferable wisdom.

The same process that guided your journey—Engage, Assess, Support, Enact—doesn't stop at the boundaries of the self. It scales with consciousness itself.

And now, that scaling faces its greatest test yet.

As technology accelerates faster than our inner capacity to adapt, the question is no longer whether individuals or systems can heal and grow—but whether humanity itself can remain whole.

CHAPTER 16

PURPOSEHOOD IN THE AGE OF AI
THE SIXTH EXTENSION OF BEING

What if the greatest threat to humanity isn't scarcity but abundance without purpose?

This sounds paradoxical because abundance has always meant salvation. For millennia, we've battled hunger, disease, isolation—struggles that have shaped every generation before us. Now, for the first time in history, we're solving them all.

Artificial intelligence that outthinks us. Genetic engineering that rewrites life itself. Robotics that transcend our physical limits. Digital tools that dissolve reality's edges. Networks that could merge individual consciousness into something planetary.

We stand at the threshold of solving everything our ancestors could only dream of overcoming. So why does something in you resist calling this abundance of solutions our greatest threat?

Because more has always meant less suffering. Because the idea that getting everything we want could destroy us feels... ungrateful? Naive?

What if that resistance is exactly what we need to examine?

Picture this: You're standing at the edge of a vast ocean. An enormous wave approaches, carrying everything humanity has ever longed for—the end of want, the defeat of death, the birth of limitless abundance. All our problems are finally over.

But waves this enormous don't only lift. They also obliterate.

This isn't the gradual progress our ancestors knew. This is total transformation—exponential, irreversible, outpacing our ability to adapt consciously. The question keeping me awake isn't whether we can build this future—we're already building it. The question is whether we'll emerge from it as recognizably human.

You sense it already. In how your phone anticipates your desires before you do. In how algorithms shape your reality so seamlessly you forget you're seeing a curated world. In that growing awareness that you're becoming more efficient but less alive, more connected but less present, more informed but less wise.

Let me share something that still haunts me, an experiment that shows what happens when beings get everything they think they need.

A PARADISE THAT BECAME A TOMB

In the 1960s, an ethologist named John B. Calhoun designed a mouse utopia—what he called Universe 25. He created a perfect world where mice had unlimited food, endless water, comfortable shelter, and complete protection from predators.

No scarcity. No struggle. No external threats. Just abundance, safety, and ease. It was paradise by every material measure.

At first the mice did exactly what you'd expect—they thrived. Their population grew rapidly, doubling every fifty-five days as they explored their new world with the joy of discovery. Social structures formed naturally, and life appeared to be harmonious and purposeful. It seemed Calhoun had indeed created utopia.

But then something chilling began to happen. Despite having access to space for thousands more, the population peaked at just half the habitat's capacity. And as it did, Calhoun observed behaviors that defied everything he thought he knew about life's drive to flourish. The mice began to exhibit what he called "the behavioral sink," a complete breakdown of normal social patterns.

What followed was what Calhoun termed the First Death. Not the death of the body but something far more devastating: the death of the soul.

Here's how Calhoun described it: "In the absence of stress from predators or lack of resources, individuals still perished, not in body but in spirit."

The males, unable to establish territories or meaningful roles, withdrew entirely from social interaction. They stopped competing for mates. They stopped defending anything worth defending. They simply gave up.

The females, overwhelmed by the breakdown of social order and unable to rely on male partnership, abandoned their maternal instincts. Mothers neglected their young. Some became aggressive, attacking the very offspring they should have protected.

But perhaps most haunting of all were the mice Calhoun called "the beautiful ones." These creatures spent their days in obsessive grooming, eating, and sleeping and avoided all social interaction. They neither fought nor mated. They were physically perfect—sleek, healthy, and unblemished.

"They became like living statues, perfect in appearance but void of purpose," Calhoun said. "Their existence had no meaning."

These beings had everything they could possibly need but lived as hollow shells of what they were meant to be. Calhoun watched as relationships collapsed, communities dissolved, and individuals retreated into isolation that was more profound than any physical death—"the complete erosion of the social fabric," as he called it.

Although physically alive and materially provided for, the mice had lost something essential: the will to live meaningfully. They'd experienced the death of connection, meaning, and Purposehood itself—the First Death.

And with no social bonds, no reproduction, no drive to continue, the population began its inexorable decline toward zero—the Second Death.

By the end of the experiment, with not a single mouse still alive, the paradise that was Universe 25 had become a tomb. And this was not the first attempt—there had been twenty-four before it.

A MIRROR FOR HUMANITY

The Universe 25 experiment haunts me because of its implications for humanity. The emerging technologies promise to solve material challenges that have defined human existence for millennia, making scarcity as we know it obsolete. Disease could be eradicated, physical limitations transcended, the need to work eliminated.

But Universe 25 revealed that abundance alone isn't enough. Without Purposehood, without meaning and connection, abundance becomes not a gift but a curse, a trap that leads to collapse.

Consider what we're already witnessing. Rising rates of depression and anxiety despite unprecedented prosperity. Social isolation in the most connected age in human history. Political polarization even as we have access to more information than ever. Climbing suicide rates in the world's wealthiest nations.

The mice in Universe 25 had everything they needed to survive, but they lost the will to thrive. They had food but forgot why eating mattered. They had shelter but abandoned the idea of home. They had potential mates but lost the drive to create new life. They had community but retreated into isolation.

When everything is provided, what's worth living for? When survival is guaranteed, what's worth striving for? When all problems are solved, what gives life meaning?

The mice had no answer. The question is whether we will.

TECHNOLOGY AS OUR SIXTH EXTENSION: THE WAVE APPROACHES

This brings us to a recognition that bridges the personal transformation you've experienced and humanity's collective challenge. In the process of building better tools, we're creating humanity's sixth extension of being.

We exist as WholeBeings across five natural extensions—Self, Family, Work, Communities, and Nature. Now we're creating a sixth extension through technology in ways that fundamentally alter what it means to be human. This sixth extension encompasses five interconnected components that are reshaping our very existence at exponential speed: artificial intelligence, genetic engineering, robotics, digital augmentation, and hyper-connectivity.

Unlike our other extensions, which evolved slowly over millennia, this one is emerging so rapidly that we risk losing ourselves before we understand what we're becoming. And each component carries the potential to accelerate humanity's journey toward our greatest flourishing or into our own version of Universe 25.

ARTIFICIAL INTELLIGENCE: THE COGNITIVE COMPANION

Artificial intelligence is becoming our cognitive companion, offering us real-time access to vast stores of knowledge, analyzing problems beyond our mental capacity, and generating solutions we could never imagine alone. AI promises breakthroughs in medicine, climate modeling, and education that could push human potential beyond all previous boundaries.

But this cognitive companion poses questions that go to the heart of what makes us human: When we outsource our decisions, our thinking, our very reasoning to machines, are we freeing ourselves for our Purposehood, or are we surrendering the essence of our agency? When AI personalizes our experiences and influences our behavior, do we risk becoming like those beautiful mice—passive recipients of algorithmic guidance rather than active creators of our own meaning?

Ask yourself this: What decisions do you make daily without consulting a device or algorithm? How might this dependency be reshaping your relationship with your own wisdom?

GENETIC ENGINEERING: REWRITING THE CODE OF LIFE

Genetic engineering offers us the power to rewrite our biological inheritance. We can now eradicate hereditary diseases, enhance our physical capabilities, and potentially extend human life span beyond anything our ancestors could imagine. For the first time in history, we aren't limited by the genetic lottery—we can design ourselves according to our aspirations.

But this power to edit the code of life raises profound questions about authenticity and identity. If we can reshape our genetic makeup at will, what defines our true self? Are we enhancing humanity or moving toward something post-human?

Purposehood reminds us that our essence transcends our biology—it's rooted in our connections, our values, and our contributions to existence itself.

Ask yourself this: If you could edit any aspect of your biological self, what would you choose? What does that choice reveal about how you define your essential nature?

ROBOTICS: EXTENDING OUR PHYSICAL PRESENCE

Robotics is expanding our physical capabilities in ways that seemed like pure science fiction just decades ago. From prosthetics that restore function to exoskeletons that amplify human strength to nanobots working inside our bodies to repair tissue and deliver targeted treatments, new technologies promise to eliminate physical limitations and free us from dangerous or repetitive labor.

But as machines take over more of our physical interactions with the world, both external and internal, we face a different kind of risk: disconnection from our embodied humanity. If robots handle our physical tasks, our manual labor, our tangible engagement with the material world, how do we maintain our grounded connection to existence? Our bodies aren't just vehicles, after all. They're integral to how we experience meaning, connection, and presence in the world.

Ask yourself this: When do you feel most embodied and present? How might increasing automation affect these moments of physical grounding?

DIGITAL AUGMENTATION: THE NEW LAYER OF REALITY

Digital tools, augmented reality, and virtual reality are creating entirely new layers of experience. We can now overlay information onto our physical reality through AR glasses, immerse ourselves in completely virtual worlds through VR headsets, and interact with others across vast distances as if they're in the same room. These technologies promise to expand our experiential possibilities beyond the constraints of physical space and time.

But as our virtual experiences become increasingly indistinguishable from reality, we risk losing our connection to the present moment, to the tangible world, to the simple but profound experience of being fully here now. When virtual becomes as compelling as real, how do we maintain our grounding in authentic existence?

Ask yourself this: How much of your daily experience happens through screens rather than direct contact with physical reality? What shifts when you step away from digital mediation?

HYPER-CONNECTIVITY: THE EMERGING GLOBAL CONSCIOUSNESS

Perhaps most profound of all is the emergence of hyper-connectivity through neural interfaces and AI-driven communication platforms. We're approaching a future where thoughts, emotions, and experiences can be shared instantly across the globe, creating a global consciousness that transcends all previous boundaries.

While this connectivity can promote unprecedented empathy and collaboration, it also raises fundamental questions about individuality and diversity. Unity without diversity isn't evolution; it's assimilation. If we can share thoughts directly, if we become part of a collective consciousness, how do we maintain the uniqueness that allows each of us to contribute something irreplaceable to existence?

Ask yourself this: In your most connected moments, do you feel more yourself or less? What would you never want to share with a collective consciousness?

UNIVERSE 26: UTOPIA OR DEMISE— WHAT FUTURE WILL WE BUILD?

We stand now at the threshold of our own Universe 26—humanity's next experiment in abundance. The technological advances approaching promise an age when material scarcity may no longer define human existence. Our sixth extension could free us from repetitive labor, eliminate preventable disease, and connect us globally in ways that transcend every previous boundary. We could witness the birth of true abundance for all.

This is humanity's moment of ultimate testing. The vision before us carries within it both the seeds of our greatest flourishing and the potential for our complete destruction. We could create a world where technology amplifies the best of human nature—our creativity, our compassion, our capacity for meaning—or we could build our own behavioral sink, a paradise that becomes a tomb.

Consider the choice we face: Will abundance serve Purposehood or will it replace it?

When artificial intelligence can solve problems we can't even comprehend, will we use that power to deepen human connection or to retreat further into isolation? When genetic engineering can perfect our bodies, will we remember that our essence transcends our biology? When robots can perform our labor, will we discover higher forms of contribution or will we lose the satisfaction of meaningful work?

The temptation will be profound. In a world where technology provides everything we need—where food appears without effort, where entertainment is endless, where comfort is guaranteed—why struggle for anything deeper? Why seek meaning when pleasure is abundant? Why build relationships when virtual connections feel sufficient? Why create when algorithms can produce whatever we desire?

This was the seduction of Universe 25: the promise that meeting physical needs is enough, that abundance equals fulfillment, that comfort equals happiness. But the mice taught us otherwise. They showed us that when survival is guaranteed but Purposehood is forgotten, existence becomes a living death. Physical paradise without existential meaning is hell disguised as comfort.

The choice before us is whether we will anchor the coming world in Purposehood or allow it to anchor us in emptiness.

If we choose wisely, our Universe 26 experiment could become humanity's greatest achievement, a world where technology serves human flourishing, where abundance enables deeper meaning, where connection transcends physical boundaries while deepening spiritual bonds—where we finally have the time, the tools, and the freedom to discover everything we're capable of becoming.

But if we choose poorly, if we allow material abundance to seduce us away from existential purpose, Universe 26 will become our final chapter—not written in a sudden destruction but in the quiet surrender of everything that made us human.

The mice of Universe 25 had no choice in their fate. They were subjects in an experiment they couldn't understand. But humans are creators. We have the power to choose. What will we do with that power?

SHARPENING OUR EXISTENTIAL INTELLIGENCE

Our future won't be shaped by algorithms. It will be shaped by the depth of our questions.

In an age when machines can process information faster than we can think, when artificial intelligence can solve problems we can't even formulate, when technology can provide answers to questions we haven't learned to ask yet, there remains one capacity that no algorithm can replicate: the ability to ask why any of it matters.

This is existential intelligence, the uniquely human capacity to grapple with life's most profound questions. Not just how to live but why to live, not just what to do but what makes doing anything worthwhile, not just how to solve problems but whether the problems we're solving are the ones that actually need solving.

As our sixth extension accelerates the pace of change beyond anything our species has ever experienced, existential intelligence becomes more than a philosophical luxury—it becomes our survival skill. When everything around us is transforming at exponential speed, the ability to anchor ourselves in timeless questions of meaning and Purposehood becomes the only stable ground we have. The same systematic approach you've mastered for personal transformation now becomes humanity's compass for navigating exponential change. The principles that guide individual healing can guide our species through this unprecedented transition.

The machines we create will soon think faster than we do, but they can't feel the weight of mortality that gives urgency to our choices. They can't experience the longing for connection that drives us to reach beyond ourselves. They can't know the quiet satisfaction of creating something meaningful from nothing or the profound joy of contributing to something larger than their own existence or what it means to simply love. And these uniquely human experiences are the sources of our greatest strength. They're what make us irreplaceable in a world of artificial intelligence.

But only if we remember to cultivate them.

The question that will define the next stage of human evolution is whether we can remain fully human in a world of thinking machines. Can we maintain our capacity for wonder in a world where everything can be explained? Can we preserve our hunger for meaning in a world where every desire can be satisfied? Can we protect our need for connection in a world where every person can be reached but true intimacy becomes increasingly rare?

This is why the evolutionary imperatives you've learned in this book matter more than ever. The ability to engage genuinely with your deepest longings. The courage to assess honestly where you are and what you truly need. The wisdom to support your growth in ways that honor your WholeBeing. The discipline to enact changes that align with your deepest values rather than your most immediate impulses.

The future won't be determined by our algorithms but by our self-awareness—by the clarity of our Purposehood.

THE NEW AGE OF PURPOSEHOOD

The choices we make in the coming years—about how we relate to technology, how we define progress, how we measure a life well lived—will determine whether humanity emerges from the pending transformation more fully human or less so.

While we can't stop the wave of change that's coming, we can choose how to surf it. We can choose to remain creators rather than becoming consumers. We can choose to deepen our humanity rather than surrender it. We can choose to use our tools rather than be used by them. But choice takes consciousness, and consciousness takes practice.

The EASE process you've learned in this book—how to engage, assess, support, and enact—is no longer just a personal framework; these are survival skills for our species. Your journey toward healing and growth, your commitment to living with Purposehood, your willingness to engineer a life worth loving—all of this has been preparation for humanity's greatest test. You're helping determine whether our species remembers what it means to be human in an age of artificial intelligence. The future depends not on our technology's sophistication but on our own existential sophistication, not on whether machines can think but on whether we can remember how to be.

This is the calling of our time: to become so fully, consciously, purposefully human that no amount of technology can diminish our irreplaceable essence.

The future belongs to those who engineer meaning, not just efficiency. The same systematic approach that guided your personal transformation—EASE, zone awareness, Purposehood-centered living—now becomes humanity's compass through exponential change.

Will we become Universe 25, or will we create something unprecedented: abundance that nurtures existential health, technology that amplifies human flourishing, connection that deepens rather than diminishes our humanity?

Universe 26 awaits. We are its architects. Together, let's build with wisdom.

THE CHOICE BEFORE YOU
A PERSONAL NOTE FROM THE AUTHOR

My friend,

You've walked with me through sixteen chapters and arrived here, at the threshold of your own transformation, ready to conduct the symphony of your life with intention and ease.

Behind you lies everything you've learned: how suffering arises not from circumstance but from misdirection, how healing requires not just intention but structure, how growth demands not perfection but practice, how your five extensions create the symphony of your existence.

Ahead lies the question that only you can answer: Will you use these tools, or will they remain elegant theories?

All your life, you've been playing fragments of music—a note here, a chord there—never hearing the full symphony you were meant to create. You've spent years, maybe a lifetime, playing someone else's music. Living by others' expectations. Adjusting to survive. Sometimes the melody soared. Often it fell apart. Always, something essential seemed to be missing.

Now you understand why. You were trying to tune single instruments while ignoring the orchestra. Fixing your work life while your relationships crumbled. Seeking personal growth while disconnecting from community. Chasing success while your soul starved for meaning.

The Purposehood Method for Existential Health showed you what you've always sensed but couldn't articulate: every extension affects the whole. A broken string distorts the whole symphony. An unplayed instrument leaves silence where music should be.

But knowing this changes everything. You now hold what you've been searching for—not another philosophy to ponder but a practice to live, not another framework to admire but a method to embody.

The Purposehood Method doesn't end with this book; it begins here. Every day offers new opportunities to practice EASE, to navigate your zones with wisdom, to conduct with growing mastery. There will be moments when old patterns resurface, when discord returns despite your best conducting—this is the music becoming real. Every master conductor knows that the most beautiful symphonies include movements of struggle that resolve into deeper harmony.

When those moments come, you'll remember you aren't just someone who survived. You're someone who's learned to navigate any zone with grace, to meet any challenge with the tools of systematic healing and growth.

In an age when algorithms compose symphonies and machines create art, there remains one composition no technology can produce: the genuine expression of your unique existence. The particular way you love. The specific gifts you carry. The irreplaceable note you add to humanity's symphony.

And you're not alone. You're part of a global Purposehood community: individuals, families, organizations, and ecosystems all learning to tune their lives to something greater. Around the world, others are applying this same method—families healing generational patterns, organizations creating cultures of flourishing, communities discovering collaborative capacity. Your individual transformation ripples outward, contributing to a global crescendo of purposeful living.

You stand now where every reader has stood—at the threshold between knowing and doing, between understanding and embodying, between reading about transformation and living it. This is your moment of choice. So I ask you, with all the urgency this moment demands, will you remain a consumer of wisdom, or will you become a creator of meaning? Will you let these insights fade into memory or will you make them muscle? Will you wait for the perfect moment, or will you recognize that this moment—this breath, this heartbeat, this now—is the only moment you need?

The orchestra of your life sits in hushed anticipation. Every extension of your being awaits your direction. The music sheet is before you, written in the ink of your deepest longings. You, my friend, aren't just a reader—you're a conductor, a composer of the possible. And the baton is in your hand.

You don't need to be ready. You need to begin.

Raise the baton. Trust the method. Conduct the symphony of your life. Live with meaning, gratitude, ease, and abundance. Let your music resound with happiness, success, and fulfillment. And in choosing to conduct your own symphony, you give others permission to conduct theirs.

The world needs your music.

Begin.

My friend, may you heal and grow with ease,

Ammar

BONUS CHAPTER

The following chapter explores how the Purposehood Method applies inside organizations, leadership, and workplace systems.

PURPOSEHOOD ORGANIZATION ENGINEERING—EXISTENTIAL LEADERSHIP FOR WORKPLACE TRANSFORMATION

In my workshops with business leaders, I often pose a direct question: "How engaged do you think your employee would be if their teenager is suicidal? Or if they're going through a painful divorce?"

The response is always the same: instant recognition that no one can fully engage at work while their WholeBeing is in crisis. Leaders immediately understand that no amount of incentives, recognition programs, or workplace perks can overcome the drain of serious struggles in other areas of life.

This isn't only true in extreme situations; it applies just as much when someone is caring for an aging parent, managing their own chronic health issue, dealing with financial pressure, or worrying about a child struggling at school. Any strain on one of the 25 components of Whole-Being inevitably carries over into the workplace.

Every Monday morning, more than three billion people around the world wake up and go to work. Most of them—79 percent, according to Gallup's State of the Global Workplace 2025 report—will spend that day contributing the minimum required and quietly counting the hours until they can leave.

This isn't just a management failure. It's not just employee apathy. It's the predictable result of a fundamental misalignment between how modern organizations operate and what human beings need to thrive.

While EASE Leadership prepares individuals to lead their own healing and growth, Existential Leadership equips organizations to create systems where human flourishing becomes the foundation of performance. This is where Existential Leadership becomes essential: leadership that aligns organizational systems with human needs for direction, meaning, and wholeness.

Think of an organization like an airplane. For any plane to fly successfully, three critical components must work together seamlessly: the engines (engagement) that move everything forward, the pilot (leadership) that navigates toward the destination, and the flight plan (strategy) that aligns everyone's efforts. Right now, most organizational "airplanes" are trying to fly with faulty engines, frustrated pilots, and a foggy flight plan that leaves teams unsure of where they're headed.

The cost of this disconnection is staggering: $438 billion in documented losses annually, with economists estimating up to $9.6 trillion in unrealized potential—representing nearly 9 percent of global gross domestic product. That's like the combined economies of Germany and Japan simply evaporating because neither managers nor employees have learned how to create mutual flourishing.

This isn't just an engagement problem or a culture issue. It's an existential crisis that requires both organizational systems and individual responsibility to solve.

But what if this crisis isn't inevitable? What if there's a systematic way to create workplaces where people naturally want to contribute their best?

Over nine years, I built and led a company that grew to over $300 million in annual sales while maintaining the kind of culture where people genuinely wanted to work. This wasn't achieved through traditional incentive structures or performance management systems. It emerged from creating an environment where personal growth and professional contribution enhanced each other, where people's work became a vehicle for their own development and a contribution to something bigger than themselves.

The company consistently achieved employee engagement scores in the top 5 percent of our industry, customer satisfaction ratings that led to more than 90 percent retention, innovation metrics that kept us ahead of larger competitors, and financial performance that attracted top talent.

This wasn't luck or charisma. It was the systematic application of the same principles that guide individual transformation: recognizing people as WholeBeings, addressing root causes rather than symptoms, and creating systems that support human flourishing rather than just extracting productivity.

THREE-PART TRANSFORMATION APPROACH

Purposehood Organization Engineering is a systemic application of The Purposehood Method for workplace transformation. It transforms organizations through three integrated approaches that address the root causes of workplace dysfunction:

EXISTENTIAL REENGAGEMENT

Using the EASE process and REVEAL360 assessment to restore alignment with Purposehood across all extensions of being for individuals within the organization

EXISTENTIAL LEADERSHIP DEVELOPMENT

Training managers in Purposehood principles to become existential leaders, equipped to navigate business challenges with ease while awakening the potentiality of those they lead, fostering whole-person flourishing alongside sustainable business results

STRATEGIC IMPLEMENTATION

Purpose-driven strategy guided by the ART framework (Attain, Retain, Train) that ensures alignment between stated values and actual choices

This isn't another piecemeal approach; it's a comprehensive methodology that addresses organizational health systematically, creating sustainable transformation.

WHY TRADITIONAL SOLUTIONS KEEP FAILING

Most organizations try to solve engagement problems with surface-level fixes: better benefits, pizza parties, employee recognition programs, or wellness initiatives that treat symptoms rather than causes. These approaches fail because they miss the deeper truth: people want their work to matter and need their contributions to align with something bigger than themselves. They don't just seek work-life balance—they seek work-life integration where their personal growth and professional contribution enhance each other.

The scope of this crisis runs deeper than most leaders realize. With only 27 percent of managers themselves engaged—meaning 73 percent of the pilots in our airplane metaphor are disengaged—it's no wonder that organizational transformation efforts consistently fail. How can disengaged managers inspire engagement in others?

Meanwhile, global well-being is slipping, with only 33 percent of employees saying they're thriving in their lives overall—clear evidence that workplace dysfunction is spilling into every aspect of human existence.

EXISTENTIAL REENGAGEMENT

Before a team can rise, it has to reconnect with its deeper why. Existential reengagement goes far beyond traditional employee satisfaction surveys or wellness programs. It addresses the fundamental disconnection between who people are and how they show up at work, restoring alignment between personal Purposehood and organizational mission across all dimensions of human existence.

TWO DRIVERS OF REENGAGEMENT

Purposehood alignment: True engagement emerges when employees discover the meaningful connection between their personal sense of purpose and the organization's deeper mission. It's about revealing the natural intersection where individual calling meets collective contribution.

When employees understand why their work matters in the context of their own Purposehood, work transforms from obligation to expression. They approach challenges with resilience because setbacks become part of a larger story they're helping to write.

WholeBeing support: Employees can't sustainably perform if they're struggling in other extensions of their lives. You could offer the best benefits package in the industry, but if someone's family is in crisis or their health is failing, they simply can't bring their full capacity to work.

This isn't about overstepping professional boundaries or becoming a therapy organization. It's about recognizing a fundamental truth: human beings are integrated systems. When the REVEAL360—Purposehood WholeBeing Assessment reveals that an employee is struggling with community isolation or spiritual emptiness, that information becomes strategic intelligence about what's preventing their full engagement.

Organizations practicing existential reengagement understand that supporting someone's relationship with their teenager or their need for meaningful community connection isn't charity, it's business wisdom. When all Five Extensions of Being are aligned, employees bring their complete capacity to their work rather than operating in survival mode.

When existential reengagement succeeds, the results extend far beyond productivity metrics. Employees become culture catalysts; their genuine engagement inspires others and creates upward spirals of collaboration, innovation, and resilience. They develop organizational ownership, caring about outcomes not because they're incentivized to but because the work has become an expression of their own Purposehood.

Most important, they develop the capacity to navigate challenges with strength rather than in survival mode, making them invaluable during times of change, crisis, or growth.

That's exactly what happened for Christophe.

CHRISTOPHE'S EXISTENTIAL LEADERSHIP

I met Christophe through a mutual connection during the Cannes Lions International Festival of Creativity. He was the founder of Innate Motion, a global consultancy that worked with some of the world's most prestigious companies. His company had already achieved something remarkable: a unique culture rooted in empathy and collaboration, with strong team bonds and regular gatherings that fostered a genuine sense of belonging. It was exactly the kind of organization many leaders aspire to create.

What impressed me most about Christophe was his commitment to continuous improvement. Even with Innate Motion's extraordinary culture and strong performance, he recognized an opportunity to deepen employee engagement. Like the most thoughtful leaders, he understood that good could become great, and he was willing to explore innovative approaches beyond traditional methods.

Christophe invited me to lead a working session for his key team, about forty talented consultants and partners who were the backbone of the company. And instead of delivering standard engagement training, we used the REVEAL360 assessment to explore a different dimension of workplace excellence.

The assessment revealed that while Christophe's consultants were highly skilled professionals, they were also navigating personal challenges—family dynamics, health concerns, community ties, and questions of life direction. Rather than treating these as distractions from performance, Christophe saw through our work together that they were integral to it. When people felt supported as whole human beings, not just as professional resources, their creativity and collaboration flourished. As he later reflected, "I realized we had an opportunity to engage people's complete potential rather than just their professional capacity. Supporting their whole lives transformed not only our work quality, but also team dynamics, client relationships, and company culture."

The approach wasn't about collapsing the distinction between personal and professional roles. It was about recognizing a fundamental truth that people perform at their highest when their work contributes to rather than competes with their overall well-being and sense of Purposehood.

Building on this success, we developed a plan to train Christophe's top leadership team in Existential Leadership modules, ensuring they could continue supporting their teams long after our work together.

THE BUSINESS CASE FOR EXISTENTIAL REENGAGEMENT

Organizations that master existential reengagement create advantages that competitors using traditional approaches simply can't match:

- Sustainable innovation: People operating in alignment with their Purposehood consistently generate creative solutions because they're contributing out of inspiration rather than obligation.

- Authentic customer connection: When employees feel genuinely supported, they naturally extend that quality of care to customer relationships, creating loyalty that transcends price competition.

- Resilient culture: Teams that have learned to navigate challenges while maintaining Purposehood can adapt to market changes without losing their identity or effectiveness.

- Talent magnetism: In an era when top performers have choices, organizations known for supporting human flourishing attract and retain the people who drive sustainable success.

This transformation of existential reengagement creates measurable advantages in employee engagement. Gallup's extensive research (456 studies across 276 organizations in 54 industries) shows that engaged employees deliver measurable advantages, including:

- Financial performance: Companies with highly engaged workforces achieve 21 percent higher profitability and 17 percent higher productivity than those with disengaged employees.

- Operational excellence: Engaged organizations see 41 percent lower absenteeism, 24 to 50 percent less turnover (depending on industry), and 20 percent higher sales performance.

- Customer impact: These organizations consistently achieve 10 percent improvement in customer ratings as engaged employees naturally extend their commitment to customer relationships.

- Competitive advantage: Organizations with high employee engagement consistently outperform those with disengaged teams, creating a performance gap that translates into sustainable market advantage.

- Cultural transformation: Beyond the metrics, engaged employees foster trust, collaboration, and accountability while eliminating silos and minimizing internal conflicts, creating environments where strategic alignment naturally emerges.

But the deeper value of existential reengagement can't be quantified: the satisfaction of building something that serves human flourishing while achieving business success, creating workplaces where people's Monday mornings feel like opportunities rather than obligations.

EXISTENTIAL LEADERSHIP: LIFE ENGINEERING IN ORGANIZATIONS

Traditional leadership development focuses on business skills—strategy, communication, decision-making. The Purposehood Method for

Existential Health introduces a deeper model: Existential Leadership. These are leaders who act as "life engineers," recognizing that their responsibility is not only to deliver results but also to support human flourishing in service of organizational mission.

The data makes this urgent: Gallup has found that managers account for about 70 percent of the variance in team engagement, yet only 44 percent of managers worldwide report receiving formal training in how to lead. When organizations do invest in manager development, the results are dramatic. Gallup's research across industries shows that performance improves by 17 to 28 percent, while manager well-being rises by 32 percent—and in some cases by as much as 50 percent when ongoing coaching and support are provided. The question isn't whether leadership development works but whether organizations will commit to the systematic approach it requires. As Harvard Business School research recently showed, the "secret ingredient" in workforce training isn't technology or budgets, but middle managers who model learning themselves. When these managers embraced training, employee participation rose by nearly 60 percent and teams became markedly more resilient. The evidence is clear: organizational culture shifts when leaders embody the very growth they ask of others.

Through training, Existential Leaders develop specialized skills for guiding people through the four zones of well-being and the different phases of healing and growth. Their ultimate goal is to prepare teams for the most challenging aspect of work: becoming their best while pursuing ambitious business objectives.

These leaders master five core capabilities:

- *Be the example:* They embody organizational values and demonstrate personal alignment with Purposehood, showing rather than telling others how to integrate well-being with performance.

- *Unleash potential:* They recognize that each person carries untapped capacity, and they see their role as nurturing both personal and professional growth so that individual development directly expands organizational capability.

- *Set clear vision:* They help people connect their personal sense of Purposehood with collective goals, creating alignment that generates energy and meaning rather than relying on constant external motivation.

- *Empower teams:* They build psychological safety where individuals can bring their full creativity and essential desires to the table, knowing that diverse voices strengthen shared success.

- *Drive resilience:* They guide teams through all four zones of well-being, equipping them to navigate contraction, healing, comfort, and growth without losing sight of direction and meaning.

This approach transforms leadership from oversight and control into facilitation and empowerment. Existential Leadership fosters environments where people are inspired to give their best—because their work is aligned with who they are, not because they are pushed to deliver under pressure.

PURPOSE-DRIVEN STRATEGY

Most strategies look good on paper and die in implementation because they lack existential coherence. Purposehood Organization Engineering solves this by grounding strategy in two integrated phases: collaborative development and intentional implementation.

EXISTENTIAL STRATEGY DEVELOPMENT PROCESS

Unlike reactive plans or trend-driven road maps, Purposehood-driven strategy begins from the inside out. It's not about chasing the future—it's about building it with intention, anchored in who we are, where we are, and what we're truly here to do.

Leaders and engaged employees co-create strategy by asking three foundational questions:

Does our strategy align with our Organizational Purposehood—our existential reason for being?

Which zone and state are we in? Are we in a moment of stabilization, repair, consolidation, or expansion, and are we designing strategy that matches that truth?

Are we enabling individuals to contribute in alignment with their values, well-being, and sense of Purposehood?

These questions form a living compass for design, reflection, and adaptation. When strategy is built through alignment and shared timing, people commit to building the future together.

EASE FRAMEWORK FOR ORGANIZATIONAL TRANSFORMATION

Just as individuals shift zones through the EASE process, so too can entire organizations. The same four steps apply:

ENGAGE: ORGANIZATIONAL READINESS.

- True change begins with a pause, not a plan. Leaders and teams must first ask:

- Are we open? Are we willing to face hard truths and consider new ways of operating?

- Do we trust? Do we trust our leadership to guide us? Do we trust the method to work? Do we trust the process enough to follow through?

- Are we committed? Are we prepared to do the daily work, not just approve it from above?

ASSESS: MAPPING THE ORGANIZATIONAL WHOLEBEING.

Diagnose each part of the organization by zone:

- Contraction – departments stuck in crisis or resignation

- Healing – teams addressing dysfunction but still fragile

- Comfort – areas coasting on adequacy without growth

- Growth – functions expanding purposefully in alignment

SUPPORT: TARGETED INTERVENTIONS.

Instead of blanket change initiatives, apply zone-specific support using the ART framework:

- Attain – Take the smallest effective actions to immediately shift negative states to positive ones within the same zone.

- Retain – Build structures and rituals to protect progress and resist regression.

- Train – Build long-term skills and shared accountability to evolve the strategy as the organization grows.

ENACT: EMBEDDING NEW PATTERNS.

Enact is the shift from planning to doing. It begins with the smallest matched action—just enough to start movement.

Repetition makes it real. Tiny daily steps become rituals. Zone-matched habits take root in teams, meetings, and decisions.

But habits alone are not enough. Sustained transformation requires collective commitment.

That's where circles come in. Purposehood Expansion Work Circles help teams reflect, adapt, and reinforce what matters together. They are one way we train cultural alignment into practice.

This is how Enact lives in organizations:

- Start with one meaningful step.

- Repeat it until it becomes a rhythm.

- Sustain it through shared commitment.

That's when strategy becomes culture—a living system of decisions that reflect what matters most.

Strategic coherence is alignment between stated values and actual choices. When that alignment is felt across every level of the organization, trust grows, ownership deepens, and momentum becomes self-sustaining.

That outcome is the signature of Existential Leadership: strategy translated into lived meaning, not just stated values.

⏸ PURPOSEHOOD PAUSE

Think of an organization you're part of—your workplace, a school, a nonprofit, or your family business.

What zone and state is the culture currently operating in?

Where is misdirection showing up—misaligned goals, confusing metrics, or a performative mission?

Which extension feels most strained—leadership vision, team dynamics, stakeholder connection?

How might your own existential alignment ripple outward to influence the system's health?

Remember: You don't have to transform the whole system, but when you align with your Purposehood, you become a catalyst. And in every living system, one shift—when anchored—can realign the whole.

EXISTENTIAL REENGAGEMENT IN THE AGE OF AI

What emerges consistently is this: organizations that master existential reengagement create sustainable advantages that traditional approaches cannot match. But as we transform our workplaces, we face an even bigger challenge—the same technological forces reshaping how we work are redefining what it means to be human.

Artificial intelligence is today's defining force, already reshaping leadership roles, reconfiguring organizational structures, and transforming how engagement happens across teams. Yet here's what's often overlooked: as machines get smarter, the human inside the system becomes more essential, not less.

When existential health is ignored in this new landscape, five critical organizational risks emerge:

Meaning collapse: As AI takes over tasks, employees question their relevance. Without Purposehood, roles feel empty, leading to disengagement or resignation.

Ethical drift: AI decisions without moral grounding erode trust. When no one is anchored in shared values, short-term wins become long-term liabilities.

Cultural fragmentation: Rapid automation fractures connection. Silos widen, belonging fades, and collaboration becomes transactional unless intentional meaning ties teams together.

Resistance and sabotage: Employees pushed into change without inner alignment often resist or quietly undermine it. Existential misalignment becomes an invisible but powerful saboteur.

Strategic blindness: AI-driven strategies can be efficient but misaligned. Without existential filters, companies chase what's possible instead of what truly matters.

Already a silent driver of disengagement, burnout, and misalignment, existential disconnection is now colliding with accelerating technology. Without a strong foundation of existential health, companies risk replacing human agency with algorithmic autopilot, draining meaning from work precisely when meaning matters most.

But Purposehood Organization Engineering offers a different path. When organizations are treated as living systems with existential needs—direction, meaning, gratitude, connection, mattering—they don't just adapt to AI. They lead it. They clarify what must never be outsourced: humanity, creativity, and ethical responsibility.

In this new landscape, Purposehood becomes strategic infrastructure. When predictability vanishes, existential alignment remains the only reliable compass. Technology is redefining what it means to be human, and if we want our systems to thrive—let alone survive—we must start where all sustainable transformation begins: with Purposehood.

Existential Leadership is how leaders keep that compass alive in daily decisions—what to automate, what to augment, and what must remain irreducibly human.

THE 25 COMPONENTS OF BEING THE ARCHITECTURE OF WHOLEBEING

WholeBeing is composed of 25 distinct yet inseparable components, organized across Five Extensions of Being: Self, Family, Work, Communities, and Nature. Together, they form the living architecture through which every human life is expressed.

These components are universal. They apply to every person, in every culture, at every stage of life. They are not roles you earn, identities you choose, or circumstances you must meet. They are structural aspects of being human.

Not everyone encounters each component in a literal or traditional form. If you do not have children, a partner, or a formal job, that does not mean those components are absent from your life. It means they may be expressed differently.

You may care for someone in a parental way without being a parent. You may contribute through unpaid, informal, or creative work without holding a job title. You may serve, influence, or support others without formal authority or recognition.

Every person participates in all Five Extensions of Being in some form.

The purpose of this framework is not to force your life into predefined categories, but to invite honest reflection: How is each component currently expressed, strained, or neglected in my lived reality?

Every person embodies all 25 components at all times. Some are visible and well-nourished. Others operate quietly, unconsciously, or under strain. None are optional. None disappear. Strength in one cannot compensate for neglect in another.

Together, these components form your WholeBeing—not as a checklist, but as a system. Healing and growth do not come from fixing parts in isolation, but from restoring coherence across the whole.

SELF

1. EXISTENTIAL SELF

The Existential Self anchors your sense of meaning, purpose, and direction. It answers life's deepest questions—Who am I? Why am I here? When unwell, life feels aimless or fragmented. When healthy, it provides clarity, resilience, and coherence across all other components.

2. PHYSICAL SELF

Your relationship with your body—sleep, movement, nutrition, and health. Neglect leads to fatigue, irritability, and cognitive decline. Care brings vitality, emotional stability, and sustained energy.

3. MENTAL SELF

Your capacity to think, focus, learn, and make sense of complexity. When strained, confusion and overwhelm rise. When nourished, creativity, clarity, and adaptability emerge.

4. EMOTIONAL SELF

Your ability to feel, process, and regulate emotions. Emotional imbalance strains relationships and self-trust. Emotional health allows resilience, empathy, and inner steadiness.

5. SPIRITUAL SELF

Your connection to something greater than yourself—through faith, spirituality, or a sense of transcendence. When neglected, life may feel empty or anxious. When alive, it brings peace, grounding, and trust in life.

FAMILY

6. PARENTS

Your relationship with those who raised you. Healing here brings grounding and emotional stability; unresolved conflict often echoes across adulthood.

7. PARTNER

Your intimate relationship, built on trust, communication, and mutual growth. When misaligned, it becomes a source of stress; when healthy, it is a powerful source of resilience.

8. CHILDREN

Your role as a caregiver, guide, or mentor. Healthy connection fosters joy and meaning; unresolved tension creates guilt, frustration, or exhaustion.

9. SIBLINGS

Relationships shaped by shared history. When healed, they offer deep support and identity; when strained, they can reopen old wounds.

10. RELATIVES

Extended family connections that shape belonging and legacy. Healthy dynamics provide continuity; unhealthy ones often require boundaries.

WORK

11. JOB

Your primary professional role. When aligned with Purposehood, work becomes meaningful contribution; when misaligned, it drains energy and identity.

12. COWORKERS

Daily professional relationships. Healthy dynamics foster collaboration and satisfaction; toxic ones create chronic stress.

13. SHAREHOLDERS

Those invested in your work's success—owners, investors, stakeholders. Alignment builds trust and stability; misalignment breeds pressure and anxiety.

14. CUSTOMERS

Those you serve through your work. Healthy relationships reinforce meaning and contribution; strained ones erode motivation.

15. SUPPLIERS

Those who support your work logistically. Reliable partnerships reduce friction; dysfunction adds invisible stress.

COMMUNITIES

16. FRIENDS

Chosen relationships that provide emotional support, honesty, and joy. Neglect leads to isolation; presence strengthens resilience.

17. NEIGHBORS

Local connections that shape safety and belonging. Even light connection improves well-being; conflict disrupts peace.

18. CIRCLES

Small groups focused on healing and growth, built on trust and confidentiality. Healthy circles provide perspective and accountability; unhealthy ones stagnate growth.

19. ASSOCIATIONS

Professional, civic, or interest-based groups. Alignment offers belonging and expansion; misalignment drains energy.

20. ACQUAINTANCES

Casual social connections that broaden perspective and opportunity. Though often overlooked, they enrich social life.

NATURE

21. AIR

The quality of the air you breathe and environments you inhabit. Clean air supports vitality and clarity; poor air undermines health.

22. PLANTS

Your relationship with plant life and green spaces. Engagement reduces stress and restores focus; disconnection contributes to fatigue.

23. ANIMALS

Connection with animals, domestic or wild. Animals offer grounding, companionship, and emotional regulation.

24. EARTH (LAND AND WATER)

Your relationship with landscapes—mountains, oceans, rivers, soil. Nature restores balance and perspective.

25. UNIVERSE

Your sense of awe and belonging within something vast. Connection here reduces existential anxiety and fosters humility and peace.

Together, these 25 components form your WholeBeing—a living system whose coherence determines your capacity to heal and grow.

At the center lies Existential Health—your relationship with meaning and direction. When it weakens, strain spreads across the system. When it's strong, healing and growth ripple naturally through every component.

APPENDIX B

GLOSSARY OF TERMS

HOW TO USE THIS GLOSSARY

This glossary is organized as a conceptual map of The Purposehood®
Method for Existential Health, reflecting how its ideas relate to one
another rather than listing terms alphabetically. Readers may use it for
quick clarification of specific terms or read it top-down to understand
how Purposehood, Existential Health, WholeBeing, RootHealing, and
EASE Leadership form an integrated system. Terms are defined in
relation to each other to preserve their intended meaning within the
method, serving as an orienting reference that complements—rather
than replaces—the chapters.

PURPOSEHOOD®

A practical philosophy for a life worth living, introduced in the book
Purposehood — Transform Your Life, Transform the World. Purpose-
hood® integrates a forward-pulling existential theory, a set of empowering beliefs, and daily practices that nourish those beliefs, supporting
personal transformation and enabling a lived sense of meaning, gratitude, ease, and abundance.

EXISTENTIAL PURPOSE

The deeper reason for being that provides direction, coherence, and
meaning beyond roles, achievements, or external expectations. It

functions as a guiding star that aligns values, decisions, and actions over time.

PURPOSEHOOD

The embodied experience of living in alignment with one's existential purpose. Purposehood refers both to the guiding existential purpose itself, and to the ongoing orientation toward it—the lived, dynamic relationship between direction and daily life.

LIFE WORTH LOVING

A life intentionally shaped around existential purpose, where happiness, success, and fulfillment arise as byproducts of living in alignment with Purposehood rather than as ends in themselves.

EXISTENTIAL HEALTH

The ability to navigate all life's challenges with ease, regardless of circumstance. Existential health underlies and shapes mental, emotional, physical, spiritual, and relational well-being.

EXISTENTIAL SUFFERING

Suffering that arises from misdirection, disorientation, limiting beliefs, stagnation, or cravings. It sits beneath many forms of emotional, mental, relational, and even physical distress, often persisting despite favorable external conditions.

EXISTENTIAL INTELLIGENCE

The human capacity to raise and reflect on fundamental questions about meaning, purpose, values, and existence itself. In the context of Purposehood, it includes the wisdom to ask meaningful questions, meaningfully question the answers, and use that awareness to guide choices, relationships, and life design with responsibility and clarity.

THE PURPOSEHOOD® METHOD FOR EXISTENTIAL HEALTH

A structured methodology for restoring and sustaining existential health by aligning life with existential purpose. It is built on three core principles—WholeBeing, RootHealing, and EASE Leadership—and applied through the EASE process (Engage, Assess, Support, Enact) to guide individuals and systems from suffering toward healing and sustainable growth.

WHOLEBEING

The understanding that a human life functions as an integrated system rather than a collection of separate parts. WholeBeing recognizes that well-being, suffering, healing, and growth emerge from the interaction of all areas of life, and that imbalance in any one area affects the whole.

FIVE EXTENSIONS OF BEING

The five primary domains through which a WholeBeing lives and expresses existential purpose: Self, Family, Work, Communities, and Nature. These extensions represent interconnected spheres of life where health, meaning, and responsibility are continuously shaped.

WHOLEBEING COMPONENTS

The twenty-five interrelated components that make up a WholeBeing, representing distinct sources of strength and vulnerability across the

Five Extensions of Being. Each component can exist in different zones and states of well-being, influencing the overall health of the whole.

ROOTHEALING

An approach to healing and growth that moves beyond symptom management to address root causes at multiple levels. It begins by identifying functional causes—biological, behavioral, relational, or systemic factors contributing to distress—then examines the deeper existential sources that sustain persistent suffering. By restoring alignment, agency, and meaning across both levels, RootHealing seeks lasting transformation rather than temporary relief.

FIVE SOURCES OF EXISTENTIAL SUFFERING

The five primary ways existential health becomes compromised, producing persistent distress across different areas of life.

MISDIRECTION

The absence or misalignment of existential purpose, resulting in a lack of clarity about where one is going and why.

DISORIENTATION

The loss of orientation in time, role, or priorities, often experienced as confusion, overwhelm, or a sense of being lost.

LIMITING BELIEFS

Internalized assumptions, labels, or narratives that constrain agency, possibility, and self-trust, often adopted unconsciously through experience or conditioning.

STAGNATION

The absence of meaningful movement or growth, where comfort, fear, or routine prevents adaptation and development.

CRAVINGS

Unregulated desires that distort priorities and decision-making, leading to excess, imbalance, or dependency on external satisfaction.

TEN PURPOSEHOOD PILLARS OF EXISTENTIAL HEALTH

Ten core existential capacities used as therapeutic and developmental interventions to restore and sustain existential health.

DIRECTION

The capacity to orient life toward existential purpose with clarity and intentionality.

ENDURANCE

The ability to remain present, committed, and steady through difficulty without collapse or avoidance.

EMPOWERMENT

The restoration of agency, responsibility, and confidence in one's capacity to influence one's life.

CONTENTMENT

A grounded sense of sufficiency and peace that supports rest and integration without disengagement from life.

AMBITION

Purpose-aligned aspiration directed toward meaningful contribution rather than comparison or accumulation.

PATIENCE

The capacity to tolerate uncertainty, delay, and gradual progress without frustration or resignation.

GRATITUDE

An appreciative awareness of what is meaningful, supportive, or sufficient in one's life, strengthening perspective and resilience.

CONNECTION

The ability to form and sustain meaningful relationships with oneself, others, and the wider world.

MATTERING

The felt sense of significance—that one's existence, presence, and contributions have value to others and to life itself.

MEANING

The integration of experience into a coherent sense of purpose, significance, and understanding across one's life.

EASE LEADERSHIP

A form of leadership grounded in existential clarity, self-regulation, and alignment with Purposehood. EASE Leadership focuses on guiding change with steadiness and coherence rather than pressure, control, or urgency, whether leading oneself, others, or systems.

EASE PROCESS

The operational four-step process—Engage, Assess, Support, and Enact—through which EASE Leadership is practiced, guiding healing and growth from readiness to sustainable integration.

ENGAGE

The first step focused on readiness and commitment, where an individual or system clarifies the desire for improvement, establishes trust in the method, and agrees to do the work required for change.

ASSESS

The diagnostic second step that maps the current state of a WholeBeing, identifying areas of strength, vulnerability, and priority for healing or growth.

REVEAL360™ — PURPOSEHOOD® WHOLEBEING ASSESSMENT

A structured assessment tool used to map the WholeBeing across its components and zones of well-being, providing a clear picture of positive and negative states to guide targeted support.

THE FOUR ZONES OF WELL-BEING

A developmental model describing four primary zones and their corresponding negative and positive states through which individuals and systems move over time.

Contraction: A zone marked by disorientation and diminished capacity, where stabilization and rebound are the primary needs.

> **Resignation:** The negative state of giving up agency or hope.

> **Endurance:** The positive state of sustaining presence and effort despite difficulty.

Healing: A zone focused on recovery and rebuilding agency after disruption or dependency.

> **Dependency:** The negative state of relying on external sources for direction or strength.

> **Empowerment:** The positive state of restored agency and self-efficacy.

Comfort: A zone of stability and rest that allows for integration and consolidation of gains.

> **Complacency:** The negative state of disengagement or resistance to change.

> **Contentment:** The positive state of grounded satisfaction and balance.

Growth: A zone of expansion, aspiration, and contribution.

Excess: The negative state of overextension driven by uncontrolled desire.

Ambition: The positive state of purpose-aligned aspiration.

SUPPORT

The third step where appropriate interventions are selected and applied based on the assessed zone and state, ensuring support is precise, proportional, and aligned with existential needs.

ART FRAMEWORK

A framework used within Support to guide intervention selection and sequencing.

Attain: Helping a person move from a negative state to a positive state within a zone.

Retain: Strengthening and stabilizing positive states to prevent regression.

Train: Building long-term capacity to navigate future challenges with greater resilience and alignment.

PATH OF EASE

The positive developmental trajectory within and across the four zones of well-being, where components remain in positive states despite changing life conditions. The path of ease reflects sustained existential health, expressed as movement from endurance to empowerment, contentment, and purpose-aligned ambition rather than repeated cycles of struggle and recovery.

PURPOSEHOOD ENGINEERING

A structured life-design discipline within the Train function of the ART framework. It provides a systematic approach for translating existential purpose into consistent patterns of thought, behavior, and decision-making across all extensions of WholeBeing. Purposehood Engineering develops the capacities required to design, implement, and sustain alignment over time.

The discipline is organized into five modules:

Realize: Clarifying existential purpose and direction.

Rebound: Stabilizing and regaining footing during contraction.

Recover: Rebuilding agency and capacity during healing.

Rest: Integrating success and restoring balance in comfort.

Rise: Expanding contribution and aspiration with alignment in growth.

PURPOSEHOOD ENGINEER

A practitioner trained in the Purposehood® Method for Existential Health who helps individuals and systems assess existential health, identify root sources of suffering, and design, support, and enact purposeful change through WholeBeing, RootHealing, and the EASE process.

ENACT

The fourth step where insight and support are translated into lived action, ensuring change becomes embodied and sustained by doing the work, repeating it habitually, and enacting it together within relational and communal contexts.

PURPOSEHOOD EXPANSION CIRCLE

A structured relational environment where individuals practice accountability, reflection, and mutual support while enacting change.

PURPOSEHOOD COMMUNITY

The broader ecosystem that supports sustained practice, learning, and shared responsibility for existential health.

SIXTH EXTENSION OF BEING

The emerging technological extension of human life, encompassing digital systems, artificial intelligence, and tools that augment cognition, communication, and decision-making. The Sixth Extension of Being recognizes technology as a powerful amplifier of human intention that must be consciously aligned with existential purpose to support, rather than erode, existential health.

PURPOSEHOOD ORGANIZATION ENGINEERING

The application of the Purposehood® Method for Existential Health to organizations, communities, and systems. Purposehood Organization Engineering focuses on designing structures, cultures, and strategies that support existential health, meaningful contribution, and sustainable performance at scale.

EXISTENTIAL REENGAGEMENT

The process of restoring meaning, agency, and commitment in the workplace when individuals or teams become disengaged, misdirected, or resigned. Existential reengagement reconnects people to purpose, responsibility, and meaningful contribution within their roles, work, and organization.

EXISTENTIAL LEADERSHIP

Leadership grounded in existential awareness, responsibility, and purpose—the ability to face work's challenges with ease while guiding decisions about direction, priorities, and values in conditions of uncertainty and change. It focuses on restoring existential health and unleashing the potential of those one leads by reconnecting stakeholders to meaning, agency, and purposeful contribution.

EXISTENTIAL STRATEGY

A strategic approach that aligns goals, structures, and actions with existential purpose, ensuring that growth, innovation, and performance serve human meaning, coherence, and long-term well-being rather than short-term optimization alone.

MIND MAP

WholeBeing
Five Extensions of Being
Self
Family
Work
Community
Nature
RootHealing
10 Purposehood Pillars of Existential Health
Direction
Endurance
Empowerment
Contentment
Ambition
Patience
Gratitude
Connections
Mattering
Meaning
The Purposehood® Method for Existential Health
EASE Leadership
Engage
Openness
Trust
Commitment
Assess
Contraction
Resignation
Endurance
Healing
Dependency
Empowerment
Comfort
Complacency
Contentment
Growth
Excess
Ambition
Support
Attain
Retain
Train
Purposehood Engineering
Realize
Rebound
Recover
Rest
Rise
Enact
Do it
Habitually
Together

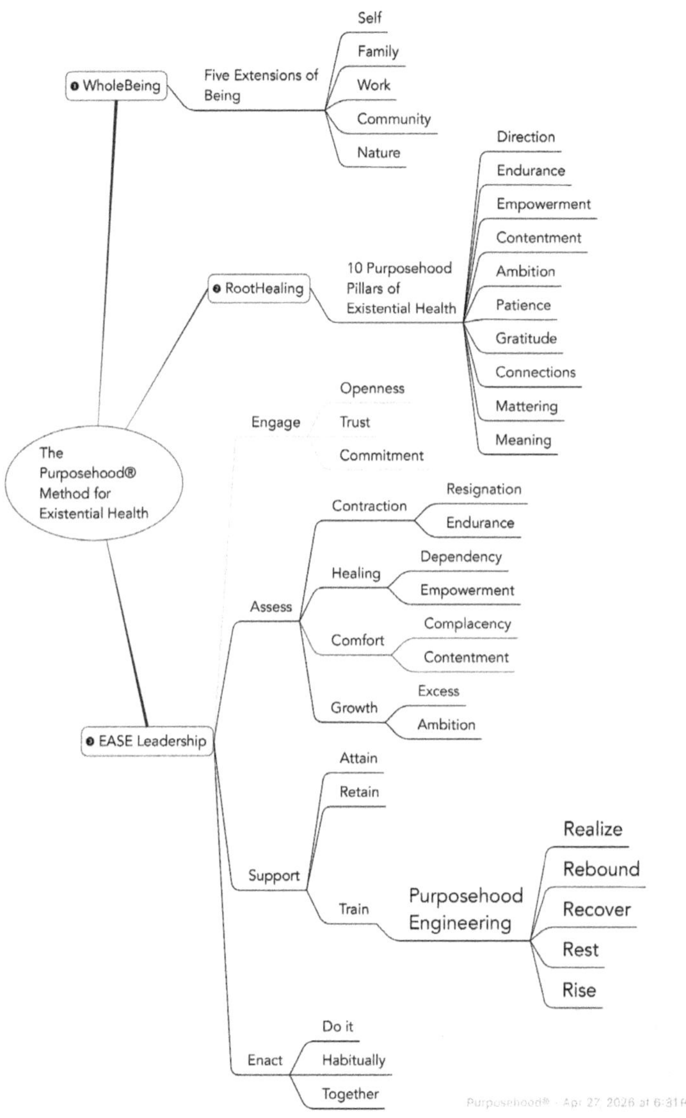

SAMPLE REVEAL360™— PURPOSEHOOD® WHOLEBEING ASSESSMENT

For personal use only. This sample version is provided for self-reflection and educational purposes. REVEAL360™ and The Purposehood® Method for Existential Health are proprietary methodologies of Purposehood® Institute. Reproduction, distribution, training, certification, or commercial use without permission is prohibited.

HOW TO USE THIS ASSESSMENT

For each of the 25 components of your WholeBeing:

Step 1 — Are You Struggling?

Check: Yes or No

Step 2 — Are You Seeking Improvement or Change?

Check: Yes or No

Step 3 — Identify Your Current Zone

Choose one: Contraction Zone, Healing Zone, Comfort Zone, or Growth Zone

Step 4 — Identify Your Current State

Use the table below to identify whether you are in the positive or negative state of that zone.

Zone	Negative State	Positive State
Contraction	Resignation	Endurance
Healing	Dependency	Empowerment
Comfort	Complacency	Contentment
Growth	Excess	Ambition

SELF

Existential Self

When it comes to your purpose, meaning, direction, identity:

Am I struggling? ☐ Yes ☐ No

Am I seeking improvement or change? ☐ Yes ☐ No

Current Zone: _______________________

Current State: _______________________

Physical Self

When it comes to your physical health and energy:

Am I struggling? ☐ Yes ☐ No

Am I seeking improvement or change? ☐ Yes ☐ No

Current Zone: _______________________

Current State: _______________________

Mental Self

When it comes to your thoughts, focus, and mental clarity:

Am I struggling? ☐ Yes ☐ No

Am I seeking improvement or change? ☐ Yes ☐ No

Current Zone: _______________________

Current State: _______________________

Emotional Self

When it comes to your emotional well-being and emotional regulation:

Am I struggling? ☐ Yes ☐ No

Am I seeking improvement or change? ☐ Yes ☐ No

Current Zone: _______________________

Current State: _______________________

Spiritual Self

When it comes to your spirituality, inner peace, or connection to something greater:

Am I struggling? ☐ Yes ☐ No

Am I seeking improvement or change? ☐ Yes ☐ No

Current Zone: _______________________

Current State: _______________________

FAMILY

Partner

When it comes to your relationship with your partner or spouse:

Am I struggling? ☐ Yes ☐ No

Am I seeking improvement or change? ☐ Yes ☐ No

Current Zone: _____________________

Current State: _____________________

Parents

When it comes to your relationship with your parents:

Am I struggling? ☐ Yes ☐ No

Am I seeking improvement or change? ☐ Yes ☐ No

Current Zone: _____________________

Current State: _____________________

Children

When it comes to your relationship with your children:

Am I struggling? ☐ Yes ☐ No

Am I seeking improvement or change? ☐ Yes ☐ No

Current Zone: _____________________

Current State: _____________________

Siblings

When it comes to your relationship with your siblings:

Am I struggling? ☐ Yes ☐ No

Am I seeking improvement or change? ☐ Yes ☐ No

Current Zone: _______________________

Current State: _______________________

Relatives

When it comes to your relationship with your relatives and extended family:

Am I struggling? ☐ Yes ☐ No

Am I seeking improvement or change? ☐ Yes ☐ No

Current Zone: _______________________

Current State: _______________________

WORK

Job and Duties

When it comes to your work, career, or responsibilities:

Am I struggling? ☐ Yes ☐ No

Am I seeking improvement or change? ☐ Yes ☐ No

Current Zone: _______________________

Current State: _______________________

Coworkers

When it comes to your relationships with coworkers or collaborators:

Am I struggling? ☐ Yes ☐ No

Am I seeking improvement or change? ☐ Yes ☐ No

Current Zone: _______________________

Current State: _______________________

Shareholders / Owners

When it comes to your relationship with owners, investors, or stakeholders:

Am I struggling? ☐ Yes ☐ No

Am I seeking improvement or change? ☐ Yes ☐ No

Current Zone: _______________________

Current State: _______________________

Customers

When it comes to your relationship with customers or clients:

Am I struggling? ☐ Yes ☐ No

Am I seeking improvement or change? ☐ Yes ☐ No

Current Zone: _______________________

Current State: _______________________

Suppliers / Partners

When it comes to your relationship with suppliers or business partners:

Am I struggling? ☐ Yes ☐ No

Am I seeking improvement or change? ☐ Yes ☐ No

Current Zone: _______________________

Current State: _______________________

COMMUNITIES

Friends

When it comes to your friendships:

Am I struggling? ☐ Yes ☐ No

Am I seeking improvement or change? ☐ Yes ☐ No

Current Zone: _______________________

Current State: _______________________

Neighbors

When it comes to your relationship with neighbors and local community:

Am I struggling? ☐ Yes ☐ No

Am I seeking improvement or change? ☐ Yes ☐ No

Current Zone: _______________________

Current State: _______________________

Circles

When it comes to your participation in circles, peer groups, or communities of belonging:

Am I struggling? ☐ Yes ☐ No

Am I seeking improvement or change? ☐ Yes ☐ No

Current Zone: _____________________

Current State: _____________________

Associations

When it comes to your relationship with associations, organizations, or causes:

Am I struggling? ☐ Yes ☐ No

Am I seeking improvement or change? ☐ Yes ☐ No

Current Zone: _____________________

Current State: _____________________

Acquaintances

When it comes to your broader social relationships and acquaintances:

Am I struggling? ☐ Yes ☐ No

Am I seeking improvement or change? ☐ Yes ☐ No

Current Zone: _____________________

Current State: _____________________

NATURE

Air

When it comes to your air quality, breathing, and the environments you inhabit:

Am I struggling? ☐ Yes ☐ No

Am I seeking improvement or change? ☐ Yes ☐ No

Current Zone: _______________________

Current State: _______________________

Animals

When it comes to your relationship with animals and other living beings:

Am I struggling? ☐ Yes ☐ No

Am I seeking improvement or change? ☐ Yes ☐ No

Current Zone: _______________________

Current State: _______________________

Plants

When it comes to your relationship with plants, greenery, and natural life:

Am I struggling? ☐ Yes ☐ No

Am I seeking improvement or change? ☐ Yes ☐ No

Current Zone: _______________________

Current State: _______________________

Earth

When it comes to your relationship with the earth, land, water, and physical environment:

Am I struggling? ☐ Yes ☐ No

Am I seeking improvement or change? ☐ Yes ☐ No

Current Zone: _______________________

Current State: _______________________

Universe

When it comes to your relationship with awe, existence, mystery, and the universe itself:

Am I struggling? ☐ Yes ☐ No

Am I seeking improvement or change? ☐ Yes ☐ No

Current Zone: _______________________

Current State: _______________________

REFLECTION

- Which areas of your WholeBeing are in negative states?

- Which areas are strongest and most aligned?

- Where are you seeking healing?

- Where are you seeking growth?

- Which areas most influence the rest of your life?

- What would happen if one important component improved?

- What is one small supportive action you can take today?

NEXT STEPS

For deeper exploration, use the full REVEAL360™—Purposehood®
WholeBeing Assessment on the Purposehood App.

Practitioners and coaches should use the professional version of the
assessment.

IMPORTANT NOTICE

This sample assessment is not a diagnostic or medical tool. It is a reflective framework designed to help individuals better understand the state
of their WholeBeing through the lens of The Purposehood® Method
for Existential Health.

REVEAL360™ and The Purposehood® Method are proprietary intellectual property of Purposehood® Institute. All rights reserved.

ACKNOWLEDGMENTS

I am a WholeBeing.

And this work was created by a WholeBeing.

This book could not have been written without every element of my WholeBeing—Self, Family, Work, Communities, and Nature—each shaping the ideas, experiences, and insights that became The Purposehood® Method for Existential Health.

I'm grateful to iSH, the mystery beyond, for this existence that I am fortunate enough to experience during my brief appearance among this evolving specimen called humans.

I'm grateful to all the components of my Self for keeping me productive in my older age, continuing to learn, question, and create.

I'm grateful to my family for keeping me connected to everyday life, despite my tendency to choose a forest over a city.

I'm grateful to all those I work with to generate value in this world. Your collaboration, challenges, and shared efforts helped shape many of the ideas in this book.

I'm especially grateful to my writing coach Toni Robino and her team at Windword Literary Services for their wisdom, patience, and professionalism. I'm grateful to the talented team at DartFrog for their help in publishing *EASE*. I'm also grateful to Kath, Catalin, Vlad, and Iura for designing and creating the accompanying technology, and to the team at bluquist, including their talented psychologists, for their advice on the REVEAL360™—Purposehood® WholeBeing Assessment.

I'm grateful to my clients who trusted me to share my experience with them, their families, and their teams, and who generously provided the stories and learning reflected throughout this book.

I'm grateful to my friends, forums, and groups for the countless discussions and surveys that helped me clarify my thoughts and make The Purposehood Method for Existential Health as practical as it is today.

I'm grateful to the beautiful nature in the South of France, which became my canvas for creativity in its plants, mountains, sea, and animals—especially Mira, my German Shepherd companion.

I shouldn't forget to be grateful to the new, emerging, and sometimes dangerous partner: AI. It gave me a window into what's to come while helping me edit in a language I'm comfortable with but not native to, often overwhelming me with options and keeping me cautious when it hallucinates. It was a very different writing experience from my previous book, Purposehood — Transform Your Life, Transform the World. An experience I learned from, though I'm not sure I'd want to repeat, as it sometimes takes away from the true pleasure of crafting your own words.

And I'm grateful to you, my dear reader, for accompanying me on this journey of healing and growth, embracing the new ideas, terms, and concepts along the way.

My friends, may you design, build, and sustain a life worth loving.

May you discover your Purposehood.

And may you heal and grow with ease.

ABOUT THE AUTHOR

Ammar Charani is the founder of the Purposehood® Institute and the creator of The Purposehood® Method for Existential Health, a structured approach that helps individuals, leaders, and organizations heal and grow by discovering and living their existential purpose. His work integrates philosophy, psychology, leadership, and systems thinking into a practical method for improving well-being across the WholeBeing—Self, Family, Work, Communities, and Nature.

A serial entrepreneur and Harvard Business School alumnus with an engineering background from the University of Central Florida, Ammar has founded and seed-invested in more than thirty companies across multiple industries and continents, creating thousands of jobs. He built one of the first community marketing companies, which grew to over 1,000 employees and supported more than 3,000 schools and relief organizations, generating over $100 million in direct contributions. He is also the cofounder of in/PACT, a social impact platform that has enabled more than one billion acts of giving through partnerships with major global brands.

A global leader within YPO, Ammar is a founding member of eleven chapters across four continents and the founder of the YPO Change Makers Club. Through his work, he has taught and trained over 1,200 CEOs, their spouses, and their next generations in Purposehood—helping them align success with meaning, responsibility, and lasting impact.

His journey began with a deep search for meaning and fulfillment. Growing up in Syria, he traveled across the country with his father, a judge, experiencing a rich mosaic of cultures, religions, and traditions. He later studied anthropology, world religions, and philosophy under Sufi masters and religious scholars, where he studied, taught, and later served as a spiritual leader. A near-death experience followed by an eleven-year exploration of life's deeper questions further shaped his path, ultimately leading to the development of Purposehood as both a philosophy and a practical life engineering approach.

Ammar is the author of Purposehood: Transform Your Life, Transform the World, an Amazon #1 new release in Humanist Philosophy and Transpersonal Psychology, and EASE—Existential Health in the Age of Overwhelm, first introduced to healthcare professionals at the 4th World Congress of Existential Therapy, which presents a structured system for healing, growth, and designing a life worth loving.

Today, Ammar is focused on expanding the Purposehood® Institute through training programs, certifications, and global collaborations. His mission is to train 20 million Purposehood Engineers, creating a worldwide movement to elevate existential health across individuals, families, organizations, and societies.

CONTINUE YOUR PURPOSEHOOD JOURNEY

You've faced contractions, healed, rested, and risen. Yet the journey of Purposehood never truly ends—it expands.

If you wish to keep deepening your practice and supporting others in theirs:

Stay connected through the <u>Purposehood App</u>, your daily companion for reflection and WholeBeing alignment, featuring the REVEAL360™ — Purposehood® WholeBeing Assessment.

Explore advanced trainings to deepen existential health and practice existential leadership as a Purposehood® Engineer—living this work through service, creation, and leadership.

Return to the source with Purposehood — Transform Your Life, Transform the World, the book that first introduced the philosophy behind this method.

Visit <u>Purposehood.org</u> for new tools, gatherings, and ongoing community exploration.

Every day is another chance to heal and grow—with meaning, gratitude, ease, and abundance.

CONTINUE THE WORK

If EASE has helped you begin to heal and grow, the next step is to go deeper into the foundation it was built on.

Purposehood: Transform Your Life, Transform the World introduces the core architecture of transformation: how a life is intentionally redesigned from the inside out.

At its foundation are three elements:

- A Forward-Pulling Theory that gives direction to your life and aligns it with your evolving being

- 27 Empowering Beliefs that reshape your internal operating system and support that direction

- Five Daily Practices that nourish those beliefs and turn them into lived reality

This is where transformation becomes structured, repeatable, and sustainable.

HOW PURPOSEHOOD ENGINEERING IS EXPERIENCED

"The world doesn't need more successful leaders. It needs more purposeful ones. Purposehood Engineering gives leaders the clarity to align achievement with meaning and use business as a force for good."

—Anastasios Economou

YPO Global Chairman Emeritus • Founder, iGrow Venture Partners • "Dragon," Dragon's Den Greece

"We're trained to grow financial capital. Purposehood Engineering shows how to grow the one asset that truly compounds: our existence. Once you see it, you stop managing life and start engineering a legacy of meaning and alignment. It's something I now consider essential to pass on to the next generation."

—Ryna Mi

Founder, The Wealth School • Former Head of Private Banking, Alfa-Bank

"I was skeptical, but the framework and step-by-step approach turned everything from fog into clarity and gave me tools I can actually use."

—Håkon Lund

Chair, IAAPA EMEA • Chair, Global Family Business Network • Owner, Lund Gruppen Holding AS

"This program exceeded my expectations. It guided me through a defined path where I could dovetail my own strengths with a clear and deliverable Purposehood. Like all great teachings, I left through a different door than I entered."

—Gene Browne
Co-Founder & CEO, The City Bin Co. • Chair, YPO IMD High Performance Leadership

"It brought a sense of absolute clarity, connecting the dots of my life into a clear purpose. It's like seeing your inner compass with a clear eye."

—Subodh Deshpande
Chief Strategy Officer, DDB

"I applied the decision-making process and turned an investment opportunity into something aligned with my Purposehood, by redirecting part of it to create real impact. It completely changed my level of motivation."

—Justin Reizes
Investor • Former Partner, KKR & Co. Inc.

"It reframed purpose in a way that is understandable, attainable, and actionable, and showed me it doesn't have to be a lofty concept, but something I can live every day."

—Megan Pratt
Partner, Innate Motion

"I'm analyzing all my plans, and if they are not aligned with my Purposehood, I exclude them, even people who steal my time. I've learned how to say no.

—Ekaterina Chernova
Founder & Managing Partner, Octagon FOAS

"The journey of life is about shared purposehood. The Purposehood Engineering training not only helps us find our purpose in life, but also how to help others find theirs."
   —Ángel García Cordero
   Chairman, SEG Ingeniería • YPO Regional Chair, Europe

"Watching 130 young people gain clarity about their purpose and the direction of their lives was one of the most powerful experiences we've seen. It's the kind of transformation every parent hopes for their child."
   —Charles Feghali
   Founder & CEO, NGE Systems • Chair, YPO Global Diplomacy Network • Chair, YNG Summit